Volume 1

Microeconomics Reading Lists

Economics Reading Lists, Course Outlines, Exams, Puzzles & Problems

Compiled by Edward Tower, September 1995
Duke University & The University of Auckland

NOTE TO USERS AND POTENTIAL CONTRIBUTORS

These teaching materials are drawn from both undergraduate and graduate programs at 105 major colleges and universities. They are designed to widen the horizons of individual professors and curriculum committees. Some include suggestions for term-paper topics, and many of the reading lists are useful guides for students seeking both topics and references for term papers and theses. Thus, they should enable faculty members to advise students more effectively and efficiently. They will also be useful to prospective graduate students seeking more detailed information about various graduate programs and to librarians responsible for acquisitions in economics. Finally, they may interest researchers and administrators who wish to know more about how their own work and the work of their department is being received by the profession.

The exams, puzzles and problems include both undergraduate and graduate exams contributed by economics departments and individual professors. They should be especially useful to professors making up exams and problem sets and to students studying for Ph.D. exams. They may also serve as the focus for study groups.

From time to time, we will reprint updated and expanded versions. Therefore, we welcome new or updated teaching materials, particularly those which complement material in this collection or cover areas we missed. Potential contributors should contact Ed Tower, Economics Department, Box 90097, Duke University, Durham, North Carolina 27708-0097, U.S.A., **tower@econ.duke.edu**

While Eno River Press has copyrighted the entire collection, authors of the various parts retain the right to reproduce and assign the reproduction of their own materials as they choose. Thus, anyone wishing to reproduce particular materials should contact their author. Similarly, those wishing to make verbatim use of departmental examinations, except as teaching materials for one's own class, should contact the department chair concerned.

Associate Compilers for this series are: **3 2280 00515 6963**

Ömer Gökçekuş, Visiting Lecturer, Duke University
Chao Jing, Graduate Instructor, University of Colorado
Wells D. Tower, Senior at Wesleyan University

Dan Tower helped produce the volumes with creativity and energy. Nancy Hurtgen and Tom Hurtgen advised on many aspects of the project. Members of the Duke Economics Department have been helpful from the inception of the project, and belated thanks go to Allen C. Kelley, who suggested in 1980 the usefulness of collecting syllabi.

Eno River Press
115 Stoneridge Drive
Chapel Hill, North Carolina 27514-9737
U.S.A.
Fax & Phone: (919) 967-8246

ISBN for the volume: 0-88024-181-0
ISBN for the series: 0-88024-160-8
Library of Congress Catalog Number: 95-061333

MICROECONOMICS READING LISTS

Contents

***

U = Undergraduate, **G** = Graduate
RE = Reading List with Exams, Problems and/ or Term Paper Topics

Introduction

Anup Wadhawan
Duke University.

Microeconomics, with its focus on the optimizing behavior of individual decision makers in an economic system, constitutes a crucial body of knowledge. It is hard to conceive of an area of Economic analysis that does not make use of these methods to some significant extent. The widespread use of the term "Micro Foundations", in diverse areas of economic analysis, highlights this fact. These two volumes could prove to be extremely useful to those seeking to familiarize themselves with the essential literature that constitutes this field. Vol. 1 contains course outlines/reading lists from Microeconomics courses taught by leading scholars. These lists are fairly comprehensive in terms of their coverage of the area and largely rely on publications that are widely known for their impact on the field. Vol. 2 contains Qualifying (Prelim) exams from various prestigious Universities. Working through them could be of invaluable assistance to serious aspirants in this area, in honing their skills and sharpening their analytical abilities.

The current volumes do not depart to a very great extent from the 1990 volumes in terms of the topics covered. The important recent developments in this area, like Game Theory, Information Economics, Experimental Economics, Search Theory etc. had acquired substantial prominence by 1990, and are well represented in the earlier edition. However, the issues and concerns to which these new concepts have been applied over the years, has shown fairly rapid progression. This fact is reflected in the contents of the current volumes. For instance, Cox (Univ. of Arizona) includes the very crucial contemporary issue of Contingent Valuation in his course on Experimental Economics. Dixit (Princeton Univ.) extends the content of his Game Theory based course beyond the basic look at equilibria, to interesting applications like Brinkmanship, Bargaining and Voting. Rosen (Univ. of Chicago) includes Spatial Economics in his course outline. Scherer (Harvard Univ.) in his course "Technology, Innovation and Economic Growth" discusses the important contemporary issue of Technology and Competitiveness.

These volumes reflect the vast knowledge, skill and experience of the contributors associated with them, and further fulfill the objectives of the 1990 edition.

UNIVERSITY OF ADELAIDE

MICROECONOMIC THEORY III and IIID

1995 COURSE OUTLINE

Lecturer-in-charge: Kym Anderson, phone 303 4712, room 128 Napier Annex
(Office hours: Monday and Wednesdays between 8.30 and 10am, or by appointment)
Tutors: Kym Anderson and Anna Strutt (room LG08)
Guest lecturer and tutor: Ian McLean (May 24 to June 5)

Welcome!

This subject is designed to round out your training in core economics as you learn to apply the tools of the profession. It assumes that the majority of you will choose careers which will make use of your skills as economic analysts in, for example, the state or federal public services, in international agencies, in business corporations, in consulting firms and the like. It also assumes that many of the undergraduates among you wish to do honours and, probably after some work experience, even higher degrees in economics. With these assumptions in mind, the course aim is to ensure you finish the degree as a dazzling practitioner of the art of economics, and have fun doing it!

Our mission in the broad is to enhance our abilities to think clearly, to be able to search and research efficiently, and to communicate ideas effectively. More specifically, the skills we seek to develop include our capacities
-- to think in the abstract;
-- to work well both individually and in groups;
-- to recognise and clearly define an issue requiring analysis or a problem requiring a solution;
-- to find and make use of theories and data for analysing that issue or problem;
-- to develop, present and defend a logical argument based on that analysis, in oral and written form, for laypersons and/or colleagues; and
-- to critique constructively the arguments of others.

Notice that none of the above skills mentions economics. One could have the same objectives for a course in philosophy, or maths, or any of the sciences. Why, then, study economics? Let me mention just four reasons as to why you might want to learn more about the *economic* way of thinking:
-- to help you make rational choices in your own personal life;
-- to help you understand and predict the behaviour of other people;
-- to enhance your prospects of an interesting and worthwhile career;
-- to help improve social welfare locally, nationally and globally;
-- to help understand why professional economists think the way they do;
-- to have fun making sense out of everyday events in the world around you.
Only a few core concepts need to be grasped to begin practicing economics. They include an understanding of:
-- how markets function and coordinate economic activity;
-- opportunity cost;
-- marginal analysis;
-- sunk costs;
-- discounting of future benefits and costs;
-- the role of competition in motivating and constraining behaviour;

-- the role of incentives on behaviour of individuals in households, firms, bureaucracies and parliaments;
-- the limited role of goverment in an economy;
-- indirect (general equilibrium) effects of market or policy changes;
-- the importance of an open-economy perspective; and
-- the importance of learning from history.

In this subject, more emphasis will be placed on how to make use of and refine our understanding of those concepts, rather than adding a lot more (less-used) concepts. Lectures will draw your attention to areas of theory that are especially relevant for analysing problems and issues confronting policy makers, business people, households and individuals, while tutorials will be spent practicing the art of economics by applying that theory in addressing contemporary issues.

The logical unit of market analysis is that of a small open economy. Partial- as well as general-equilibrium modes of analysis will be used, and much of the time an economy-wide perspective will be required to ensure that indirect as well as direct effects are included in the analysis.

The lectures will be structured as follows, with some examples of questions that could be addressed (to which you might add some of your own):

Lectures 1-5 (February 27 to March 13): **Review of partial-equilibrium analysis**
Why are drinks and food dearer in theatres?
Who bears the burden of a sales tax?
Why shouldn't farmers pay for agricultural research?
Why do economists almost invariably argue against import tariffs?

Lectures 6-9 (March 15 to 27): **Extension to general equilibrium analysis**
Should exporters be compensated for the presense of tariffs?
If *laissez faire* is so good, why do so few countries practice it?
How are different sectors and factor owners affected by a mining boom? an export price slump? the unionization of some labour?

Lectures 10-12 (March 29 to April 5): **More on economic growth and income distribution**
Why have the real prices of primary products and their share of GNP declined over the long term?
Even though the quantity and quality of available labour relative to natural resources keeps rising, so too does the wage/rental ratio and the share of labour in GNP. Why?
Why do some people/countries remain poor?

Mid-semester break, followed by Lecture 13 (April 24): mid-semester test

Lectures 14-20 (April 26 to May 22): **Other applications: economics of law, time, behaviour of households, the environment**
How can economics be applied to the law when the purpose of the law is to be just, not efficient?
Why do people tend to get more harried as they get richer?
What can economics say about the age of people when they marry and have children, and the number of and the amount of time they spend with their children?
Is a global carbon tax needed to slow global warming?

Lectures 21-24 (May 24 to June 5: **Economic methodology** (led by Ian McLean)

-- introduces students to developments in the philosophy of science in recent decades, compares the methodology of economics with that of science more broadly, and assists thinking about the design and conduct of economic research, such as for the honours thesis.

Lecture 25 (June 7): **Review/wrap-up**

Class times

Two 50-minute lectures will be given each week throughout Semester I, at 12.10 p.m. each Monday and Wednesday in LG28 of the Napier Annex. In addition, you are invited to participate in a 50-minute tutorial/discussion session each week, where you will have the opportunity to practice the art of economics in a sympathetic environment, before you have to do so in the workplace after this year.

Assessment

There will be a 50-minute exam in the first class following the mid-semester break (on Monday, April 24), as well as a final 2-hour exam at the end of the semester. The smaller exam will be worth one fifth of the total grade, the larger exam will be worth one half of the final grade, and the remaining 30 per cent is for performance in tutorial discussion.

You will be asked to form into groups of 3 students for the purpose of preparing for, and presenting material at, tutorials. A group will be chosen at random each week to open the discussion with a 10-15 minute presentation. As an incentive for continual participation by each member of each group, one third of the grade for each week will be given to those members of the group chosen to make the opening presentation who show up, with zero for any absent group member.

Students are reminded that a credit in Microeconomic Theory III is a necessary (but not sufficient) condition for enrolling in Honours.

Textbooks

No single textbook is capable of serving the needs of this course. Instead, reliance is on the myriad intermediate and advanced microeconomic textbooks in the library, and on the Course Reader (purchasable from the bookstore for $20.50). All starred references in the list below are required reading and are in the Course Reader.

READING LIST

I. REVIEW OF PARTIAL EQUILIBRIUM ANALYSIS

*Corden, W.M. (1974), *Trade Policy and Economic Welfare*, Oxford: Clarendon Press, pp. 9-33 and 42-54.

Friedman, D.D. (1990), *Price Theory: An Intermediate Text*, Cincinnati: South-Western, 2nd edition (a lively text full of stimulating puzzles).

McCloskey, D.N. (1985), *The Applied Theory of Price*, New York: Macmillan, 2nd edition (another lively text with great puzzles and answers to the odd-numbered ones -- try yourself out).

Varian, H.R. (1993), *Intermediate Microeconomics: A Modern Approach*, New York: Norton, 3rd edition (a classic text for acquiring the tools needed for PE closed-economy microeconomic analysis).

II. EXTENSIONS TO GENERAL EQUILIBRIUM ANALYSIS

*Jones, R.W. (1965), "The Structure of Simple General Equilibrium Models", *Journal of Political Economy* 73(6): 557-72, December.

*Mussa, M. (1974), "Tariffs and the Distribution of Income: The Importance of Factor Specificity, Substitutability and Intensity in the Short and Long Run", *Journal of Political Economy* 82(6): 1191-1203, December.

*Corden, W.M. (1974, pp. 42-54).

*Bhagwati, J.N. (1971), "The Generalized Theory of Distortions and Welfare", in *Trade, Balance of Payments and Growth*, edited by J. Bhagwati et al., Amsterdam: North Holland, 1971. Reprinted as Ch. 12 in the readings volume edited by J.N. Bhagwati (1981), *International Trade: Selected Readings*, Cambridge: MIT Press.

*Corden, W.M. (1984), "Booming Sector and Dutch Disease Economics: Survey and Consolidation," *Oxford Economic Papers* 36(3): 359-80, November.

*Warr, P.G. (1978), "The Case Against Tariff Compensation", *Australian Journal of Agricultural Economics* 22(2):85-98, August.

*Anderson, K. (1994), "Lobbying Incentives and the Patterns of Protection in Rich and Poor Countries", *Economic Development and Cultural Change* 42 (forthcoming).

Jones, R.W. (1971), "A Three-Factor Model in Theory, Trade and History", Ch. 1 in *Trade, Balance of Payments and Growth*, edited by J. Bhagwati et al., Amsterdam: North Holland.

Bator, F.M. (1957), "The Simple Analytics of Welfare Maximization", *American Economic Review* 47(1): 22-59, March.

Lloyd, P.J. (1974), "A More General Theory of Price Distortions in an Open Economy", *Journal of International Economics* 4(4): 365-86, November.

Corden, W.M. (1983), "The Normative Theory of International Trade", Ch. 2 in *Handbook of International Economics*, Vol. 1, edited by R.W. Jones and P.B. Kenen, Amsterdam: North Holland.

Important milestones in the history of thought on distortions and welfare in open economies are:

Meade, J.E. (1955), *The Theory of International Economic Policy, Volume 2*: London: Oxford University Press, Ch. 14.

Lipsey, R.G. and K. Lancaster (1956), "The General Theory of the Second Best", *Review of Economic Studies* 24(1): 11-32.

Fishlow, A. and P.A. David (1961), "Optimal Resource Allocation in an Imperfect Market Setting", *Journal of Political Economy* 69(6): 529-46, December.

Bhagwati, J. and V.K. Ramaswami (1963), "Domestic Distortions, Tariffs and the Theory of the Optimal Subsidy", *Journal of Political Economy* 71(1):44-50, February.

Johnson, H.G. (1965), "Optimal Trade Intervention in the Presence of Domestic Distortions", in R.E. Caves, H.G. Johnson and P.B. Kenen (eds.), *Trade, Growth and the Balance of Payments*, Amsterdam: North Holland.

III. MORE ON ECONOMIC GROWTH AND INCOME DISTRIBUTION

*Johnson, H.G. (1964), "Towards a Generalized Capital Accumulation Approach to Economic Development", pp. 219-27 in *The Residual Factor and Economic Growth*, Paris: OECD.

*Schultz, T.W. (1972), "The Increasing Economic Value of Human Time", *American Journal of Agricultural Economics* 54(5): 843-50, December.

*Schultz, T.W. (1975), "The Value of the Ability to Deal With Disequilibria", *Journal of Economic Literature* 13(3): 827-46, September.

*Schultz, T.W. (1980), "Nobel Lecture: The Economics of Being Poor", *Journal of Political Economy* 88(4): 639-51, August.

Browning, E.K. and W.R. Johnson (1984), "The Trade-Off Between Equity and Efficiency", *Journal of Political Economy* 92(2): 175-203, April.

Dowrick, S. (1993), "New Theory and Evidence on Economic Growth, and their Implications for Australian Policy", *Economic Analysis and Policy* 23(2), September.

Harberger, A.C. (1962), "The Incidence of the Corporate Income Tax", *Journal of Political Economy* 70(3):215-40, June.

Mieszkowski, P.M. (1969), "Tax Incidence Theory: The Effects of Taxes on the Distribution of Income", *Journal of Economic Literature* 7(3): 1103-24 September.

IV. OTHER APPLICATIONS

*Becker, G.S. (1976), *The Economic Approach to Human Behaviour*, Chicago: University of Chicago Press, Ch. 1.

Johnson, H.G. (1968), "The Economic Approach to Social Questions", *Economica* 25(127): 1-21, February. (Reprinted as Ch. 2 in his *On Economics and.Society*, Chicago: University of Chicago Press, 1975.)

1. Economics of law

*Friedman, D.D. (1990), *Price Theory: An Intermediate Text*, Cincinnati:South-Western, 2nd edition, Ch. 20.

*Varian, H.R. (1993), *Intermediate Microeconomics: A Modern Approach*, New York: Norton, 3rd edition, Ch. 32.

Becker, G.S. (1968), "Crime and Punishment: An Economic Approach", *Journal of Political Economy* 76(2): 169-217, April. (Reprinted in his *The Economic Approach to Human Behaviour*, Chicago: University of Chicago Press, Ch. 4.)

2. Economics of time

*Becker, G.S. (1965), "A Theory of the Allocation of Time", *Economic Journal* 75(299): 493-517, September. (Reprinted in his *The Economic Approach to Human Behaviour*, Chicago: University of Chicago Press, Ch. 5.)

*Schultz, T.W. (1972), "The Increasing Economic Value of Human Time", *American Journal of Agricultural Economics* 54(5): 843-50, December.

3. Economics of households

*Becker, G.S. and R.T. Michael (1965), "On the New Theory of Consumer Behaviour", *Swedish Journal of Economics* 75: 378-95. (Reprinted in his *The Economic Approach to Human Behaviour*, Chicago: University of Chicago Press, Ch. 7. See also his Chs. 9-11 on the economics of marriage, fertility, and the interaction between quality and quantity of children.)

4. Economics of the environment

*Anderson, K. (1992), "The Standard Welfare Economics of Policies Affecting Trade and the Environment", Ch. 2 in *The Greening of World.Trade Issues* edited by K. Anderson and R. Blackhurst, London: Harvester Wheatsheaf and Ann Arbor: University of Michigan Press.

Coase, R. (1960), " The Problem of Social Cost", *Journal of Law and.Economics* 3: 1-44, October.

V. METHODOLOGY OF ECONOMICS

1. Introduction to Scientific Methodology: induction; hypothesis testing and logical positivism/empiricism; falsification (Popper); paradigms (Kuhn) and research programs (Lakatos).

A.F. Chalmers, *What is this Thing Called.Science?* (U. of Queensland Press, 1976).

M. Blaug, *The Methodology of Economics*, (Cambridge U. P., 1980); or B. Caldwell, *Beyond.Positivism: Economic Methodology in the Twentieth Century,* (Allen and Unwin, 1984).

2. Economic Methodology I: The Logical Empiricist Legacy: verification, assumptions and predictions - Machlup, Friedman and their critics; fact/value split and role of ideology; are economists the slaves of defunct philosophers?

* M. Friedman, "The Methodology of Positive Economics", in *Essays in Positive Economics*, (Chicago U. P. 1953).

* T. Mayer, "Friedman's Methodology of Economics: A Soft Reading", *Economic Inquiry* (April 1993).

3. Economic Methodology II: Theory Choice: paradigms, scientific revolutions, research programs and methodological pluralism in economics; is economics a science?; rhetoric and persuasion; what do economists do? From theory to practice: undertaking economic research.

* D.M. Hausman, "Economic Methodology in a Nutshell", *J. of Econ. Perspectives*, Spring 1989.

* D. Colander, "The Lost Art of Economics", *J. of Econ. Perspectives* (Summer 1992).

D.N. McCloskey, "The Rhetoric of Economics", *J. of Econ. Literature*, June 1983. (Note: key sections for this topic are I, V, VI and VIII.)

ADDENDUM: (1) on quantifying the effects of shocks and policy interventions

Corden, W.M. (1971), *The Theory of Protection*, London: Oxford University Press, especially Chs. 2-5.

Clements, K.W. and L.A. Staastad (1984), *How Protection Taxes Exporters*, Thames Essay No. 39, London: Trade Policy Research Centre.

Dixon, P.B., B.R. Parmenter, J. Sutton and D.P. Vincent (1982), *Orani: A Multisectoral Model of the Australian Economy*, Amsterdam: North Holland.

Harris, R. (1984), "Applied General Equilibrium Analysis of Small Open Economies with Scale Economies and Imperfect Competition", *American Economic Review* 74(5): 1016-32, December.

Industries Assistance Commission (1987), *Assistance to Agricultural and. Manufacturing Industries*, Canberra: Australian Government Publishing Service (and annual reports of the IAC/Industry Commission).

(2) On reasons for seemingly inappropriate policies

Corden, W.M. (1974, pp. 54-57, 107-114, 231-235).

Breton, A. (1974), *The Economic Theory of Representative Government*, Chicago: Aldine.

Buchanan, J.M., R.D. Tollison and G. Tullock (eds.) (1980), *Toward. a Theory of the Rent-Seeking Society*, College Station: Texas A and M University Press.

Buchanan, J.M. and G. Tullock (1962), *The Calculus of Consent*, Ann Arbor: University of Michigan Press.

Colander, D.C. (ed.) (1984), *Neoclassical Political Economy*, Cambridge: Ballinger.

Downs, A. (1957), *An Economic Theory of Democracy*, New York: Harper and Row.

Krueger, A.O. (1974), "The Political Economy of the Rent-Seeking Society", *American Economic Review* 69(3):291-303.

Mueller, D.C. (1989), *Public Choice II*, Cambridge: Cambridge University Press.

Olson, M. (1965), *The Logic of Collective Action*, Cambridge: Harvard University Press.

Rowley, C.K., R.D. Tollison and G. Tullock (eds.) (1988), *The Political Economy of Rent-Seeking*, Boston: Kluwer Academic Publishers.

Stigler, G.J. (1975), *The Citizen and. the State*, Chicago: University of Chicago Press, Introduction and Chs. 1, 2 and 8.

ANALYTIC METHODS

RGS Winter 1993

Syllabus

Instructors: Bart Bennett and Jim Hammitt

Office hours: By appointment: x7695 and x7247

Time of Course: Mondays and Wednesdays, 12:00 - 2:00; Room 1748

Texts: A *Primer for Policy Analysis*, Stokey and Zeckhauser, Norton, 1978.
STORM: Quantitative Modeling for Decision Support, Version 3.0, Emmons, Flowers, Khot and Mathur, Holden-Day, 1992.
Introduction to Operations Research, Hillier and Lieberman, Holden-Day, 1990, Fifth Edition. (Only for those with good math skills).

Optional: *Decision Analysis*, Raiffa, Addison-Wesley, 1968, (the classic) or
Quick Analysis, Behn & Vaupel, Basic Books, 1982 (more conversational and accessible).
Applied Operations Research: Examples from Defense Assessment, Shephard, Hartley, Haysman, Thorpe, and Bathe, Plenum Press, 1988 (20 cases with solutions).
Quantitative Methods For Public Decision Making, McKenna, McGraw-Hill, 1980. (Slightly more technical than S and Z, with good brief examples of applications).

Reserve: *Fire Department Deployment Analysis*, The RAND Fire Project, North Holland, 1979.
Analysis For Public Decisions, Quade, North Holland, 1989 (3rd edition).
Urban Operations Research, Larson and Odoni, Prentice-Hall, 1981.
Decisions with Multiple Objectives, Keeney and Raiffa, John Wiley, 1976
Decision Making, Models and Algorithms, Gass, John Wiley, 1985.

Objectives: To introduce students to several tools for policy analysis that are not taught in other RGS courses. By the end of the course, students should be able to formulate models using these tools, solve simple problems, interpret the results, and understand the limitations of the tools.

Assignments: Students will be asked to prepare written assignments on a regular basis. Some exercises will involve use of operations research programs on a diskette. These assignments will either help the student understand the mechanics of the techniques being studied or develop skills in evaluating specific applications of the techniques. You may discuss any problems with your classmates (or anyone else), but the final write-up should be independently done. Other texts are held on reserve in the RGS collection. These are helpful to provide additional insights into subjects discussed in this course.

There are eight sections to the course. Readings in each section are numbered according to class session, and should be read before that class. Some of the optional readings are very long--you could skim for future reference.

Exams: There will be a final. It will be straightforward and simply designed to check your understanding of the material. It will count for approximately 50 percent of the grade. Homework assignments will be graded, and will count for the other 50 percent. Participation, especially in the class discussions, will be used to decide close grading decisions.

Part A.   Framework For Policy Analysis (1 class)

Goal: Become interested in policy analysis and in models

Reading: 1. Stokey and Zeckhauser, Chap. 1-3.
             Hillier and Lieberman, pp. 1-25.
             Fire Department Deployment Analysis, Chap. 3.

Optional: McKenna, Chapter 1

Part B.   Prescriptive Models

Part B.1   Decision Analysis (4 classes)

Goal: Learn how to set out and solve decision trees, using utility theory, subjective probability, and Bayes Theorem. Understand the value of information and how it affects data-gathering. Improve your guesses. Understand the pros and cons of subjective probability and of maximizing expected utility.

Reading: 1. Shed Load case.
             Learn basic probability if necessary (McKenna Chap 2)

             2. Stokey and Zeckhauser, pp. 201-219.
             Raiffa, Chapters 0, 1, 2; or Behn and Vaupel, Chaps. 1-5.

             3. Stokey and Zeckhauser, pp. 217-236;
             Raiffa, Chap. 5, pp. 104-114, Chap. 7, pp. 157-172; or Behn and Vaupel, Chaps. 7, 10.
             Tversky, Amos, and Daniel Kahneman, "Judgment under Uncertainty: Heuristics and Biases," *Science* 185: 1124-1131,1974.

             4. Stokey and Zeckhauser, pp. 237-254.
             Raiffa, Ch. 3 and Ch. 4, pp. 51-88; or Behn and Vaupel, Chaps. 6, 8.
             Tversky, Amos, and Daniel Kahneman, "The Framing of Decisions and the Psychology of Choice," *Science* 211:453-458,1981.

Optional: Easy: *The Value of a Test* (RAND P-5603).
             Raiffa, rest of Chapter 4 (more on risk aversion).

15

Raiffa, rest of Chap. 5, Chap. 6, rest of Chap. 7 (the classic argument for using expected utility).

Machina, Mark J., "Choice Under Uncertainty: Problems Solved and Unsolved," pp. 134-188 in National Research Council, *Valuing Health Risks, Costs, and Benefits for Environmental Decision Making*, National Academy Press, Washington, D.C., 1992.

Phelps, Dale L., and Charles E. Phelps, "Cryotherapy in Infants with Retiopathy of Prematurity: A Decision Model for Treating One or Both Eyes," *JAMA* 231: 1751-1756, 1989 (a medical decision analysis).

Schoemaker, Paul J. H., "The Expected Utility Model: Its Variants, Purposes, Evidence and Limitations," *Journal of Economic Literature* 20: 529-563, 1982 (critiques of expected utility theory).

Thaler, R., "Toward A Positive Theory of Consumer Choice," *Journal of Economic Behavior and Organization* 1: 39-40, 1980.

Thompson, Mark S., "Decision-Analytic Determination of Study Size: The Case of Electronic Fetal Monitoring," *Medical Decision Making* 1:165-179, 1981 (Using EVSI to design a study).

Part B.2   Multi-attribute Outcomes (3 classes)

Goal: Understand the systems approach to multi-attribute problems. Learn to do cost-benefit and cost-effectiveness analysis. Think about how to trade off diverse attributes such as lives and dollars, and when discounting is appropriate.

1. Stokey and Zeckhauser, Chapters 3, 8.

2. Stokey and Zeckhauser, Chapters 9, 10.
Raiffa, pp. 239-255; or Behn and Vaupel Chap. 11.

3. Acton, Jan Paul, "Measuring the Monetary Value of Lifesaving Programs," *Law and Contemporary Problems*, 40: 46-72, 1976.

Goodin, Robert E., "Discounting Discounting," *Journal of Public Policy* 2: 53-72, 1982.

Keeler, Emmett B., and Shan Cretin, "Discounting of Life-Saving and Other Nonmonetary Effects," *Management Science* 29: 300-306, 1983.

Kelman, Steven, "Cost-Benefit Analysis: An Ethical Critique," *Regulation*, 5:33-40, January/February 1981.

Optional: Keeney and Raiffa, Chaps. 3-5 (Technical details of MAUT).

Lind, Robert C., "A Primer on the Major Issues Relating to the Discount Rate for Evaluating National Energy Options," pp. 21-94 in Lind et al., *Discounting for Time and Risk in Energy Policy*, Resources for the Future, Washington, D.C., 1982.

Quade,. 1989 (on reserve) or the classic Quade and Boucher, Systems Analysis and Policy Planning, R-439-PR, 1968

Part B.3   Linear Programming (4 classes)

Goal: Learn the elements of an LP problem. Understand how to obtain graphical solutions. Discussion of duality and sensitivity analysis. Be able to use the computer to solve LP problems. Discussion of other classes of Linear Programming problems.

Reading: 1. Stokey and Zeckhauser, Chap. 11.
             STORM, Chaps. 1 - 4.
             Hillier and Lieberman, pp. 29-52.

             2. *STORM,* Chap. 5.
             Hillier and Lieberman pp. 58-71, 94-100.

             3. & 4. *Applied Operations Research*, Chap. 15 (to be handed out)

Optional: Gass, Parts II and III.
             McKenna, Chap. 8 and 9.

Part C   Descriptive Models

Part C.1   Probabilistic Models—Queueing Theory (3 classes)

Goals: Understand the need for probabilistic analysis; the Poisson Process; components of a queueing system; performance measures; how queueing is used in policy analysis.

Reading: 1. Stokey and Zeckhauser, Chap. 5.
             STORM, Chap. 2.

             2 & 3. Case: Riverview Medical Center Hospital.

Optional: Hillier and Lieberman, Chaps. 16-17 (technical).
             Larson and Odoni, Chap. 4.

Part C.2   Simulation (3 classes)

Goals: Understand the use of simulation as an analytic tool; simulation languages; random number generation; statistical analysis

Reading: 1. Stokey and Zeckhauser, Chap. 6.

             2. Hillier and Lieberman, Chap. 23.

17

3. *Fire Department Deployment Analysis,* Chap 13 (to be handed out).

Part C.3   Deterministic Models—Difference Equations (1 class)

Goals: Understand how to model simple dynamic systems with difference equations. Understand stocks, flows, and equilibrium. Understand life tables.

Reading: 1. Stokey and Zeckhauser, Chap 4.

Part D   Synthesis (1 class)

Goals: Understand the purposes, strengths, and limits of each of the techniques covered in the course; how they are related and how they differ; how to choose an appropriate one; what other tools, methods, classes of problems exist.

Reading: Simon, et al., *Decision Making and Problems Solving,* 1987. Gass, *Managing the Modeling Process,* 1987.

             Hodges, James S., "Six (or So) Things You Can Do with a Bad Model," *Operations Research* 39: 355-365, 1991 (reprinted as N-3381-RC).

FINAL EXAM

Economics 288
Fall 1992

Marcus Berliant

Washington University-St. Louis
Introduction to Individual Decision Theory, Game Theory and Social Choice
COURSE DESCRIPTION

This course is an introduction to individual decision theory, game theory, and social choice.

Individual decision theory is the study of how individuals make choices when facing uncertainty. Its study is a prerequisite to the study of game theory, which is a theory of how these individuals interact.

The emphasis of the course will be on elementary game theory. Game theory is a branch of mathematics that has important applications to statistics, biology, political science, economics, and other areas. Here we will focus on applications to economics and political science.

Social choice is an application of game theory to the mechanisms that groups of individuals use to make choices.

This course is self–contained, so there are no prerequisites. However, students taking this course in the past have indicated that knowledge of basic calculus (Math 141–142 or 161–162) greatly facilitates comprehension of the material. The following courses are helpful and will make this course easier to understand:

Math 207, Economics 207, 208, 256, 274.

COURSE REQUIREMENTS

By the end of this course, you are expected to understand basic game theory, to be able to solve simple games, and to know about the fundamental applications of game theory to economics and political science. There will be four homework sets during the term, each worth 5% of the grade (for a total of 20%). A midterm worth 30% of the grade will be given in class. The final exam is scheduled for Monday, December 21 at 12:30 and is worth 50% of the grade. There will be 500 total points possible in the course. Points will be allocated to homework sets and exams according to the percentages.

WARNING: Students taking this course in the past have often waited until the last moment to start work on their homework, and as a consequence have found that they have had insufficient time to complete it. Game theory problems are generally much more difficult than they might appear to be at first glance. You will have approximately two weeks to complete each homework set.

This course is cross listed as Political Science 288 and 488. Those students taking the course as 488 are required to write a paper of 10 pages or less on material related to the course. The paper topic must be cleared with the instructor. This paper will be graded pass/fail, and a passing grade is required to pass this course. In this manner, 488 students can be included on the same curve as others.

OFFICE HOURS

My office is located at 213 Harkness.

Office hours are tentatively:
                                        Tuesday   1–2 pm
                                          Thursday 1–2 pm

I hope to have a TA for this course. The functions of the TA will be to grade homework sets, help grade exams, and hold office hours and recitations.

READINGS

The homework and exams will be based on both the lectures and readings, but primarily on the lectures.

Undergraduate game theory courses are relatively new, so there is a general lack of decent texts. The main textbook for the course, which is an order of magnitude better than any of the others available and was just recently published, is

Fun and Games by K. Binmore. (Abbreviation B)

Binmore is very good at explaining things, but does not cover the very basic material (decision theory) or our applications. An alternative text to Binmore is

Games and Information by Rasmusen. (Abbreviation G&I)

This was the first textbook written for an undergraduate game theory course, and was published only two years ago. I think that Binmore is superior to Rasmusen, but you might feel otherwise. A persistent problem with this course is that the available texts are adequate, but not good.

Games and Decisions by Luce and Raiffa (Abbreviation L+R)

This textbook is considered a well–written classic and contains the essential material of the field. It is written for graduate students, and therefore should be used with caution.

The text for decision theory is

Decision Analysis: Introductory Lectures on Choices Under Uncertainty by Raiffa. (Abbreviation: R)

This paperback will be used for the first few weeks of the course.

The text for social choice and the important interactions between game theory and economics is

Welfare Economics and Social Choice by A. Feldman. (Abbreviation: F)

All of these texts are on reserve at the library, and have been ordered by the bookstore; I suspect that some are out of print. You should use them to supplement and clarify lectures. **There is no need to buy all of the texts.** I would suggest purchasing Binmore and perhaps Raiffa.

A list of topics and associated readings follows. We will not spend exactly one lecture on each topic or sub–topic, nor will we cover any text completely. The texts are listed from best to worst for each topic.

Topic	Textbook Chapters
I. Introduction	B ch. 0; R Ch. 0; L+R Ch. 1
II. Individual Decision Theory	
A. Basic Decision Theory: The Extensive Form	R Ch. 1, 2
B. Expected Utility Theory	R Ch. 4,5; B ch. 3; L+R Ch. 2, Appendix 1
C. The Normal Form	R Ch. 6
III. Game Theory	
A. Noncooperative Game Theory	
1. Two Players	B ch. 1, 2, 4, 6, 7, 8; L+R Ch. 3, 4, 5, Appendices 2–6
2. n Players	B ch. 10; G&I Part I; L+R Ch. 7.1 – 7.8
B. Cooperative Game Theory	
1. Two Players	B ch. 5.1 – 5.5; G&I ch.10.1 – 10.2; L+R Ch. 6
2. n Players	L+R Ch. 7.9, 8, 11.4
IV. Applications to Economics	
A. Noncooperative Theory and Imperfect Competition	B ch. 7.2; G&I Ch. 12.1 – 12.2
B. The Core of a Market Economy (Cooperative)	F Ch. 1, 2, 3 Hildenbrand & Kirman, on reserve for ECO 541 in the Management Library, or may be borrowed from instructor
V. Application to Political Science (Noncooperative)	F Ch. 9
VI. Social Choice and Mechanism Design	F Ch. 10, 11; G&I pp. 173 – 175; L+R Ch. 14
VII. Application to Public Finance	F ch. 6

Lecture Outline for the Semester

Caution: We might deviate from this, but it is provided for your use.

0. Organizational Matters

I. Introduction
    A. What is Game Theory?
    B. A Brief History

II. Individual Decision Theory
    A. Basic Decision Theory: The Extensive Form
        1. Trees
        2. Backwards Induction: Dynamic Programming
        3. Conditional Probabilities and Bayes' Rule
    B. Expected Utility Theory
        1. Introduction
        2. Preferences and Utility
        3. Preferences over Lotteries and Subjective Probability
        4. Risk Aversion
        5. Application to Trees
        6. Certainty Equivalents
        7. The Allais Paradox
    C. The Normal Form

III. Game Theory
    A. Introduction
    B. Noncooperative Game Theory
        1. Extensive and Normal Forms
        2. Two Player Zero Sum Games
            a. The Normal Form
            b. The Extensive Form
        3. Two Player Non–Zero Sum Games
            a. The Normal Form
            b. Repeated Normal Form Games
            c. The Extensive Form
            d. Refinements
        4. n – Player Games
            a. The Normal Form
            b. The Extensive Form
            c. Kuhn's Theorem
    C. Cooperative Game Theory
        1. Introduction
        2. Two Player Games
        3. n – Player Games

22

Washington University-St Louis

ECO 506: SELECTED TOPICS IN GENERAL EQUILIBRIUM THEORY

Marcus Berliant
Spring 1994

Thursdays 9:00–12:00 am
Harkness 208

Course Syllabus and Reading List

This course will cover topics of interest in mathematical economics, with particular emphasis on topics in general equilibrium theory. A selection of both classical and contemporary material will be covered. Much of the course will be devoted to studying smooth economies.

Organization of the Course

This will be a lecture course. A homework set will account for 20% of the grade, while an in–class final examination will account for the remainder. The homework and exam will be based on both the lectures and readings, but primarily on the lectures.

Each student taking the course for credit will be required to present a research paper (by someone famous) in class. A fine selection of such papers is available in my office. Students should choose their papers in the first two weeks of class. Presentations will then be scheduled for the last few class meetings and the selected papers will be distributed to the entire class. Presentations will be limited to 90 minutes and will be graded on a pass/fail basis. It is necessary to pass this component of the course in order to pass the course.

Mathematics

Those students who have had Economics 505 or a course in mathematical analysis have an adequate mathematics background. The additional mathematics needed to understand this material will be presented in class in a relatively superficial manner. Students who wish to write papers on smooth economies or who want to have a deep understanding of the material should take (or have taken) a course on differential topology, such as Mathematics 541. Mathematics texts containing the material are listed below. They are on reserve and will be discussed further at the first class meeting.

The texts for the main part of the course are as follows. They are on reserve in the management library.

Andreu Mas–Colell, <u>The Theory of General Economic Equilibrium: A Differentiable Approach</u>, Cambridge University Press, 1985.

Egbert Dierker, <u>Topological Methods in Walrasian Economics</u>, Springer–Verlag, 1974.

Overviews of the requisite mathematics can be found in Chapter 1 of Mas–Colell's book and chapters 2–3 of Dierker's book.

Useful mathematics texts (in order of increasing difficulty):

V. Guillemin and A. Pollack, <u>Differential Topology</u>, Prentice–Hall, 1974.

J. Milnor, <u>Topology from a Differentiable Viewpoint</u>, University of Virginia Press, 1965.

M. W. Hirsch, <u>Differential Topology</u>, Springer–Verlag, 1976.

M. Golubitsky and V. Guillemin, <u>Stable Mappings and Their Singularities</u>, Springer–Verlag, 1973.

These are on reserve in the small mathematics library.

The reading list is flexible. If the class is either uninterested in or has already seen some topics, they can be skipped. Others can be added, if desired.

We will start with some topics in consumer theory, as I believe strongly that it is very important to have a firm classical foundation in this area. The main part of the course on smooth economies will then be covered. Finally, a lecture or two will address computation of equilibria. We will then proceed with paper presentations.

The sections marked with an asterisk (*) will not be covered in class due to time constraints. However, students taking the qualifying exam in general equilibrium should be aware that this material is covered on the qualifying examination.

These readings by no means form a complete list, but are merely a subjective selection of some of the important work in each area. (I would be happy to supply a more extensive reading list on a topic to anyone interested.) They will be on reserve in the management library.

I.   Topics in Consumer Theory

   A.   Representation of Preferences by Utility Functions

Debreu, G., "Continuity Properties of Paretian Utility," IER 5:3, September 1964.

Bowen, R., "A New Proof of a Theorem in Utility Theory," IER 9:3, October 1968.

Peleg, B., "Utility Functions for Partially Ordered Topological Spaces," Econometrica 38, January 1970.

B. Expected Utility Theory

Herstein, I. and J. Milnor, "An Axiomatic Approach to Measurable Utility," Econometrica 21, 1953, reprinted in Newman, Readings in Mathematical Economics.

C. Risk Aversion

Arrow, K.J., "The Theory of Risk Aversion," chapter 3 in Essays in the Theory of Risk Bearing, 1971.

Pratt, J.W., "Risk Aversion in the Small and Large," Econometrica 32, 1964.

Rothschild, M. and J.E. Stiglitz, "Increasing Risk I: A Definition," JET 3, 1971.

D. Non – Expected Utility Theory

Machina, M., "'Expected Utility' Analysis without the Independence Axiom," Econometrica 50, 1982, pp. 277–323.

E. Subjective Probability Theory

Savage, L., The Foundations of Statistics, Wiley, 1954 (Second Edition, Dover, 1972).

Arrow, K.J., "Exposition of the Theory of Choice under Uncertainty," chapter 2 of Decision and Organization, ed. by McGuire and Radner, North Holland, 1972.

F. Separable Utility

Debreu, G., "Topological Methods in Cardinal Utility Theory," Chapter 1 of Mathematical Methods in the Social Sciences, Stanford University Press, 1959.

Gorman, T., "The Structure of Utility Functions," ReStud 53, 1968.

Koopmans, T., chapter 3 of <u>Decision and Organization</u>, ed. by McGuire and Radner, North Holland, 1972.

G. Intertemporal Preferences

Koopmans, T., chapter 4 of <u>Decision and Organization</u>.

H. Revealed Preferences

Richter, M., "Revealed Preference Theory," <u>Econometrica</u> 34, July 1966.

I. Spaces of Preferences

Hildenbrand, W., <u>Core and Equilibria of a Large Economy</u>, Princeton University Press, 1974, Part I.B.3.

J. Concave Representations

Hildenbrand and Kirman, <u>Introduction to Equilibrium Analysis</u>, Appendix to ch. 2.

Kannai, Y., "Approximation of Convex Preferences," <u>JME</u> 1 (1974).

II. Existence*

Weintraub, E. Roy, "On the Existence of Competitive Equilibrium: 1930 – 1954," <u>Journal of Economic Literature</u> 21, March 1983, pp. 1–39.

Debreu, G., "Market Equilibrium," <u>Proceedings N.A.S.</u> 42, 1956, pp. 876–878.

McKenzie, L., "On the Existence of General Equilibrium for a Competitive Market," <u>Econometrica</u> 27, 1959, pp. 54–71.

Debreu, G., "New Concepts and Techniques for Equilibrium Analysis," <u>IER</u> 3:3, September 1962.

Bergstrom, T., "How to Discard 'Free Disposability' – At No Cost," <u>JME</u> 3, 1976, pp. 135–139.

Mas–Colell, A., "Equilibrium Theory with Possibly Satiated Preferences," mimeo., 1988.

III. Welfare*

Debreu, G., "Valuation Equilibrium and Pareto Optimum," <u>Proceedings N.A.S.</u>, 1954, reprinted in <u>Readings in Welfare Economics</u>, Arrow and Scitovsky, eds.

IV. Smooth Economies

Here we will use the two texts as well as the following articles.

A. Preferences

Debreu, G., "Smooth Preferences," _Econometrica_ 40, 1972.

Debreu, G., "Smooth Preferences: A Corrigendum," _Econometrica_, 1976.

B. Exchange Economies

Debreu, G., "Economies with a Finite Set of Equilibria," _Econometrica_ 38, 1970.

Dierker, E., "Two Remarks on the Number of Equilibria of an Economy," _Econometrica_ 40, 1972.

C. Production Economies

Kehoe, T., "Regularity and Index Theory for Economies with Smooth Production Technologies," _Econometrica_ 51, July 1983, pp. 895–918.

D. Incomplete Markets

Cass, D., "Incomplete Financial Markets and Indeterminacy of Competitive Equilibrium," CARESS Working paper #90–23 (1990), University of Pennsylvania.

Hirsch, M.D., M. Magill, and A. Mas–Colell, "A Geometric Approach to a Class of Equilibrium Existence Theorems," _Journal of Mathematical Economics_ 19 (1990) 95–106.

V. Computation of Equilibria

Debreu, G., "Four Aspects of the Mathematical Theory of Economic Equilibrium," _Proceedings of the International Congress of Mathematicians_ in Vancouver, 1974.

Scarf, H.E., "Computation of General Equilibria," in _The New Palgrave: A Dictionary of Economics_, edited by J. Eatwell, M. Milgate, and P. Newman (1987).

Eaves, B.C., "Properly Labelled Simplexes," in _Studies in Optimization_, Mathematical Association of America Studies in Mathematics vol. 10, G.B. Dantzig and B.C. Eaves, eds.

Todd, M.J., _The Computation of Fixed Points and Applications_, Springer – Verlag Lecture Notes in Economics and Mathematical Systems no. 124, 1976.

Smale, S., "A Convergent Process of Price Adjustment and Global Newton Methods," _Journal of Mathematical Economics_ 3 (1976), 107–120.

28

Marcus Berliant

LECTURE OUTLINE

I. Consumer Theory

    A. Representations of Preferences by Utility Functions

        1. Binary Relations
        2. Preference Relations
        3. Utility Representations for Partial Orders
        4. Utility Representations for Complete Preorders

    B. Expected Utility Theory

    C. Risk Aversion

        1. Introduction

        2. Measures of Risk Aversion

        3. Uncertain Prospects

            a. Mean – Variance
            b. Rothschild – Stiglitz

    D. Non – Expected Utility Theory

    E. Subjective Probability Theory

    F. Separable Utility

    G. Intertemporal Preferences

    H. Revealed Preferences

    I. Spaces of Preferences

        1. The Topology of Closed Convergence
        2. Continuity Properties of Correspondences
        3. Preferences

    J. Concave Representations

IV. Smooth Economies

    A. Introduction and Mathematics

UNIVERSITY OF CANTERBURY   DEPARTMENT OF ECONOMICS

ECON 301

ALLOCATION THEORY

1995

Objective

The objective of this course is to establish the foundations of modern economic analysis and techniques. The course operates on two levels. On one level, the course provides a rigorous analysis of how resources and output are allocated in decentralized economy. The first half of the course is devoted to a detailed analysis of the economic behaviour of individual consumers and producers. Then, we examine the coordination of consumption and production decisions in decentralized markets, and the outcomes for social welfare. We also analyse the impact of imperfect competition on market behaviour using recent developments in game theory.

At a deeper level, ECON 301 is a course about how economists *do* economics. In the course, you will learn how to model mathematically issues in economics. You will be expected to master the fundamental analytical tools of economics - constrained optimization, comparative statics and elementary game theory. Assignments and tutorials will give you the opportunity to hone these analytical skills and to apply them to questions of topical interest.

Lecturer   Michael Carter
                    Room 409   Phone   364 2524
                    Office hours   Monday   2-3 pm
                                    Wednesday 9-11 am

Lectures   Tuesday 1.10 - 3.00 pm, Lecture Theatre S6

Tutorials Monday   3.10 - 4.00 pm   Room 444 (Economics)
               Another tutorial stream may be held if demand warrants.

Tutorial exercises will be distributed and students will be expected to complete the exercises **before** the tutorial.

Assessment

Assessment in the course comprises five assignments (5% each), a test (20%) and a final examination (50%). The remaining 5% will be earned in tutorials where your preparation and contribution will be assessed. The timetable for assessment is:

	Weight	Due Date
Assignment 1	5	April 4
Assignment 2	5	May 16
Test	20	June 13
Assignment 3	5	July 11
Assignment 4	5	August 8
Assignment 5	5	October 3
Final examination	50	October 27

Assignments must be submitted no later than the beginning of the lecture on the date due, and no credit will be given for assignments which are submitted late. As senior students, you are expected to be able to timetable your work to meet deadlines in spite of the exigencies of life. In exceptional circumstances, exemption may be granted for individual assignments.

References

The course will follow closely the first half of the text

Varian, H   *Microeconomic Analysis*, 3rd edition (Norton, 1992)

This is the advanced version of the ECON 204 text. You are **strongly recommended** to also acquire

Binger, B & Hoffman, E *Microeconomics with Calculus* (Scott-Foresman, 1988)

which will help bridge the gap from ECON 204. In particular, the concrete examples presented in Binger and Hoffman will elucidate the more general theory presented in lectures and provide some guidance to answering the tutorial questions and assignments. Although both texts are available on 3 hour loan from the Restricted Loans Unit in the Main Library, you are encouraged to purchase personal copies. (Note: Varian is also used Honours/Masters course.)

Frequent reference will also be made to

Carter, M   *Foundations of Mathematical Economics* (forthcoming, MIT Press)

Some sections will be distributed for use in class, although arrangements for this have not yet been finalised. A draft copy of the manuscript will be placed in the Restricted Loans unit of the Library.

The following references will be helpful as supplementary reading for various parts of the course:

Birchenhall, C & Grout, P *Mathematics for Modern Economics* (Philip Allan, 1984)

Chambers, R *Applied Production Analysis: A Dual Approach* (Cambridge University Press, 1988)

Chiang, A *Fundamental Methods of Mathematical Economics* 3rd. edition (McGraw-Hill, 1984)

Deaton, A & Muellbauer, J. *Economics and Consumer Behaviour* (Cambridge University Press, 1980)

Dixit, A *Optimization in Economic Theory* 2nd. edition (Oxford University Press, 1990)

Kreps, D *A Course in Microeconomic Theory* (Princeton University Press, 1990)

Silberberg, E *The Structure of Economics: A Mathematical Analysis* 2nd. edition (McGraw-Hill, 1990)

They should be available for 3 day loan in the Restricted Loans Unit.

Outline and Reading List

The numbers in brackets are the approximate number of lecture hours devoted to each topic. Topics will not necessarily be presented sequentially. For example, Constrained Optimization (Topic 1) will integrated with the rest of the course; similarly Oligopoly Theory (Topic 4.3) will be presented concurrently with Game Theory (Topic 5).

1. Constrained Optimization (4)

Carter	Ch. 4
Varian	Ch. 27
Binger & Hoffman	Ch. 2, 3
Dixit	Ch. 1-8, Appendix
Birchenhall & Grout	Ch. 5, 8, 9, 12.2, 13
Chiang	Ch. 21
Silberberg Ch.	Ch. 7, 14

2. Theory of the Producer (15)

2.1. Technology

Varian	Ch. 1
Binger & Hoffman	Ch. 10
Chambers	Ch. 1

2.2. Profit Maximization

Varian	Ch. 2
Binger & Hoffman	Ch. 12
Silberberg	Ch. 1,4

2.3 The Profit Function

Varian	Ch. 3
Birchenhall & Grout	Ch. 11.4, 12.4
Chambers	Ch. 4
Silberberg	Ch. 7.1-7.3

2.4. Cost Minimization

Varian	Ch. 4
Binger & Hoffman	Ch. 11
Birchenhall & Grout	Ch. 11.3
Silberberg	Ch. 8.5-8.7, 8.9

2.4. Cost Functions

Varian	Ch. 5
Binger & Hoffman	Ch. 11
Birchenhall & Grout	Ch. 12.4
Silberberg	Ch. 8.1-8.4, 8.8, 8.10
Chambers	Ch. 2

2.5. Duality

Varian	Ch. 6
Silberberg	Ch. 9.3

3. Theory of the Consumer (12)

3.1. Utility maximization

Varian	Ch. 7
Binger & Hoffman	Ch. 5.1-5.5, 8.1-8.4, 8.10
Birchenhall & Grout	Ch. 10, 11.2, 12.3
Silberberg	Ch 10.1-10.3, 10.5-10.6
Deaton & Muellbauer	Ch. 2.1-2.5

3.2. Choice

Varian	Ch.8
Binger & Hoffman	Ch. 5.6-5.8, 6,8.6, 8.7
Silberberg	Ch. 10.4, 11.1-1.2
Deaton & Muellbauer	Ch. 2.6, 3

3.3. Consumer Demand

Varian	Ch. 9
Binger & Hoffman	Ch. 9, 17.2-17.4
Carter, M	"An expository note on the composite commodity theorem", *Economic Theory*, forthcoming
Silberberg	Ch 10.7, 11.3
Deaton & Muellbauer	Ch. 4.1, 5, 6

3.4 Consumers' surplus

Varian	Ch. 10
Binger & Hoffman	Ch. 8.8-8.9
Silberberg	Ch. 11.5

Microeconomics

Economics 411

Spring 1995

University of Arizona
Professor James Cox
401NN McClelland Hall
621-2164

Course Syllabus

<u>Objectives</u>: The primary objective of this course is to develop students' understanding of microeconomic theory. We will study mathematical models of economic agents and both market and nonmarket institutions. We will study the ability of some of the models to predict outcomes in laboratory experiments with human decisionmakers. Students will participate in experiments, and hence "observe" their own behavior, in addition to reading about experiments with other real decisionmakers. This course is designed to help prepare students for graduate study in economics and related disciplines.

<u>Prerequisites</u>: Prerequisites for this course are Mathematics 125b and Economics 300 or 361. Any student who has not satisfied these prerequisites will be dropped from the course unless he has convinced the instructor that he is adequately prepared to undertake the course material.

<u>Participation</u>: Students are expected to attend class regularly, to participate in experiments in the Economic Science Laboratory, to do assigned problem sets, and to actively participate in classroom discussion.

<u>Grading</u>: Course grades will be based on cumulative points earned in experiments, two midterm exams, and a final exam. You can elect to drop any one exam or the cumulative experimental points as a determinant of your grade. The remaining exams and/or cumulative experimental points will be given equal weight in determining your grade. Any missed experiment cannot be made up. Make-up exams will only be given for good cause, such as illness, and by prior arrangement with the instructor.

<u>Reading</u>: There is no required textbook for this course. Instead, several books and articles have been put on reserve in the reserve book room of the main library. Additional articles may be put on reserve or distributed during the semester.

<u>Topics</u>: Course topics include competitive markets, monopoly, duopoly, revealed preference, public goods, noncooperative games, uncertainty, information asymmetry, auction markets, and rational expectations.

<u>Office Hours</u>: Mondays 3:15 - 5:00 PM, Thursdays 1:00 - 2:30 pm, and by appointment

Economics 411
University of Arizona

Professor Cox
Spring 1995

First Examination

INSTRUCTIONS: Answer four out of the following five questions. The questions are weighted equally.

1. Explain (a) the price-taking hypothesis, (b) the complete knowledge hypothesis, and (c) the Hayek hypothesis. What was learned about these hypotheses from the experiments reported by Vernon Smith on this topic? Explain how the experiments support the author's conclusions.

2. Explain the standard textbook theory of monopoly using either graph(s) or equations. What are the key assumptions about information and behavior contained in this model? What was learned about monopoly pricing and allocative efficiency from the experiments reported in the article by Vernon Smith on this topic? Explain how the experiments support the author's conclusions.

3. Explain what it means for a utility function to "rationalize a set of observations." Explain what it means for a utility function to be "locally nonsatiated." What is the necessary condition for the existence of a locally nonsatiated utility function that rationalizes a set of observations? Prove that your answer is correct.

4. Assume that an economic agent's preferences satisfy the axioms of expected utility theory. Also assume that the agent prefers the binary lottery $[\frac{1}{2}x, \frac{1}{2}y,]$ to the binary $[\frac{1}{2}a, \frac{1}{2}b]$.

   Then do you know which of the following two lotteries the agent prefers: $[\frac{1}{3}x, \frac{1}{3}y, \frac{1}{3}z]$ or $[\frac{1}{3}a, \frac{1}{3}b, \frac{1}{3}z]$? Use the axioms to prove that your answer is correct.

5. What are the testable implications of the strong axiom of revealed preference? Derive them.

37

Second Examination

INSTRUCTIONS: Answer all of the questions. The questions are weighted equally.

1. Consider a market with two firms that produce quantities y_1 and y_2 of a homogeneous commodity. Let the market inverse demand function be $p = 108 - 3y_1 - 3y_2$. Let the firms' cost functions be $c_1(y_1) = 36y_1$ and $c_2(y_2) = 36y_2$. Then:

    a. Find the Stackelberg equilibrium quantities and equilibrium price.

    b. Find the Cournot-Nash equilibrium quantities and equilibrium price.

2. Consider a market with two firms that produce quantities y_1 and y_2 of a homogeneous commodity. Let the market inverse demand function be $p = 30 - \frac{1}{2}y_1 - \frac{1}{2}y_2$. Let the firms' cost functions be $c_1(y_1) = \frac{1}{2}(y_1)^2$ and $c_2(y_2) = \frac{1}{2}(y_2)^2$. Then:

    a. Find the collusive monopoly quantities and price.

    b. Is there an incentive for the firms to cheat on the cartel agreement? Prove that your answer is correct.

3. Does the following game have one or more pure strategy Nash equilibria? Does it have a Nash equilibrium that is Pareto-optimal? Does it have a Nash equilibrium that is not Pareto-optimal? Explain.

	Left	Middle	Right
Top	8, 10	8, 8	2, 6
Middle	10, -2	6, 2	4, 6
Bottom	6, 4	2, 8	-2, 10

Was the behavior in the in-class matrix game experiment consistent with the prediction of Nash equilibrium outcomes? Explain.

4. There are two bidders. Both are risk neutral. The bidders values for the auctioned item are independently drawn from the uniform distribution on $[0, 5]$. Then:

    a. Derive the Nash equilibrium bid function for the first-price sealed-bid auction.

    b. Was bidding behavior in the in-class first-price auction experiment consistent with this model? Explain.

    c. Derive the Nash equilibrium bid function for the second-price sealed-bid auction.

Final Examination

INSTRUCTIONS: Answer all of the questions. The four numbered questions are weighted equally.

1. Consider a model with two types of workers. Type 1 workers have productivity v_1 and can acquire education at cost c_1 per unit. Type 2 workers have productivity v_2 and can acquire education at cost c_2 per unit. Assume that the workers know their own productivities. Also assume that a prospective employer cannot observe the workers' productivities. Then:

    (a) Under what condition(s) will there be a pooling equilibrium in which all workers are hired at the same wage?
    (b) Under what condition(s) will there ba a separating equilibrium in which the more productive workers are hired at a higher wage?

2. C. Garcia and J. Smith have the following utility functions:

    | | Utility Functions | |
Prizes	Garcia	Smith
$ 0	0	0
$ 4	2	10
$12	6	12.25
$16	8	20
$25	12.5	25
$36	18	30
$49	24.5	35

    In this table, the left column lists the dollar amounts of several possible prizes or payoffs. The middle column shows the utility of each of the prizes to C. Garcia. The right column shows the utility of the prizes to J. Smith. Assume that Lottery A offers a 1/3 chance of winning a prize of $36 and a 2/3 chance of no prize (or $0).

    (a) What is the maximum amount of money that Garcia would be willing to pay to play Lottery A? What is the maximum amount that Smith would pay to play this lottery?

    (b) What are Garcia's and Smith's risk premiums for Lottery A?

    (c) Who is more risk averse, Garcia or Smith? Explain.

3. Consider the following game matrix.

	Left	Middle	Right
Top	a,b	c,d	e,f
Middle	g,h	i,j	k,l
Bottom	m,n	o,p	q,r

    Answer the following questions.

    (a) If (Middle,Right) is a Nash equilibrium, then what inequalities must hold among the payoff amounts a, b, c, ...q,r?

    (b) If (Middle,Right) is Pareto optimal then what inequalities must hold among the payoff amounts a, b, c, ..., q,r?

    (c) If (Middle,Right) is a dominant strategy equilibrium, then what inequalities must hold among the payoff amounts a, b, c, ..., q,r?

4. Assume that a monetary loss in the amount, 3, can occur with probability, P. The economic agent can influence P by exercising caution, but this will be costly. Let the cost, C, required to achieve probability P be given by $C=4(1-P)^3$. Assume that the agent is risk neutral.

(a) If insurance is <u>not</u> available, what probability of a loss will the agent choose?

An insurance policy that pays the full amount of the loss (if it occurs) is now available at a total premium or price Φ (i.e., the policy cost is Φ, not ΦL).

(b) If insurance has already been purchased, what probability of a loss will the agent choose?

(c) Given your answer to part (b), what premium must an insurance company charge in order to "break even" (i.e., to have zero expected profit)?

(d) Using your answers to parts (a) and (c), prove that a risk neutral agent will not purchase any insurance at the premium which must be charged in order for the insurance company to break even.

(e) What feature of actual insurance policies does result (d) explain?

Introduction to Experimental Economics
SYLLABUS
ECONOMICS 506
PROFESSOR JAMES C. COX   **G**
FALL 1994

<u>Course Objectives</u>

This course is an introduction to experimental economics that is intended to:

a.   expose you to a varied set of experimental research papers;

b.   guide you to think about economic theory from the perspective of an empirical science; and

c.   provide you with a working knowledge of techniques for conducting laboratory experiments in economics.

<u>Course Requirements</u>

There are four graded requirements, each of which counts for 25% of your course grade:

1.   a midterm exam;

2.   a survey paper on experimental research, due on the last day the class meets;

3.   an experimental research proposal, due during the scheduled final exam period for this course; and

4.   a class presentation based on your survey paper, your experimental research proposal, or both.

Nongraded course requirements include participation in class discussions and in laboratory experiments during the scheduled class period. During participation in experiments, each of you will accumulate a subject payoff amount. These are the amounts that are paid to the subjects in U.S. currency ("cold cash") when the subjects' responses are to be used in research papers. Your subject payoff amounts from class-period experiments will not be paid to you in cash; instead, they will be paid in "priority rights" in the following way. The student with the highest cumulative (over all experiments) payoff amount will have first choice from the scheduled days for student class presentations. The student with the second-highest cumulative payoff will have second choice, and so on.

Class assignments for the first part of the semester are listed on "Course Outline I" and on the "Core Reading List." Class assignments for the second part of the semester will consist of student presentations and discussion of topics that we all will select.

The class will meet on Tuesdays and Thursdays, 3:30-4:45 p.m. The regular classroom is room 119 in McClelland Hall. On days when we are conducting experiments we will meet in the old laboratory, room 100 in the Economics Building.

The instructor's office is room 401-NN in McClelland Hall. His office hours are 10:00-11:30 on Mondays and Wednesdays, and by appointment (phone #621-2164).

a. Discussion of course content and some elementary economic models.

b. Laboratory experiment.

c. Discussion of papers 1 and 2 on the core reading list.

d. Discussion of papers 3 and 4 on the core reading list.

e. Discussion of papers 5 and 6 on the core reading list.

f. Laboratory experiment.

g. Discussion of papers 7, 8, and 9 on the core reading list.

h. Laboratory experiment.

i. Discussion of papers 10 and 11 on the core reading list.

j. Laboratory experiment.

k. Discussion of papers 12 and 13 on the core reading list.

l. Laboratory experiment.

m. Discussion of papers 14 and 15 on the core reading list.

n. Laboratory experiment.

o. Discussion of papers 16 and 17 on the core reading list.

p. Discussion: integration and wrap-up.

q. Midterm exam.

ECON 506: CORE READING LIST

1. V. Smith, "Markets as Economizers of Information: Experimental Examination of the Hayek Hypothesis," Economic Inquiry, vol. 20, April 1982, pp. 165-179.

2. V. Smith, "An Empirical Study of Decentralized Institutions of Monopoly Restraint," pp. 83-106 in G. Horwich and J. Quirk (eds.), Essays in Contemporary Fields of Economics (West Lafayette: Purdue University Press, 1981).

3. V. Smith, "Theory, Experiment, and Economics," Journal of Economic Perspectives, vol. 3, Winter 1989, pp. 151-169.

4. V. Smith, "Economics in the Laboratory," Journal of Economic Perspectives, vol. 8, Winter 1994, pp. 113-131.

5. R. Battalio, et al., "A Test of Consumer Demand Theory Using Observations of Individual Consumer Purchases," Western Economic Journal, vol. 11, December 1973, pp. 411-428.

6. J. Cox, "On Testing the Utility Hypothesis," discussion paper, University of Arizona, August 1994.

7. D. Grether and C. Plott, "Economic Theory of Choice and the Preference Reversal Phenomenon," American Economic Review, vol. 69, September 1979, pp. 623-638.

8. J. Cox and M. Isaac, "Experimental Economics and Experimental Psychology: Ever the Twain Shall Meet?" pp. 647-669 in A.J. MacFadyen and H.W. MacFadyen (eds.), Economic Psychology: Intersections in Theory and Application (New York: North-Holland, 1986).

9. J. Cox and D. Grether, "The Preference Phenomenon: Response Mode, Markets and Incentives," discussion paper, University of Arizona, August 1992, revised July 1993.

10. J. Cox, B. Roberson, and V. Smith, "Theory and Behavior of Single Object Auctions," pp. 1-43 in V. Smith (ed.), Research in Experimental Economics, vol. 2 (Greenwich: JAI Press, 1982).

11. J. Cox, V. Smith, and J. Walker, "Theory and Behavior of First-Price Auctions," Journal of Risk and Uncertainty, vol. 1, March 1988, pp. 61-100.

12. R. Forsythe, T. Palfrey, and C. Plott, "Asset Valuation in an Experimental Market," Econometrica, vol. 50, May 1982, pp. 537-567.

13. V. Smith, G. Suchanek, and A. Williams, "Bubbles, Crashes and Endogenous Expectations in Experimental Spot Asset Markets," Econometrica, vol. 56, September 1988, pp. 119-1151.

14. V. Smith, "Experiments with a Decentralized Mechanism for Public Goods Decision," American Economic Review, vol. 70, September 1980, pp. 584-599.

15. M. Isaac and J. Walker, "Group Size Effects in Public Goods Provision: The Voluntary Contributions Mechanism," Quarterly Journal of Economics, February 1988, vol. 103, pp. 179-199.

16. R. Cooper, D. Dejong, R. Forsythe, and T. Ross, "Forward Induction in the Battle of the Sexes Games," American Economic Review, vol. 83, December 1993, pp. 1303-1316.

17. E. Hoffman, K. McCabe, K. Shachat, and V. Smith, "Preferences, Property Rights, and Anonymity in Bargaining Games," discussion paper, University of Arizona, Jan. 1993; forthcoming in Games and Economic Behavior.

Mid-term Exam

Answer four out of the following five questions. The questions are weighted equally.

1. What is a "heuristic experiment"? Choose a paper from the reading list that reports heuristic experiments. (Why were the experiments conducted?) How were they designed? What was learned from these heuristic experiments? In what sense are these experiments not heuristic but, rather, theory-testing experiments?

2. What is a theory-testing experiment? Choose a paper from the reading list that reports theory-testing experiments. (Why were the experiments conducted?) How were they designed? What was learned from these theory-testing experiments? In what sense are these experiments not theory-testing but, rather, heuristic experiments?

3. The results from individual choice experiments are often inconsistent with the predictions of expected utility theory while the results from market experiments are often consistent with the predictions of that theory. What insights into this apparent inconsistency are provided by the Cox-Grether paper on preference reversal experiments.

4. Explain the Smith auction (SA) and the voluntary contributions mechanism (VCM) for public goods allocation. What have experiments with the SA and VCM revealed about their properties?

5. What questions were addressed in the Forsythe, Palfrey, and Plott paper on asset valuation? How were their experiments designed? What was learned from these experiments?

Economics 696a
Spring 1995

Professor James Cox
University of Arizona

Experimental Economics
READING LIST

A.   Methodology

1.   V. Smith, "Microeconomic Systems as an Experimental Science," American Economic Review, December 1982, pp. 923-955.

2.   V. Smith, "Experimental Methods in Economics," in J. Eatwell, et al. (eds.), The New Palgrave: A Dictionary of Economics (New York: The Stockton Press, 1987).

3.   V. Smith, "Theory, Experiment, and Economics," Journal of Economic Perspectives, Winter 1989, pp 151-169.

4.   J. Cox and M. Isaac, "Experimental Economics and Experimental Psychology: Ever the Twain Shall Meet?", in A.J. MacFadyen and H.W. MacFadyen (eds.), Economic Psychology: Intersections in Theory and Application (New York: North-Holland, 1986).

5.   V. Smith, "Rational Choice: The Contrast between Economics and Psychology," Journal of Political Economy, 99, 1991, pp. 877-897.

B.   Markets

1.   V. Smith, "Bidding and Auctioning Institutions: Experimental Results," in Y. Amihud (ed.) Bidding and Auctioning for Procurement and Allocation (New York University Press, 1976).

2.   V. Smith, "Markets as Economizers of Information: Experimental Examination of the Hayek Hypothesis," Economic Inquiry, April 1982, pp. 165-179.

3.   A. Williams, "Intertemporal Competitive Equilibrium," in V. Smith (ed.), Research in Experimental Economics, vol. 1 (Greenwich: JAI Press, 1979).

4.   V. Smith and A. Williams, "Cyclical Double-Auction Markets with and without Speculators," Journal of Business, Jan. 1984, pp. 1-33.

5.   D. Gode and S. Sunder, "Allocative Efficiency of Markets with Zero-Intelligence Traders: Market as a Partial Substitute for Individual Rationality," Journal of Political Economy, 101, Feb. 1993, pp. 119-137.

6.   S. Mestelman and D. Welland, "Advance Production in Experimental Markets," Review of Economic Studies, 55, Oct. 1988, pp.

C.   Market Dynamics

1.   M. Isaac and C. Plott, "Price Controls and the Behavior of Auction Markets," American Economic Review, June 1981, pp. 448-459.

1

2.   V. Smith and A. Williams, "On Nonbinding Price Controls in a Competitive Market," American Economic Review, June 1981, pp. 467–474.

3.   D. Coursey and V. Smith, "Price Controls in a Posted Offer Market," American Economic Review, March 1983, pp. 218–221.

D.   Market Power

1.   V. Smith, "An Empirical Study of Decentralized Institutions of Monopoly Restraint," in G. Horwich and J. Quirk (eds.), Essays in Contemporary Fields of Economics (West Lafayette: Purdue University Press, 1981).

2.   C. Holt, L. Langan, and A. Villamil, "Market Power in Oral Double Auctions," Economic Inquiry, Jan. 1986, pp. 107–123.

3.   V. Smith and A. Williams, "The Boundaries of Competitive Price Theory: Convergence, Expectation, and Transaction Costs," in L. Green and J Kagel (eds.), Advances in Behavioral Economics, vol. 2 (Norwood, NJ: Ablex Publishing, 1990).

E.   Incentive Mechanisms for Control of Monopolies

1.   M. Loeb and W. Magat, "A Decentralized Method for Utility Regulation," Journal of Law and Economics, Oct. 1979, pp. 399–404.

2.   J. Cox and M. Isaac, "Incentive Regulation: A Case Study in the Use of Laboratory Experimental Analysis in Economics," in S. Moriarity (ed.), Laboratory Market Research (Norman: The University of Oklahoma, Center for Economic and Management Research, 1986).

3.   J. Cox and M. Isaac, "Mechanisms for Incentive Regulation: Theory and Experiment," Rand Journal of Economics, Autumn 1987, pp. 348–359.

4.   J. Cox and M. Isaac, "Incentive Regulation and Innovation," in M. Isaac (ed.), Research in Experimental Economics, vol. 5 (Greenwich: JAI Press, 1992).

F.   Experimental Evaluation of Econometric Estimators

1.   J. Cox and R. Oaxaca, "Using Laboratory Market Experiments to Evaluate Econometric Estimators of Structural Models," discussion paper, University of Arizona, revised 1991.

G.   Individual Choice Under Certainty

1.   R. Battalio, J. Kagel, et.al., "A Test of Consumer Demand Theory Using Observations of Individual Consumer Purchases," Western Economic Journal, Dec. 1973, pp. 411–428.

2.   J. Cox, "On Testing the Utility Hypothesis," unpublished paper, Department of Economics, University of Arizona, revised 1994.

2

3. D. Brookshire, D. Coursey and W. Schulze, "The External Validity of Experimental Economics Techniques: Analysis of Demand Behavior," Economic Inquiry, 25, April 1987, pp. 239-250.

4. J. Kagel, R. Battalio, et al., "Experimental Studies of Consumer Demand Behavior Using Laboratory Animals," Economic Inquiry, 13, March 1975, pp. 22-38.

5. R. Battalio, L. Green, and J. Kagel, "Income-Leisure Tradeoffs of Animal Workers," American Economic Review, Sept. 1981, pp. 621-632.

6. R. Battalio, J Kagel, et al., "Commodity Choice Behavior with Pigeons as Subjects," Journal of Political Economy, 89, Feb. 1981, pp. 67-91.

7. R. Battalio, G. Dwyer, and J. Kagel, "Tests of Competing Theories of Consumer Choice and the Representative Consumer Hypothesis," Economic Journal, 97, Dec. 1988, pp. 842-856.

8. R. Battalio, J. Kagel, and C. Kogut, "Experimental Confirmation of the Existence of a Giffen Good," American Economic Review, 81, Sept. 1991, pp. 961-970.

H. Theories of Choice Under Uncertainty

1. P. Schoemaker, "The Expected Utility Model: Its Variants, Purposes, Evidence and Limitations," Journal of Economic Literature, June 1982, pp. 529-563.

2. M. Machina, "Choice under Uncertainty: Problems Solved and Unsolved," Journal of Economic Perspectives, 1, Summer 1987, pp. 121-154.

3. D. Kahneman and A. Tversky, "Prospect Theory: An Analysis of Decision Under Risk," Econometrica, 47, March 1979, pp. 263-291.

I. Individual Choice Under Uncertainty

1. D. Grether, "Bayes Rule as a Descriptive Model: The Representativeness Heuristic," Quarterly Journal of Economics, Nov. 1980, pp. 537-557.

2. D. Grether and C. Plott, "Economic Theory of Choice and the Preference Reversal Phenomenon," American Economic Review, Sept. 1979, pp. 623-638.

3. C. Holt, "Preference Reversals and the Independence Axiom," American Economic Review, June 1986, pp. 508-515.

4. J. Cox and S. Epstein, "Preference Reversals Without the Independence Axiom," American Economic Review, June 1989, pp 408-426.

5. G. Loomes, C. Starmer, and R. Sugden, "Observing Violations of Transitivity By Experimental Methods," Econometric, 59, 1991, pp. 425-439.

6. C. Starmer and R. Sugden, "Testing for Juxtaposition and Event - Splitting Effects," Journal of Risk and Uncertainty, 6 June 1993, pp. 235-254.

3

7. R. Battalio, J. Kagel, and D. MacDonald, "Animals' Choices Over Uncertain Outcomes: Some Initial Experimental Results," <u>American Economic Review</u>, 75, Sept. 1985, pp. 597-613.

8. C. Camerer, "An Experimental Test of Several Generalized Utility Theories," <u>Journal of Risk and Uncertainty</u>, 2, April 1989, pp. 61-104.

9. R. Battalio, J. Kagel, and K. Jiranyakul, "Testing Between Alternative Models of Choice Under Uncertainty: Some Initial Results," <u>Journal of Risk and Uncertainty</u>, 3, March 1990, pp. 25-50.

10. J. Quiggin, "Testing Between Alternative Models of Choice Under Uncertainty - Comment," <u>Journal of Risk and Uncertainty</u>, 6 April 1993, pp. 161-164.

11. J. Kagel, D. MacDonald, and R. Battalio, "Tests of 'Fanning Out' of Indifference Curves: Results from Animal and Human Experiments," <u>American Economic Review</u>, 80, Sept. 1990, pp. 912-921.

J. Willingness to Accept, Willingness to Pay, and Contingent Valuation

1. J. Knetsch and J. Sinden, "Willingness to Pay and Compensation Demanded: Experimental Evidence of an Unexpected Disparity in Measures of Value," <u>Quarterly Journal of Economics</u>, Aug. 1984, pp. 507-521.

2. W. M. Hanemann, "Willingness to Pay and Willingness to Accept: How Much Can they Differ?", <u>American Economic Review</u>, 81, June 1991, pp. 635-647.

3. R. Boyce, et. al., "An experimental Examination of Intrinsic Values as a Source of the WTA - WTP Disparity," <u>American Economic Review</u>, 82, December 1992, pp. 1366-1373.

4. J. Irwin, et. al., "Preference Reversals and the Measurement of Environmental Values," <u>Journal of Risk and Uncertainty</u>, 6 January 1993, pp. 5-18.

5. J. Shogren, et. al., "Resolving Differences in Willingness to Pay and Willingness to Accept," <u>American Economic Review</u>, 84, March 1994.

6. R. Cummings, G. Harrison, and E. Rutstrom, "Homegrown Values and Hypothetical Surveys: Is the Dichotomous - Choice Approach Incentive - Compatible?" <u>American Economic Review</u>, forthcoming.

K. Market Feedback and Choice Under Uncertainty

1. D. Coursey, J. Hovis, and W. Schulze, "The Disparity Between Willingness to Accept and Willingness to Pay Measures of Value," <u>Quarterly Journal of Economics</u>, Aug. 1987, pp. 679-690.

2. C. Camerer, "Do Biases in Probability Judgment Matter in Markets? Experimental Evidence," <u>American Economic Review</u>, Dec. 1987, pp. 981-997.

3.   C. Camerer, G. Loewenstein, and M. Weber, "The Curse of Knowledge in Economic Settings: An Experimental Analysis," Journal of Political Economy. 97, Oct. 1989, pp. 1232-1254.

4.   J. Cox and D. Grether, "The Preference Reversal Phenomenon: Response Mode, Markets and Incentives," Economic Theory, forthcoming.

L.   Insurance, Ambiguity, and Risk

1.   C. Camerer and H. Kunreuther, "Experimental Markets for Insurance," Journal of Risk and Uncertainty, 2 September 1989, pp. 265-299.

2.   E. Johnson, et. al., "Framing, Probability Distortions, and Insurance Decisions," Journal of Risk and Uncertainty, 7 August 1993, pp. 35-51.

3.   G. McClelland, W. Schulze, and D. Coursey, "Insurance for Low-Probability Hazards: A Bimodal Response to Unlikely Events," Journal of Risk and Uncertainty, 7 August 1993, pp. 95-116.

4.   R. Sarin and M. Weber, "Effects of Ambiguity in Market Experiments."

M.   Search Decisions

1.   Y. Braunstein and A. Schotter, "Economic Search: An Experimental Study," Economic Inquiry, 19, Jan. 1981, pp. 1-25.

2.   Y. Braunstein and A. Schotter, "Labor Market Search: An Experimental Study," Economic Inquiry, 20, Jan. 1982, pp. 133-144.

3.   J. Cox and R. Oaxaca, "Laboratory Experiments with a Finite Horizon Job Search Model," Journal of Risk and Uncertainty, 2, Sept. 1989, pp. 301-329.

4.   J. Cox and R. Oaxaca, "Tests for a Reservation Wage Effect," in John Geweke (ed.), Decision Making Under Risk and Uncertainty: New Models and Empirical Findings. Dordrecht: Kluwer Academic Publishers (in press).

5.   J. Cox and R. Oaxaca, "Direct Tests of the Reservation Wage Property," Economic Journal, 102, Nov. 1992, pp. 1423-1432.

6.   J. Cox and R. Oaxaca, "Finite Horizon Search Behavior with and without Recall," discussion paper, University of Arizona 1991.

7.   J. Cox and R. Oaxaca, "Search Behavior with an Unknown Distribution of Offers," discussion paper, University of Arizona, 1992.

8.   D. Grether, A. Schwartz, and L. Wilde, "Uncertainty and Shopping Behavior: An Experimental Analysis," Review of Economic Studies, April 1988, pp. 239-250.

9.   G. Harrison and P. Morgan, "Search Intensity in Experiments," Economic Journal, 100, June 1990, pp. 478-486.

5

N.   Auction Markets

1.   V. Smith, "Auctions," forthcoming in J. Eatwell, et al. (eds.), The New Palgrave: A Dictionary of Economics (New York: The Stockton Press, 1987).

2.   J. Cox, B. Roberson, and V. Smith, "Theory and Behavior of Single Object Auctions," in V. Smith (ed.) Research in Experimental Economics, vol. 2 (Greenwich: JAI Press, 1982).

3.   J. Cox, V. Smith, and J. Walker, "Theory and Individual Behavior of First Price Auctions," Journal of Risk and Uncertainty, March 1988, pp. 61-99.

4.   V. Harlow and K. Brown, "Understanding and Assessing Financial Risk Tolerance: A Biological Perspective," Financial Analysts Journal, Nov.-Dec. 1990, pp. 50-62, 80.

5.   J. Cox, V. Smith, and J. Walker, "Theory and Behavior of Multiple Unit Discriminative Auctions," Journal of Finance, Sept. 1984, pp. 983-1010.

6.   G. Miller and C. Plott, "Revenue Generating Properties of Sealed-Bid Auctions: An Experimental Analysis of One-Price and Discriminative Processes," in V. Smith (ed.), Research in Experimental Economics. vol. 3 (Greenwich: JAI Press, 1985).

7.   J. Cox, V. Smith, and J. Walker, "Expected Revenue in Discriminative and Uniform Price Sealed Bid Auctions," in V. Smith (ed.), Research in Experimental Economics, vol. 3 (Greenwich: JAI Press, 1985).

8.   M. Isaac and J Walker, "Information and Conspiracy in Sealed Bid Auctions," Journal of Economic Behavior and Organization, 6, 1985, pp. 139-159.

9.   J. Kagel, R. Harstad, and D. Levin, "Information Impact and Allocation Rules in Auctions with Affiliated Private Values: A Laboratory Study," Econometrica, Nov. 1987, pp. 1275-1304.

10.   J. Kagel and D. Levin, "The Winner's Curse and Public Information in Common Value Auctions," American Economic Review, Dec. 1986, pp. 894-920.

11.   J. Cox, S. Dinkin, and V. Smith, "Endogenous Entry and Exit in Common Value Auctions," discussion paper, University of Arizona, revised 1995.

12.   J. Cox, R. M. Isaac, P. Cech, and D. Conn, "Moral Hazard and Adverse Selection in Procurement Contracting," discussion paper, University of Arizona, revised 1994.

13.   J. Cox and R. Oaxaca, "Is Bidding Behavior Consistent with Bidding Theory in Private Value Auctions?" forthcoming in R. M. Isaac (ed.), Research in Experimental Economics, vol. 6 (Greenwich: JAI Press).

O.   Methodology: Lottery Payoffs and the Random Decision Selection Procedure

1.   J. Berg, et al., "Controlling Preferences for Lotteries on Units of Experimental Exchange," Quarterly Journal of Economics, 101, pp. 281-306.

2.   J. Walker, V. Smith, and J. Cox, "Inducing Risk-Neutral Preferences: An Examination in a Controlled Market Environment," Journal of Risk and Uncertainty, 3, March 1990, pp. 5-24.

3.   T. Rietz, "Implementing and Testing Risk-Preference-Induction Mechanisms in Experimental Sealed - Risk Auctions," Journal of Risk and Uncertainty, 7, Oct. 1993, pp. 199-213.

4.   J. Cox and R. Oaxaca, "Inducing Riks Neutral Preferences: Further Analysis of the Data," Journal of Risk and Uncertainty, forthcoming.

5.   C. Starmer and R. Sugden, "Does the Random-Lottery Incentive System Elicit True Preferences? An Experimental Investigation," American Economic Review, 81, Sept. 1991, pp. 971-978.

P.   Methodology: The Metric War

1.   G. Harrison, "Theory and Misbehavior of First-Price Auctions," American Economic Review, 79, Sept. 1989, pp. 749-762.

2.   D. Friedman, "Theory and Misbehavior of First-Price Auctions: Comment," American Economic Review, 82, Dec. 1992, pp.1374-1378.

3.   J. Kagel and A. Roth, "Theory and Misbehavior of First-Price Auctions: Comment," American Economic Review, 82, Dec. 1992, pp. 1379-1391.

4.   J. Cox, V. Smith, and J. Walker, "Theory and Misbehavior of First-Price Auctions: Comment," American Economic Review, 82, Dec. 1992, pp. 1392-1412.

5.   A. Merlo and A. Schotter, "Theory and Misbehavior of First-Price Auctions: Comment," American Economics Review, 82, Dec. 1992, pp. 1413-1425.

6.   G. Harrison, "Theory and Misbehavior of First-Price Auctions: Reply," American Economic Review, 82, Dec. 1992, pp. 1426-1443.

Q.   Expectations and Asset Valuation

1.   R. Forsythe, T. Palfrey, and C. Plott, "Asset Valuation in an Experimental Market," Econometrica, May 1982, pp. 537-567.

2.   C. Plott and S. Sunder, "Efficiency of Experimental Security Markets with Insider Information: An Application of Rational Expectations Models," Journal of Political Economy, Aug. 1982, pp. 663-698.

3.   D. Friedman, G. Harrison, and J. Salmon, "The Informational Efficiency of Experimental Asset Markets," Journal of Political Economy, June 1984, pp. 349-408.

4.   T. Copeland and D. Friedman, "The Effect of Sequential Information Arrival on Asset Prices: An Experimental Study," Journal of Finance, 42, 1987, pp. 763-797.

5. V. Smith, G. Suchanek, and A. Williams, "Bubbles, Crashes and Endogenous Expectations in Experimental Spot Asset Markets," Econometrica, Sept. 1988, pp.1119-11151.

6. C. Plott and S. Sunder, "Rational Expectations and the Aggregation of Diverse Information in Laboratory Security Markets," Econometrica, 56, Sept. 1988, pp. 1085-1118.

7. T. Copeland and D. Friedman, "Partial Revelation of Information in Experimental Asset Markets," Journal of Finance, 46, 1991, pp. 265-295.

8. T. Copeland and D. Friedman, "The Market Value of Information: Some Experimental Results," Journal of Business, 65, 1992, pp. 241-266.

9. S. Sunder, "Market for Information: Experimental Evidence," Econometrica, 60, May 1992, pp. 667-695.

R. Learning to Play Nash Equilibrium

1. J. Cox and M. Walker, "Learning to Play Cournot Duopoly Strategies," Department of Economics, University of Arizona, 1994.

2. J. Cox and M. Walker, "Experiments on Bayesian Learning of Nash Equilibrium Play," Department of Economics, University of Arizona, 1995.

S. Political Stock Markets

1. R. Forsythe, F. Nelson, G. Neumann, and J. Wright, "Anatomy of an Experimental Political Stock Market," American Economic Review, 82, December 1992, pp. 1142-1161.

8

De Alessi   Economics 634   University of Miami
Fall 1994   TuTh 10:50-12:05

Office Hours (Jenkins 517A): TuTh 10-10:40am, 1:00-1:30pm, and by appointment.

The course is organized as a seminar: students present and discuss assignments.
The final grade is determined by class performance adjusted for the quality of written work.

TEXT
Although a text is not required, most students will find it helpful to read one along with the assignments. Consider Becker, G. Economic Theory, Knopf: 1971; it is excellent and terse.

ASSIGNED READINGS
Available in the reserve room. Several are reprinted in:
Breit, Hochman & Saueracker, Readings in Microeconomics, Dryden, (2d / 3d ed: B-2 /B-3)

INTRODUCTION
1.(Aug 25) Administrative comments.

2.(Aug 30) Scope of economics.
     Schumpeter, J.A. "Nature & Necessity of a Price System," Ch. 6 (1-4) in Economic
         Reconstruction (1934).
     Hayek, F.H. "Use of Knowledge in Society," AER Sep 1945.
     Stigler, G.J. "Nobel Lecture: The Process and Progress of Economics," JPE Aug 1983.
     Hirshleifer, J. "The Dark Side of the Forces," EI Jan 1994.
     Suggested
     Knight, F.H. Economic Organization (1933, reprinted 1951), 3-15.
     Robbins, L. Nature and Significance of Economic Science (1935, reprinted 1962).
     Alchian, A.A. "How Should Prices Be Set?" Il Politico Jun 1967.
     Brunner, K. "The Perception of Man and the Conception of Society," EI Jul 1987.

CONSUMPTION CHOICE
3.(Sep 1) Methodology.
     Friedman, M."Methodology of Positive Econ," in his Essays in Positive Econ (1953).B-3
     Nagel, E. "Assumptions in Economic Theory," AER May 1963. B-2
     De Alessi, L. "Nature and Methodological Foundations of Some Recent Extensions of Econ
         Theory," in Radnitzky & Bernholz (eds.), Economic Imperialism (1987): 51-57.
     Suggested
     Keynes, J.N. Scope and Method of Political Economy (1890), Ch. 1, 2 (31-35).
     Blaug, M. The Methodology of Economics (1980), esp. Ch. 1.
     Caldwell, B. Beyond Positivism (1982), esp. Ch. 2-3.
     Hausman, D.M. "Economic Methodology in a Nutshell," JEP Spr 1989.

4.(Sep 6) Utility: historical perspective; Marshallian and indifference curve analyses.
     Marshall, A. Principles of Economics (8th ed. 1948), Bk III, Ch. 3.
     Hicks, J.R. Value and Capital (2d ed., 1957), Ch. 1 (11-16).
     Suggested
     Stigler, G.J. "Development of Utility Theory," JPE Aug & Oct 1950.
     Hirshleifer, J. "Economics from a Biological Viewpoint," JLE Apr 1977.
     Riley, J.G. "Well-Behaved Preferences: An Expository Note," EI Jul 1977.
     Frank, R.H. "If Homo Economicus Could Choose His Own Utility Function, Would He
         Want One with a Conscience?" AER Sep 1987.

5.(Sep 8) Utility: axioms; bilateral (fixed stock of goods) and market (fixed budget) exchange.
Radford, R.A. "The Economic Organization of a P.O.W. Camp," Ec Nov 1945.
Newman, P. The Theory of Exchange (1965), Ch. 2 (44-45), Ch. 3 (50-64).
Hicks, J.R. Value and Capital (2d ed., 1957), Ch. 1 (16-25).
Suggested
Enke, S. "Some Economic Aspects of Fissionable Materials," QJE May 1954.
Wilson, E.O. "The Economics of Caste in Social Insects," AER Index Subs. Dec 1978.
Samuelson, P.A. Foundations of Economic Analysis (1958), Ch. 5.
Working, E.J. "What Do Statistical Demand Curves Show?" QJE 1927. AEA
Houthakker, H.S. "The Present State of Consumption Theory," Em Oct 1961.
Sen, A. "Behaviour and the Concept of Preferences," Ec Aug 1973.

6.(Sep 13) Demand curves: real, apparent, and money income constant.
Hicks, J.R. Value and Capital (2d ed., 1957), Ch. 2 (26-35).
Kagel, J.H. et al. "Demand Curves for Animal Consumers," QJE Feb 1981. B-3
Suggested
Friedman, M. "Marshallian Demand Curve," JPE Dec 1949, Sect. I. B-3
Bailey, M.J. "Marshallian Demand Curve," JPE Jun 1954. B-3
Friedman, M. Price Theory (1976), Ch. 2 (Sect: "Deriv of D Curves from Indiff Curves").

7.(Sep 15) Reversibility of indifference curves; Giffen, snob, bandwagon, and Veblen effects.
Knetsch, J.L. "Endowment Effect and Evidence of Nonreversible Indifference Curves," AER
    Dec 1989.
Dwyer, G.P. Jr. & Lindsay, C.M. "Robert Giffen and the Irish Potato," AER Mar 1984.
Leibenstein, H. "Bandwagon, Snob, & Veblen Effects ...," QJE May 1950. B-2
Suggested
Dougan, W.R. "Giffen Goods and the Law of Demand," JPE Aug 1982 (esp. 809-810).
Gilley, O.W. "In Search of Giffen's Behavior," EI Jan 1991.

8.(Sep 20) Demand to buy and to hold (flow-stock); consumer's and consumers' surplus.
Alchian, A.A. & Allen, W.R. Production and Exchange (3d ed., 1983), Ch.4 (57-63).
Marshall, A. Principles of Economics (8th ed., 1948), Book III, Ch. 6 (124-30).
Hicks, J.R. Value and Capital (2d ed., 1957), Ch. 2 (38-41).
Suggested
Morey, E.R. "Confuser Surplus," AER Mar 1984.
Becker, G.S. "A Theory of Rational Addiction," JPE Aug 1988.

9.(Sep 22) Irrational behavior; household production.
Becker, G.S. "Irrational Behavior and Economic Theory," JPE Feb 1962, Sect I-II.
Lancaster, K. "Change & Innovation in the Theory of Consumption," AER May 1966:14-17.
Becker, G.S. Economic Theory (1971), Ch. 3 (45-47).
Suggested
Lancaster, K. "A New Approach to Consumer Theory," JPE Apr 1966. B-3
Becker, G.S. "A Theory of the Allocation of Time," EJ Sep 1965. B-3

10.(Sep 27) Choices under uncertainty; utility.
Friedman,M. & Savage,L. "Utility Analysis of Choices Involving Risk," JPE Aug 1948. AEA
Alchian, A.A. "Meaning of Utility Measurement," AER Mar 1953, Sect. I-III. B-2
Suggested
Weitzman, M. "Utility Analysis of Group Behavior: An Empirical Study," JPE Feb 1965.
Brookshire, D.S. et al. "Test of the Expected Utility Model: Evidence from Earthquake ..,"
    JPE Apr 1985.
Plott, C. R. & Sunder, S. "Efficiency of Experimental Security Markets with Insider
    Information: An Application of Rational Expectations Models," JPE Aug 1982.

PRODUCTION CHOICES

11.(Sep 29) Production functions: output isoquants, returns to scale. variable proportions.
Review a text: production functions.
Knight, F.H. Risk, Uncertainty and Profit (1921), Ch. 4 (98-104).
Borts, G.H. & Mishan, E.J. "Exploring the 'Uneconomic' Region of the Production
Function," REStud Oct 1962, Sect. I-IV.
Alchian, A.A. & Allen, W.R. Production and Exchange (3d ed., 1983), Ch. 8 (163-171).
Suggested
Beattie, B.R. "Asymmetric Stages, Ridgelines and the Econ Region..," SEJ Jan 1988.

12.(Oct 4) Prod. possibility curve, equilibrium w/fixed resource stock. Aggregate PPC. Cost.
Bator, F.M. "Simple Analytics of Welfare Maximization," AER Mar 1957: Sect. IA. B-3
Alchian, A.A. "Cost," Internt'l Encyclopedia Social Sciences (1968):up to "Law of Cost."
Suggested
Buchanan, J.M. Cost and Choice (1969): Ch. 3.
De Alessi, L. & Staaf, R.J. "Property Rights and Choice," in Mercuro (ed.) Law and
Economics (1989): 184-193.

13.(Oct 6) Derivation of cost and supply curves in short and long run.
Review a text: derivation of cost curves.
Viner, J. "Cost Curves and Supply Curves," Zeitschrift ... 1931. AEA: 198-216.
Suggested
Robinson, J. "Rising Supply Price," Ec Feb 1941. AEA
Ellis, H.S. & Fellner, W. "External Economies and Diseconomies," AER Sep 1943.
AEA

14.(Oct 11) Rate and volume of output. Short run. Fixed and variable costs.
Alchian, A.A. "Costs & Outputs," in M. Abramovitz, Alloc of Econ Res (1959). B-2
De Alessi, L. "The Short Run Revisited," AER Jun 1967. B-3
Suggested
Oi, W.Y. "Neoclassical Foundations of Progress Functions," EJ Sep 1967: Sect II-III.
Hirshleifer, J. "The Firm's Cost Function: A Successful Reconstruction?" JB Jul 1962.

15.(Oct 13) Intertemporal choices; speculation and usury.
Fisher, I. The Theory of Interest (reprinted 1954). Ch. 10-11.
Hirshleifer, J. "On the Theory of Optimal Invest. Decisions," JPE Aug 1958: 329-336.
Suggested
Galenson, D.W."Market Evaluation of Human Capital: Indentured Servitude," JPE Jun 1981.

16.(Oct 18) Information & transaction costs.
Coase, R.H. "The Problem of Social Cost," JLE Oct 1960 (pp. 1-19). B-3
Stigler, G.J. "The Economics of Information," JPE Jun 1961. B-3
Akerlof, G.A."The Market for 'Lemons': Qualitative Uncertainty & the Market
Mechanism," QJE Aug 1970.B-3
Suggested
Cheung, S.N.S."Transaction Costs, Risk Aversion & the Choice of Contractual
Arrangement," JLE Apr 1969.B-3
Becker, G. S. & Stigler, G. J."Law Enforcement, Malfeasance, & Compensation of
Enforcers," JLS Jan 1974.
Williamson, O.E. "Transaction Cost Economics: The Governance of Contractual Relations,"
JLE Oct 1979.
Stiglitz, J.E. "Information and Economic Analysis: A Perspective," EJ Suppl 1985.

17.(Oct 20) Property rights; specialization and exchange.
Demsetz, H. "Toward a Theory of Property Rights," AER May 1964.
Alchian & Demsetz "Production, Inf Costs, and Econ Organization," AER Dec 1972. BHS-3
North, D. "Institutions & Credible Commitments," JITE, March 1993.
Suggested
De Alessi, L. "The Economics of Property Rights: A Review of the Evidence," ResLE 1980.
Demsetz, H. "The Exchange and Enforcement of Property Rights," JLE Oct 1964.
Buchanan, J.M. & Stubblebine, W.L. "Externality," Ec Nov 1962: 371-5, 380-4. BHS-3

18.(Oct 25) Choice of business organization.
Williamson, O.E. "The Evolving Science of Organization," JITE, March 1993.
Joskow, P.L. "Asset Specificity & Structure of Vertical Relationships," JLEO Spr 1988.
Suggested
Coase, R.H. "The Nature of the Firm," Ec Nov 1937. AEA
Knight, F.H. Risk, Uncertainty and Profit (1921, reprinted 1965).
Klein, Crawford, & Alchian "Vertical Integration, Appropriable Rents, &..,"JLE Oct 1978.
Jensen, M.C. & Meckling, W.H. "Theory of the Firm:...," JFinE Oct 1976.
Fama, E.F. "Agency Problems and the Theory of the Firm," JPE Apr 1980.
Williamson, O.E. "Credible Commitments: Using Hostages ...," AER Sep 1983.
De Alessi, L. & Fishe, R.P.H. "Why Do Corporations Distribute Assets?" JITE Mar 1987.
Baumol,W.J"Entrepreneurship: Productive, Unproductive, & Destructive,"JPE Oct 1990.

OUTPUT MARKETS
19.(Oct 27) Price takers' markets: competition.
Review a text: competition.
Alchian, A.A. "Uncertainty, Evolution, and Economic Theory," JPE Jun 1950.

20.(Nov 1) Price searchers' markets: monopoly.
Review a text: monopoly.
Harberger, A.C. "Monopoly and Resource Allocation," AER May 1954.
Tullock, G. "The Welfare Costs of Tariffs, Monopolies, & Theft," WEJ (EI) Jun 1967.
Suggested
Lerner, A.P. "..Monopoly and the Measurement of Monopoly Power," REStud Jun
1943.BHS-3
Fisher, F.M. & McGowan, J.J. "Misuse of Accounting Rates of Return to Infer Monopoly
Profits." AER Mar 1983
Littlechild, S.C. "Misleading Calculations of the Social Cost of Monopoly," EJ Jun 1981.

21.(Nov 3) Price searchers' markets: duopoly, oligopoly, monopolistic competition.
Chamberlin, E.H. Theory of Monopolistic Competition (7th ed., 1960), Ch. 3, 5(71-81).
Demsetz, H. "Do Compet and Monopolistic Compet Really Differ?" JPE Jan/Feb 1968.
Haddock, D "Basing-Point Pricing: Compet v Collusive Theories," AER Jun 1982, Sect.I-II.
Suggested
Stigler, G.J. Five Lectures on Economic Problems (1949), Ch 2.
Margolis, S.E. "The Excess Capacity Controversy," EI Apr 1985.

22.(Nov 8) Price discrimination, sources of market power; self enforcing contracts.
Robinson, J. Economics of Imperfect Competition (2d ed 1969), Ch. 15(179-188).
Demsetz, H. "Barriers to Entry," AER Mar 1982.
Klein, B. & Leffler, K.B. "The Role of Market Forces in Assuring Contractual
Performance," JPE Aug 1981.
Suggested
McGee, J. "Predatory Price Cutting: The Standard Oil (NJ) Case," JLE Oct 1958.
Baumol,W.J."Contestable Mkts: An Uprising in Industry Structure," AER Mar 1982. BHS-3

Telser, L. "Some Aspects of the Economics of Advertising," JB Apr 1968.
Nelson, P. "Advertising as Information," JPE Jul/Aug 1974.
Kwoka, J.E. "Advertising & the Price and Quality of Optometric Services," AER Mar 1984.

INPUT MARKETS
23.(Nov 10) Derived demand for inputs.
Review a text: derived demand for inputs.
Alchian, A.A. "Information Costs, Pricing, and Resource Unemployment," WEJ Jun 1969.
Klein,B."Transaction Cost Det. of 'Unfair' Contractual Agreements,"AER May 1980.

24.(Nov 15) Supply of inputs; market equilibrium.
Battalio, Green, & Kagel "Income-Leisure Tradeoffs of Animal Workers," AER Sep 1981.
Bronars, S.G. & Deere, D.R. "Unionization, Incomplete Contracting, & Capital Investments," JB Jan 1993.

Suggested
Welch, F. & Cunningham, J."Minimum Wages.. Level & Age Composition of Youth Empl" REStat Feb 1978.
Ruback, R.S. & Zimmerman, M.B. "Unionization and Profitability," JPE Dec 1984.
Robins, P.K. "Labor S Findings from 4 Neg Income Tax Experiments," JHumRes Fall 1985.
Biddle,J.E. & Hammermesh, D.S. "Sleep and the Allocation of Time," JPE Oct 1990.
Carmichael, H.L. "Incentives in Academics: Why Is There Tenure?" JPE Jun 1988.

WELFARE/EFFICIENCY/GOVERNMENT
25.(Nov 17) Public goods. Welfare criteria.
Minasian, J.R. "Television Pricing and the Theory of Public Goods," JLE Oct 1964.
Mishan, E.J. "Reappraisal of the Principles of Resource Allocation," Ec Nov 1957: I-IV.
Suggested
Knight, F.H. "Some Fallacies in the Interpretation of Social Cost," QJE 1924. AEA
Bator, F.M. "Simple Analytics of Welfare Maximization," AER May 1957. BHS-3
Lipsey, R.G. & Lancaster, K. "General Theory of the Second Best," REStud 1956:11-18.
Samuelson, P.A. "Public Goods & Subscr. TV: Correction of the Record," JLE Oct 1964.

26.(Nov 22) Economic efficiency.
Demsetz, H. "Information and Efficiency: Another Viewpoint," JLE Apr 1969: I-II.
De Alessi, L. "Efficiency Criteria for Optimal Laws: Objective Standards or Value Judgments?" CPE Fall 1992.
Klein, D. B. "Coase, Kirzner, Schumpeter, and Alchian: Four Facets of Economic Freedom," University of California, Irvine, mimeo, 1994.
Suggested
Leibenstein, H. "On the Basic Propositions of X-Efficiency," AER May 1978.
Stigler, G.J. "The Xistence of X-Efficiency," AER Mar 1976.
De Alessi, L. "Property Rights, Transaction Costs, and X-Efficiency:..," AER Mar 1983.

27.(Nov 29) Government regulation.
Averch, H.D. & Johnson, L.L. "Firm under Regulatory Constraint," AER Dec 1962.
Alchian,A.A. & Kessel,R.A. "Competition, Monopoly, & Pursuit of Gain," Aspects of Labor Economics 1962.
Eckert, R.D. "On the Incentives of Regulators: The Case of Taxicabs." PubC Spr 1973.
Suggested
Baumol, W.J. & Klevorick, A. "Input Choices & Rate-of-Return Reg.," Bell J Spr 1971.
Coase, R.H. "Theory of Public Utility Pricing," Bell J Spr 1970.
Stigler, G.J. "Theory of Economic Regulation," Bell J Spr 1971.
Demsetz, H. "Why Regulate Utilities?" JLE Apr 1968.
Jarrell, G.A. "The Demand for State Reg. of the Electric Utility Industry," JLE Oct 1978.

28.(Dec 1) Antitrust. Government ownership.

Coate, Higgins, & McChesney, "Bureaucracy and Politics in FTC Merger Cases," JLE Oct 1990.

Davies, D.G. "Efficiency of Public vs Pvt Firms: The Case of Australia's Two Airlines," JLE Apr 1971.

Lindsay, C.M. "A Theory of Government Enterprise," JPE Oct 1976.

Suggested

Faith, R.L., Leavens & Tollison. "Antitrust Pork Barrel," JLE Oct 1982.

McKean, R.N. "Property Rights in Government," SEJ Sep 1972.

Buchanan, J.M. "Market Failure and Political Failure," Cato Spr/Sum 1988.

ABBREVIATIONS

AEA	AEA Readings in Price Theory, Stigler and Boulding, eds. (1952).
AER	American Economic Review
Bell J	Bell Journal
CPE	Constitutional Political Economy
Ec	Economica
Em	Econometrica
EI	Economic Inquiry
EJ	Economic Journal
IRLE	International Review of Law & Economics
JB	Journal of Business
JFinE	Journal of Financial Economics
JITE	Journal of Institutional & Theoretical Economics
JHumRes	Journal of Human Resources
JLE	Journal of Law & Economics
JLEO	Journal of Law, Economics, & Organization
JLS	Journal of Legal Studies
JPE	Journal of Political Economy
PubC	Public Choice
QJE	Quarterly Journal of Economics
REStat	Review of Economics & Statistics
REStud	Review of Economic Studies
ResLE	Research in Law & Economics
SEJ	Southern Economic Journal
WEJ	Western Economic Journal (now EI)

Peter Diamond
14.213: Microeconomic Theory III
Spring 1995

The central topic of this course is the theory of general equilibrium and its applications and extensions. We will start with the basic theory including existence, optimality and uniqueness of equilibrium. We will then discuss the core; Arrow's impossibility theorem; externalities and public goods; intertemporal competitive equilibrium and insurance; and incomplete markets.

Readings marked * are highly recommended and cover core topics that will be examined. Other readings are supplementary, but you should look at at least some of them. The Kreps and Varian readings are substitutes, depending on the style you prefer.

1. Existence, Optimality and Uniqueness of General Equilibrium
* D. Kreps, A Course in Microeconomic Theory, Chapters 6 and 8.
* H. Varian, Microeconomic Analysis, 3rd Edition, Chapters 17, 18, 21.2 and 21.3.
G. Debreu, Theory of Value.
K. Arrow and F. Hahn, General Competitive Analysis.
A. Mas-Colell, The Theory of General Economic Equilibrium: A Differentiable Approach.
P. Diamond and D. McFadden, "Some Uses of the Expenditure Function in Public Finance", Journal of Public Economics 3, February 1974, 3-21.
W. Moss, "Some uses of the Expenditure Function in Public Finance: A Comment," Journal of Public Economics (5) 1976: 373-379.

2. The Core and Convergence Theorems
* W. Hildenbrand and A. Kirman, Equilibrium Analysis, Chapter 1.
G. Debreu and H. Scarf, "A Limit Theorem on the Core of an Economy," International Economic Review, 4, 1963.

3. Arrow's Impossibility Theorem
* D. Kreps, Chapter 5.
K. Arrow, Social Choice and Individual Values, 2nd edition.
A. Sen, "Social Choice, in The New Palgrave, Vol 4, 1988.

4. Externalities and Public Goods
* D. Kreps, Chapters 6 and 8.
* H. Varian, Chapters 23 and 24.
* P. Dasgupta and G. Heal, Economic Theory and Exhaustible Resources, Chapter 3.
M. Weitzman, "Free Access vs. Private Ownership as Alternative Systems for Managing Common Property", Journal of Economic Theory, pp.225-234, 1974.
* J. Farrell, "Information and the Coase Theorem," Journal of Economic Perspectives 1 (Fall 1987), 113-129.
M. Weitzman, "Prices vs. Quantities," Review of Economic Studies, October 1974, 477-492.
R. Coase, "The Problem of Social Cost," Review of Economic Studies, October 1974, 477-776.
J.-J. Laffont, Fundamentals of Public Economics, Chapter 1.
* P. Diamond, "Consumption Externalities and Imperfect Corrective Pricing", Bell Journal of Economics and Management Science 4(2), Autumn 1973, 526-538.

5. Intertemporal Competitive Equilibrium, Capital Theory and Insurance Markets
* D. Kreps, Chapter 6.
* H. Varian, Chapters 19 and 20.
K. Arrow, "The Role of Securities in the Optimal Allocation of Risk-Bearing," Review of Economic Studies 31 (1963-1964), 91-96.
G. Debreu, Chapter 7.
P. Dasgupta and G. Heal, Chapters 4 and 6.
E. Malinvaud, "The Allocation of Small Risks in Large Markets," Journal of Economic Theory 4 (1972), 312-328.
J.J. Laffont, The Economics of Uncertainty and Information, MIT Press, Fourth Edition, 1993.

6. Incomplete Markets
* P. Diamond, "The Role of a Stock Market in a General Equilibrium Model with Technological Uncertainty," American Economic Review 57 (1967), 759-776.
O. Hart, "On the Optimality of Equilibrium When the Market Structure Is Incomplete," Journal of Economic Theory, December 1975, 418-443.
R. Radner, "Existence of Equilibrium of Plans, Prices, and Price Expectations in a Sequence of Markets," Econometrica 40 (1972), 289-303.
P. Diamond, "Efficiency with Uncertain Supply," Review of Economic Studies XLVII, July 1980, 645-651.
Loong, L.H. and R. Zeckhauser, "Pecuniary Externalities do Matter When Contingent Claims Markets are Incomplete, Quarterly Journal of Economics 47, 1982, pp.171-186.
J. Stiglitz, "The Inefficiency of Stock Market Equilibrium, Review of Economic Studies 49, 1982, pp.241-261.
J. Geanakoplos and H. Polemarchakis, "Existence, Regularity, and Constrained Suboptimality of Competitive Portfolio Allocations when the Asset Market is Incomplete", in: W.P. Heller, R.M. Ross and D.A. Starrett, eds., Uncertainty, Information and Communication. Essays in Honor of Kenneth J. Arrow, Vol.III Cambridge University Press, 1986.
J. Geanakoplos et.al., "Generic Inefficiency of Stock Market Equilibrium when Markets are Incomplete", Journal of Mathematical Economics 19, 1990, pg.113-151.
J. Hirshleifer, "The Private and Social Value of Information and the Reward to Inventive Acticity", American Economic Review, LXI, No.4, 1971.
L. Makowski, "Perfect Competition, The Profit Criterion, and the Organization of Economic Activity, " Journal of Economic Theory, 22, 1980, pp. 222-242.
D. Acemoglu, "Was Prometheus Unbound by Chance? Risk, Diversification and Growth," MIT Working Paper, September 1994.
A. Bisin, "General Equilibrium and Endogenously Incomplete Financial Markets," MIT Working Paper, October 1994.

Spring, 1995   **Qualifying Exam**
ANSWER ALL THREE QUESTIONS
1. (35 points) "Nonconvexities destroy both parts of the Fundamental Welfare Theorem."
Discuss this quotation, being careful with your definitions and precise in your discussion of its accuracy.

2. (45 points) Consider a competitive economy with two periods and two states of nature. The probability of state 1 is 1/3 and the probability of state 2 is 2/3. There are three goods

60

in this economy, first period consumption, a, and second period consumption in each state of nature, b_1 and b_2. There are 2 consumers, both of whom are expected utility maximizers, using the correct probabilities. The utility function of consumer A (for expected utility maximization) is $u^A = (1/2)\ln[a] + (1/2)\ln[b]$, where a is consumption of consumer A in the first period and b is consumption of consumer A in the second period. The utility function of consumer B (for expected utility maximization) is $u^B = (1/2)a + (1/2)b$, where a is consumption of consumer B in the first period and b is consumption of consumer B in the second period. The endowment of each consumer is 12 units of the first period consumption good and none of the second period consumption good in either state of nature.

There are two types of firms in this economy. There are large numbers of each type of firm. All firms have constant returns to scale. Firms of type 1 can convert units of the first period consumption good into units of the second period consumption good that only are produced in state of nature 1, with 1.25 units of output for each unit of input. Firms of type 2 can convert units of the first period consumption good into units of the second period consumption good that are produced in fixed proportions in the two states of nature. For a firm of type 2, one-half unit of output in each state is produced for each unit of input. Production decisions are made before the state of nature is known. Each firm is owned in equal shares by the two consumers.

a. Assume there is a complete set of contingent commodity markets. Determine competitive equilibrium prices and quantities.

b. Assume that instead of the utility function $u^A = (1/2)\ln[a] + (1/2)\ln[b]$, consumer A had the utility function $u^A = a^{1/2}b^{1/2}$. Does this change equilibrium? Explain your answer.

3. (20 points) "When the set of markets is incomplete, adding a market makes at least one person better off." "When the set of markets is incomplete, adding a market makes at least one person worse off." Discuss the validity of these two statements.

PROBLEM SET #1

1. Consider the picture of price equilibrium (e.g., Kreps, pg. 192) in the two-consumer, two-good case. For each set of relative prices, we can mark the point that consumer 1 would demand. (Assume that consumers have strictly convex preferences so their maximization problems always have unique solutions.) As we vary the relative prices of the goods, we trace out a curve -- the so-called <u>offer curve</u> of consumer 1. This is shown for you below

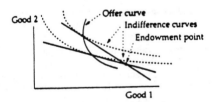

The offer curve of a consumer in two-commodity world.

We can create a similar offer curve for consumer 2, and rotating the picture for consumer 2 by 180 degrees and putting his origin at the location of the social endowment in her (consumer 1's) coordinate system, we get the Edgeworth box with two offer curves. Consider the assertion: <u>Walrasian equilibrium allocations correspond to points where the two offer curves intersect</u>. This is not quite correct as it stands. Why not? If you see why not, try to repair the assertion. (Kreps, 6.1.)

2. Consider the following exchange economy. There are two goods and two consumers. The two goods are called tillip and quillip and the two consumers are called 1 and 2. Consumer 1 has utility function $U_1(t,q) = .4 \ln(t) + .6 \ln(q)$ (where t is the amount of tillip 1 consumes, and q is the amount of quillip). Consumer 2 has utility function $U_2(t,q) = .5 \ln(t) + .5 \ln(q)$. Consumer 1 is endowed with 10 units each of quillip and tillip. Consumer 2 is endowed with 10 units of quillip and 5 units of tillip.

    (a) What is the Walrasian equilibrium of this economy? (If there is more than one equilibrium, gtive them all.)

    (b) Suppose a social dictator wished to implement an allocation that makes $U_1(t,q) + U_2(t,q)$ as large as possible at the equilibrium. Give <u>all</u> the possible reallocations of the endowment that give the dictator's optimal endowment as a Walrasian equilibrium. (Kreps, 6.2.)

3. A particular social planner I know is very big on mellow consumers. Specifically, she hopes to prevent her consumers from envying each other. To this end, she defines an <u>envy-free</u> allocation of resources as one in which no consumer would rather have the consumption bundle assigned to another consumer instead of his or her own. Our social planner wishes to implement an envy-free allocation. She also wishes the allocation to be efficient.

    This social planner is also lazy. She isn't willing to figure out the utility functions of her consumers. (She does have a good list of all their endowments.) She is blessed with an economy that functions well as an exchange economy; however she reassigns endowments, the economy finds a Walrasian equilibrium.

    Can you help out this social planner? Specifically, describe how to reallocate endowments and shares so that the resulting Walrasian equilibrium is guaranteed to be both efficient and envy free. (Hint: the trick is to find some way to redistribute endowments and shareholdings so that, <u>at every set of prices</u>, consumers all begin with the same level of wealth to spend on consumption. There is a way to redistribute endowments and shareholdings so this is true: What is it?) (Kreps, 6.3.)

4. Give examples of the following (illustrate using an Edgeworth box).
    (i) An exchange economy with no competitive equilibrium relative to particular initial endowments.
    (ii) An exchange economy with an infinite number of competitive equilibria relative to particular initial endowments.
    (iii) A Pareto optimum which cannot be sustained as a competitive equilibrium.
    (iv) A competitive equilibrium which is not Pareto optimal. (Do not use externalities to produce this example.)

PROBLEM SET #2

1. Consider the following social choice problem in the setting of consumption of two goods by two consumers. The two goods are called tillip and quillip and the two

consumers are called 1 and 2. Consumer 1 has utility function $U_1(t,q) = 6 + .4 \ln(t) + .6 \ln(q)$ (where t is the amount of tillip 1 consumes and q is the amount of quillip). Consumer 2 has utility function $U_2(t,q) = 8 + \ln(t) + \ln(q)$. The social endowment consists of 15 units of tillip and 20 units of quillip.
What is the set of all feasible, Pareto efficient allocations of the consumption good for this society? (Kreps, 5.2b.)

2. In a perfectly competitive pure exchange economy, there are two classes of persons, denoted by A and B, with equal numbers in each. They consume goods X and Y, with utility functions:
$U^A = X - 100\ e^{-Y/10} + 47$ for class A
$U^B = Y - 100\ e^{-X/10} + 100$ for class B
and they have endowments of 40X for class A and 50Y for class B.

   (i)   Writing p for the relative price of Y, derive the demand functions of the two groups, and comment on their properties. (Watch for corner solutions.)
   (ii)   Graphically, or otherwise, show that there are multiple competitive equilibria. (Hint: consider the local behavior of excess demand at $p=1$.)

3. There are two goods X and Y and two consumers A and B with the following utility functions and endowments:
$U^A = a \ln X^A + (1-a) \ln Y^A, \quad E^A = (0,1)$
$U^B = \min (X^B, Y^B), \qquad\qquad E^B = (1,0).$

Calculate the competitive equilibrium prices and allocation. (Varian 17.4)

4. We have two agents with <u>indirect</u> utility functions:
$\quad v^A(p_1,p_2,y^A) = \ln y^A - a \ln p_1 - (1-a) \ln p_2$
$\quad v^B(p_1,p_2,y^B) = \ln y^B - a \ln p_1 - (1-a) \ln p_2$

and initial endowments
$\quad E^A = (1,1),\ E^B = (1,1).$
Calculate the competitive market clearing prices. (Varian 17.6)

5. Consider an economy with 15 consumers and 2 goods. Consumer 3 has a Cobb-Douglas utility function $U^3 = \ln X + \ln y$. At a certain Pareto efficient allocation, consumer 3 has an allocation (10,5). What are the competitive prices that support this Pareto optimal allocation? (Varian 17.9.)

6. Either prove or find a counterexample to the following proposition:

In an economy with identical consumers, an increase in the endowment of one good will lead to a reduction in the price of that good relative to all other goods.

PROBLEM SET #3

1. Consider an economy with two goods and two individuals with identical (continuous, strictly monotonic) preferences and identical endowments. Describe the core of this economy and illustrate it in an Edgeworth box in the following three cases. (Make a clear argument that you have found the core.)
(a) Preferences are strictly convex.

(b) Preferences are convex but not strictly convex and the initial endowment point lies on a section of indifference curve that is linear.

(c) Preferences are not convex and the initial endowment point lies on a part of an indifference curve that is not on the frontier of the convex hull of the set better than the endowment point. Assume that there are no more than three intersections between an indifference curve of person A and an indifference curve of person B when the indifference curves are drawn in an Edgeworth Box. Also assume that there are no linear sections of indifference curves.

2. A two-good exchange economy has equal numbers of two types of consumers. Type A has initial endowment $(1,0)$ and utility function
$ax_1 + bx_2$.
Type B has initial endowment $(0,1)$ and utility function
Min $\{cx_1, dx_2\}$.
$(a, b, c, d > 0.)$

(a) Determine the competitive equilibrium prices and quantities. (Are prices unique? Are quantities unique?)

(b) Calculate the core of this economy if there is only one consumer of each type.

(c) Assume $a = b$ and $c = d$. Assuming that there are at least two individuals of each type, show that the competitive equilibria are the only members of the core.

3. Does an exchange economy with identical consumers with strictly monotonic, strictly convex preferences have unique competitive equilibrium prices?

4. Consider the following economy: There are three goods, legume, tillip and quillip, two consumers (called 1 and 2), and two firms (called x and y). Firm x is owned entirely by consumer 1 and makes tillip out of legume according to the simple linear production technology $t \leq 31$. That is, for every unit of legume input, this firm produces three times as many (or less) units of tillip. Firm y is owned entirely by consumer 2 and makes quillip out of legume according to the production technology $q = 41$. Each consumer initially owns 5 units of legume. Consumer 1 has utility function $u_1(t,q) = 6 + .4\ln(t) + .6\ln(q)$. Consumer 2 has utility function $u_2(t,q) = 8 + \ln(t) + \ln(q)$.

(a) What is the general equilibrium of this economy? Assume that firms take prices as given and are profit maximizers, and consumers take prices as given. When you give prices, normalize them so the price of legume is $1. What would be the general equilibrium if the shareholdings were reversed? If each consumer held a half-share in each firm?

(b) What is the set of all feasible, Pareto efficient allocations for this economy? (Kreps, 8.11)

5. With regard to proposition 6.1: *If consumer preferences are continuous, aggregate demand is upper semi-continuous. If consumer preferences are convex, aggregate demand is convex valued.*

(a) Prove that if consumer preferences are convex, aggregate demand is convex valued. This should be rather easy.

(b) Prove that if consumer preferences are continuous, aggregate demand is upper semi-continuous. This is done by mimicking the argument made for proposition 2.13(b).

64

(c) Use (b) to give a fast proof that if consumer preferences are continuous and single-valued, aggregate demand is given by a continuous function.
In all parts of this problem, we are dealing with strictly positive prices only.
(Kreps, 6.8.)

PROBLEM SET #4

1. In a perfectly competitive economy there are 2 goods, X and Y, produced using capital, K, and labor L, according to the following production functions:

    $$X = \min [K_x, L_x] \text{ and } Y = \min [K_y, L_y/4]$$

    where K_x, L_x are the inputs of K and L into the production of X, and K_y, L_y are defined similarly. There is a fixed total supply of capital (200 units) and of labor (440 units), fully mobile between sectors. All consumers are identical and have preferences represented by the utility function $U = \sqrt{XY}$.

    (a)   Describe the conditions for a general equilibrium, paying particular attention to the possibility that one factor may be less than fully employed.
    (b)   Calculate the equilibrium quantities of X and Y, the relative price P_x/P_y and the factor price ratio w/r.
    (c)   A regulation is introduced by the government requiring industry X to use an extra 3 units of capital per unit of output to clear up pollution damage. How will this policy affect the equilibrium of the economy? Will both factors be fully employed in the new equilibrium?

2. Consider an economy with a continuum (of unit measure) of identical consumers with utility function

    $$u = (1/3) \ln(x_1) + (2/3) \ln(24 + x_2), \ 0 \le x_1, \ 0 \le 24 + x_2 \le 24.$$

    Assume that there are a continuum of private firms, all of which have access to a CRTS technology that can convert units of good 2 into units of good 1 with A units of good 1 per unit of good 2.

    (a)   Find competitive equilibrium. Why didn't I bother to tell you who owns the firms?
    Assume that the government has access to a technology that uses B units of good 2 as a fixed cost and then can convert any number of units of good 2 into good 1, with 2A units of good 1 produced per unit of good 2.
    (b)   Considering only Pareto optima where everyone receives the same allocation, for what values of B should the government's technology be used? How can such an equilibrium be decentralized?
    (c)   Assuming the government has no access to revenues except from the sale of good 1, for what values of B is it feasible for the government to use its

7

technology? (Do not forget the existence of the competitive suppliers.) Show your answer in an x_1 - x_2 diagram. For what values should the government use its technology?

(d) Explain why the values of B for which the government should use its technology are different in parts (b) and (c).

3. There are N fishers in a community. Some of them fish in the ocean. The ocean is so large that each fisher can catch w fish no matter how many fishers go to sea. Some of the fishers fish in a lake. (Lake fish and ocean fish are perfect substitutes in consumption.) If there are x fishers on the lake, each of them catches $x^{-1/2}$ fish (i.e., $x^{1/2}$ fish are caught in total and each worker catches the same number).

(a) If each fisher is free to choose whether to go to the ocean or the lake and no one will go where he expects to catch fewer fish, how many fishers will go to the lake, how many to the ocean, and what will be the average catch? If the government restricts access to the lsake, how many fishers should it allow on the lake to maximize the total catch in the community? What size lake fishing license supports this equilibrium?

(b) Assume the demand for fish is:

$$Q = A - BP$$

Compare the price of fish in the free access and efficient allocations.

(c) We now assume that ocean fish and lake fish are <u>not</u> perfect substitutes. The demand for ocean fish is such that each fish is worth \$2. The demand for lake fish is

$$Q_L = A' - B'P_L$$

How many lake fishers are there in free access equilibrium? If a positive license fee is charged for fishing in the lake, does the price of lake fish go up or down? What makes this case different from that in (b)?

4. Imagine a three-person economy in which the first commodity is gardening services, the consumption of which makes one's yard more beautiful, and the second good is food. Imagine that two of the consumers in this society live in adjacent houses, while the third lives on the other side of a particularly large mountain. Consumption by the third consumer of gardening services generates no externality for the other consumers, but each of the others generates a positive externality for her neighbor through the consumption of gardening services. To be precise, imagine that consumers 1 and 2 have utility functions of the form

$$V^i(x) = w(x^1_1) + w(x^2_1) + x^i_2$$

where $w : [0, \infty) \to R$ is a strictly increasing, strictly concave, and differentiable function. Note well that consumers 1 and 2 get just as much utility out of their neighbor's yard as they do out of their own, and their utility for food is linear. (You

8

were warned that this is a very special setting.) Also imagine that consumer 3 has a utility function of the form $V^3(x) = w(x^3_1) + x^3_2$. there is a social endowment of gardening services and food.

(a) Suppose the social endowment is initially allocated evenly among the three consumers. What will be the corresponding Walrasian equilibrium (with externalities)?

(b) Characterize the set of Pareto efficient allocations of the social endowment. Is the equilibrium allocation in (a) Pareto efficient? (Kreps, 6.5.)

PROBLEM SET #5

1. Consider an economy with 2 individuals, Ms.1 and Ms.2. There is one non-produced good (labor) in the economy and each individual has an endowment of 3 units of labor. There are 2 firms in the economy -- firm F_A and F_B. Ms.1 owns firm F_A while Ms.2 owns firm F_B. The firms convert 'labor' (ℓ) into good x. The production functions are as follows:

Firm F_A: $x_A = \ell_A$

Firm F_B: $x_B = 2 \sqrt{\ell_B}$

Also, production by firm F_B creates pollution where pollution $z = x_B$ (i.e. output of firm F_B). Finally, utility of Ms. i is $U^i (\ell^i, x^i) = (3-\ell^i)^{1/2} \cdot (x^i)^{1/2} - z/8$; $i = 1,2$ (note: ℓ^i represents i's 'labor supply').

a) Derive the competitive equilibrium of this economy (i.e., equilibrium prices, production and consumption plans). [Restrict your attention to an interior allocation where (i) both firms are producing positive amounts of good x and (ii) consumers consume positive amounts of both goods].

b) Is the equilibrium a Pareto Optimum? Explain.

c) Assume the government fixes a limit z^* on the amount of pollution emitted by firm F_B. As a function of z^* solve for the resulting "competitive equilibrium". [Assume also that z^* is set at a value less than that obtained in (a)].

2. Consider an economy with many identical consumers. The economy lasts two periods. The consumers have (identical) endowments of trees (T). Each tree yields f_1 units of fruit in period 1 and f_2 units of fruit in period 2. Each consumer has utility function $u(x_1, x_2)$, where x_i is fruit eaten in period i. There are competitive markets in trees, fruit in period 1 and fruit in period 2 that all clear before period 1. Derive the equation for the price of trees relative to the price of fruit in terms of the preferences and endowment.

3. Consider a competitive economy in continuous time with a continuum of unit measure of identical households. Assume that all consumers have the utility function

$$u = \int_0^T e^{-rs} \log (c(s))\, ds$$

where T is the (known) end of time.

Assume that the economy begins with a (nondepreciating, nonaugmentable) stock A of consumer goods owned equally by all consumers. Derive the equations for competitive equilibrium per capita consumption as a function of time. Derive the price of a unit of consumer goods as a function of time.

4.   Consider a competitive economy in continuous time with a continuum of unit measure of identical households. Assume that all consumers have the utility function

$$u = \int_0^T e^{-rs} \log (c(s))\, ds$$

where T is the (known) end of time.

Assume that the economy begins with a stock A of (edible) bushes owned equally by all consumers. At time t each bush is of size $f(t)$, with $f(0) > 0$ $f'(t) > 0$, $f''(t) < 0$. No new bushes can be planted. Derive the equations for competitive equilibrium per capita consumption as a function of time. Derive the value of a standing bush as a function of time. (Hint: make use of the fact that some bushes are cut at each moment of time.)

5.   Consider an exchange economy with one physical good and two states of nature. Assume that there are a complete set of Arrow-Debreu markets. Assume that all consumers are expected utility maximizers and all consumers have the same subjective probabilities, with π as the probability of state one. Consumer h has utility u^h and endowment e^h. Show that if the aggregate endowment is the same in both states of nature, then the relative price of the commodity in the two states is $\pi/(1-\pi)$.

6.   Consider the set of date-event pairs depicted in figure 6.7. Recall the following data given before:

At date zero, a claim paying \$1 at date 1 in event $\{s_3, s_4, s_5\}$ costs \$.50
At date 1 in event $\{s_3, s_4, s_5\}$, a claim paying \$1 at date 2 in event $\{s_4, s_5\}$ will cost \$.60
At date 2 in event $\{s_4, s_5\}$, a claim paying \$1 at date 3 in event $\{s_4\}$ will cost \$.40
Broccoli at date zero costs \$2.00 per unit
Artichokes at date 3 in event $\{s_4\}$ will cost \$.67 per unit

Add to this the following addition data:

At date zero, a claim paying \$1 at date 1 in event $\{s_1, s_2\}$ costs \$.40
At date 1 in event $\{s_1, s_2\}$, a claim paying \$1 at date 2 in event $\{s_1, s_2\}$ will cost \$.90
At date 2 in event $\{s_1, s_2\}$, a claim paying \$1 at date 3 in event $\{s_1\}$ will cost \$.40
At date 3 in event $\{s_1\}$, artichokes will cost \$1.33

10

Suppose a consumer wished to sell some date 3-event $\{s_1\}$ artichokes with which she is endowed and use the proceeds to buy date 3-event $\{s_4\}$ artichokes. For every unit of date 3-event $\{s_1\}$ artichokes she sells, how many units of date 3-event $\{s_4\}$ artichokes can she purchase? What is the strategy she follows for affecting such a trade? (This strategy should involve changing her "position" in vegetables at these two date-event pairs only. The key is the first step. She sells date 1-event $\{s_1, s_2\}$ dollars and uses the proceeds from that sale to buy date 1-event $\{s_3, s_4, s_5\}$ dollars.) (Kreps 6.9)

PROBLEM SET #6

1. Consider a competitive stock market economy with a continuum of identical agents of measure one and a continuum of states of nature. Consumers are expected utility maximizers. They own equal shares in the two firms that exist in the economy. Firms one and two produce outputs $y^1(s)$ and $y^2(s)$ as functions of the states of nature, $s, 0 \le s \le 1$. Derive an equation for the relative values of the two firms in the stock market.

2. Consider a competitive stock market economy with 2 consumers, 2 firms and 3 states of nature. Assume that firm 1 has output $y^1 = (1,1,1)$ across the three states, while firm 2 has output $y^2 = (2,0,0)$. the consumers own equal shares in the two firms. Both are expected utility maximizers with $u = \log(c)$. However, they have different beliefs about the states of nature with consumer one having subjective probabilities $(1/3, 1/3, 1/3)$ while consumer two has subjective probabilities $(1/2, 1/4, 1/4)$. Derive the relative price of the two firms in stock market equilibrium.

   If the government makes a market for a bond that pays the same amount in all 3 states of nature, what happens to the relative price of the shares of the two firms in stock market equilibrium?

3. Consider an economy with a continuum (of measure 1) of identical households. There are two states of nature, each with equal probability. Each household is an expected utility maximizer using the known probabilities with $u(c) = \log(c)$. Assume that each household can produce 1 unit of output in state 1 or 2 units in state 2. Find competitive equilibrium with a complete set of Arrow-Debreu markets.

4. Consider a perfect foresight incomplete market economy with 2 goods and 2 states of nature with equal probabilities. Assume there is a continuum of consumers of measure 2. All consumers are expected utility maximizers, using the known probabilities. Half of the consumers have utility function $u^A(c_1, c_2) = (c_1 c_2)^a$, $0 < a < 1$ and are endowed with 2 units of good 1 in both states of nature. Half of the consumers have utility function $u^B(c_1, c_2) = (c_1)^b$, $0 < b < 1$. These consumers can choose between two different production plans. With plan 1 a consumer has 1 unit of good 2 in both states. With plan 2 a consumer has e_1 units of good 2 in state 1 and e_2 units of good 2 in state 2. Assume that there are only markets for trading good 1 against good 2 after the state is realized. Consider only equilibria where all type B's

11

choose the same plan (uniform equilibria).

a.   Calculate the price of good 2 in the ex-post market as a function of the endowment of good 2 in the state.

b.   Show that the expected utility of each person of type B is equal to 1 if they all follow the same plan.

c.   Show that having all type B's follow plan 1 is the unique uniform incomplete market competitive equilibrium if

$$(e_1^b + e_2^b)/2 \leq 1 \leq (e_1^{-b} + e_2^{-b})/2$$

d.   Show that having all type B's follow plan 2 is the unique uniform incomplete market competitive equilibrium if

$$(e_1^{-b} + e_2^{-b})/2 \leq 1 \leq (e_1^b + e_2^b)/2$$

e.   Show that having the government order all the B's to follow plan 1 (followed by competitive markets) Pareto dominates having all the B's follow plan 2 if 1 > $(e_1^a + e_2^a)/2$. Do not confuse e_1 raised to the power a with A's endowment.

f.   Show that ordering all the B's to follow plan 2 (followed by competitive markets) Pareto dominates having all the B's follow plan 1 if $(e_1^a + e_2^a)/2 > 1$.

g.   Show that the competitive equilibrium might be Pareto dominated by another allocation if the government can costlessly induce all type B's to change their production plan.

Spring, 1994   **Final Exam**

Answer <u>all</u> <u>three</u> questions. Some are easier using algebra, some are easier using geometry. Do not confuse exponents with individual indexes, marked A, B.

1. (40 points)
    a. Consider a two-person two-good exchange economy. Person A has an endowment of (1,0) and preferences $u^A = c_1^A c_2^A$. Person B has an endowment (1,2) and preferences u^B = Min$[2c_1^B, 3c_2^B]$. Using an Edgeworth Box draw their offer curves. Find competitive equilibrium prices and quantities.

    b. Consider an economy with 15 consumers and 2 goods. Consumer 3 has utility function $U^3 = x_1 + x_2$. At a certain Pareto efficient allocation, consumer 3 has an allocation (10,0). What can you say about the competitive prices that support this Pareto optimal allocation? Explain your answer.

    c. Consider a two-person two-good exchange economy. Assume that both persons have identical preferences, given by $u = c_1 + c_2$. Assume that the aggregate endowment of this economy is (1,2). Derive the set of Pareto optimal allocations.

    d. Consider an economy with two identical consumers. Each consumer <u>strictly</u> prefers the consumption bundle (x_1, x_2) to the bundle (y_1, y_2) if $\{x_1 + x_2 > y_1 + y_2$ <u>or</u> if $\{x_1 + x_2 = y_1 + y_2$ <u>and</u> $x_1 > y_1\}$. Assume that the aggregate endowment is (1,2). Derive the set of Pareto optimal allocations. Is there any problem achieving any of these allocations as competitive equilibria?

e. Consider an economy with equal numbers of two types of consumers. Assume that persons of type A have an endowment of $(1,1)$ and preferences $u^A = c_1^A c_2^A$. Assume that persons of type B have an endowment $(1,2)$ and preferences $u^B = c_1^B + c_2^B$. Assuming one person of each type, derive the core. Assuming two persons of each type, derive the core.

f. (Extra credit) Reconsider question a. with the following change. Person B has an endowment $(1,2)$ and preferences $u^B = \text{Min}[2c_1^B, c_2^B]$. Using an Edgeworth Box draw their offer curves. Can you find competitive equilibrium prices and quantities?

2. (30 points)

Consider a competitive economy with three goods, two consumers and one firm. Consumer A has the utility function $u^A = x_1^A + \ln[24 + x_2^A]$ and the consumption possibility set $\{x_1^A \geq 0, -24 \leq x_2^A \leq 0, x_3^A = 0\}$. Consumer A owns 100% of the firm. Consumer B has the utility function $u^B = (1/3)\ln[x_1^B] + (2/3)\ln[24 + x_3^B]$ and the consumption possibility set $\{x_1^B \geq 0, -24 \leq x_3^B \leq 0, x_2^B = 0\}$. The production set of the firm is $\{ (y_1, y_2, y_3) \mid y_1 \geq 0, y_2 \leq 0, y_3 \leq 0, y_1 - \ln[-y_2-y_3] \leq 0\}$.

a. Find the competitive equilibrium prices and quantities. What are the firm's profits in equilibrium?

Now assume that there is an externality in that consumer B is bothered by the supply of good 2 by consumer A. That is, the utility function of consumer B is now $u^B = (1/3)\ln[x_1^B] + (2/3)\ln[24 + x_3^B] + (0.1)x_2^A$.

b. Find the competitive equilibrium prices and quantities. Is equilibrium Pareto optimal? Explain how you would use taxes to achieve a Pareto optimum. (Describe a mathematical approach or an equation for determining taxes, do not derive a tax level.)

Now return to the formulation as in part a. (without externalities). Assume that for no apparent reason, the government decrees that for any consumer, labor supply is limited by the rule $x_2 \geq -6$. There is no restriction on x_3.

c. Find the competitive equilibrium prices and quantities. Is Consumer B better off in this equilibrium than in the one you found in answer to part a? What can you say about the Pareto optimality of this equilibrium? Explain carefully.

3. (30 points)

Consider a competitive economy with two periods and two states of nature. The probability of state 1 is 1/3 and the probability of state 2 is 2/3. There is a continuum of identical consumers each of whom is an expected utility maximizer, using the correct probabilities. Consumers learn which state of nature has occurred at the start of period 2. The utility function of each consumer (for expected utility maximization) is $u = (1/2) \ln[a] + (1/2) \ln[b]$, where a is consumption in the first period and b is consumption in the second period. The endowment of each consumer is 12 units of the first period consumption good and none of the second period consumption good in either state of nature. There are two types of firms in this economy. There are large numbers of each type of firm. All firms have constant returns to scale. On a 1 for 1 basis, firms of type 1 can convert units of first period consumption good into units of the second period consumption good that only are produced in state of nature 1. On a 1 for 1 basis, firms of type 2 can convert units of first period consumption good into units of the second period consumption good that only are produced in state of nature 2. There is a complete set of contingent commodity markets.

13

a. Determine competitive equilibrium prices and quantities.

Now assume that the government has the opportunity to invest z units of first period consumption good in order to improve the production possibilities of firms of type 1. Completing this investment means that these firms can convert each unit of first period consumption good into 2 units of second period consumption good if state of nature 1 happens.

b. Assume that the government wants to maximize the expected utility of the representative consumer and that the government can finance its investment by lump sum taxes. Derive an equation showing the values of z for which the government should use its investment opportunity.

Now assume that the government does not have the ability to levy lump sum taxes. If the government carries out its investment it levies taxes at the same proportional rate on the purchase of period two consumption in each state of nature in order to finance its investment.

c. Describe how you would approach determining the values of z for which the government should use its investment opportunity.

d. Extra credit

Derive an equation showing the values of z for which the government should use its investment opportunity.

e. Extra credit

Return to the setting in part a with no government investment. Assume that instead of the utility function $u = (1/2) \ln[a] + (1/2) \ln[b]$, consumers had the utility function $u = a^{1/2}b^{1/2}$. Does this change equilibrium? Explain your answer.

14

U

Princeton University
Department of Economics
Spring Term 1994

ECONOMICS 199 (U) - GAMES OF STRATEGY

Lectures: Tuesday and Thursday, 1.30 - 2.20, Comp. Sci. 104
Precepts: Wednesdays 10, 11 and 1.30, Thursdays 10, 11, Fisher Hall B-04
Professor: Avinash Dixit, 212 Fisher Hall, 8-4013, dixitak@pucc
          Office hours Tuesday 3-4, Wednesday 11.30-12.30
Preceptors: David Saettone, B-08 Fisher Hall, 8-5409, saettone@pucc
          Office hours Wednesday 2.30-4
          Norman Thurston, B-09 Fisher Hall, 8-2911, thurston@pucc
          Office hours Thursday 9-10

COURSE DESCRIPTION

This course is about strategically interdependent decisions. In such situations, the outcome of your actions depends also on the actions of others. When making your choice, you have to think what the others will choose, who in turn are thinking what you will be choosing, and so on. Game Theory offers several concepts and insights for understanding such situations, and for making better strategic choices. This course will introduce and develop some basic ideas from game theory, using illustrations, applications, and cases drawn from business, politics, sports, and even fiction and movies. There will be little formal theory, and the only pre-requisite is some high-school algebra. The course will *NOT* count as an economics departmental.

ASSESSMENT

There will be three short assignments during the term, each counting 10% toward the course grade. These will combine problem-set type material and more open-ended inquiries. The schedule is as follows:
    No.1: Handed out on February 24, due on March 3
    No.2: Handed out on March 31, due on April 7
    No.3: Handed out on April 21, due on April 28
Two game-playing projects can substitute for part or all of these assignments. Details of the projects are at the end of this syllabus.

An in-class mid-term examination to be held on March 10 will count 20% toward the course grade, and a scheduled final examination will count 50%.

BOOKS

The following two books are major components of the required reading, and are available for purchase at the U-store
Avinash Dixit and Barry Nalebuff, *Thinking Strategically*, Norton, 1991
Thomas Schelling, *The Strategy of Conflict*, Oxford, 1960
    Also significant in the required reading, but out of print, is
Morton Davis, *Game Theory: A Nontechnical Introduction*, Basic Books, 1983
several copies are on reserve in the Firestone library.

1

The following books are useful sources of examples and additional readings; they are cited for specific topics below. These and some other readings are on reserve in the Firestone library.

Economics: Robert Gibbons, *Game Theory for Applied Economists*, Princeton, 1992
Politics: Peter Ordeshook, *A Political Theory Primer*, Routledge, 1991
           Steven Brams, *Rational Politics*, Academic Press, 1985
Biology: John Maynard Smith, *Evolution and the Theory of Games*, Cambridge, 1982
Mathematics: Robert Luce and Duncan Raiffa, *Games and Decisions*, Wiley, 1957

COURSE OUTLINE

1. *INTRODUCTION AND MOTIVATION*

Topics:

Decisions (impersonal environment) and games (environment has other strategic actors whose choices interact with ours).

Some dimensions of classification of strategic interaction: (a) Games with fixed rules v. games where the players have freedom to set some rules. (b) Games with sequential moves v. simultaneous moves. (c) Single play v. repeated interaction. (d) Games of pure conflict (zero sum) v. games where the players have some common interests. (e) Games where the players have full information v. those with limited information.

Reading:

Dixit and Nalebuff, Chapter 1
Davis, Chapter 1

Optional additional readings:

Luce and Raiffa, Chapter 1

2. *SOME BASIC CONCEPTS AND TECHNIQUES*

Topics:

Games with sequential moves - Backward induction. Simultaneous-move games - Dominant strategies. Dominated strategies. Nash equilibrium.

Reading:

Dixit and Nalebuff, Chapters 2, 3
Davis, Chapters 2, 3 (pp.24-37)

Optional additional reading:

Ordeshook, Chapters 1-3
Luce and Raiffa, Chapters 2, 3
Gibbons, pp. 1-14, 57-61

2

74

3. RANDOMIZATION

Topics:

Mixed strategies. Their role in zero-sum games. Informal discussion of the von Neumann-Morgenstern theory. Examples from sports.

Readings:

Dixit and Nalebuff, Chapter 7
Davis, Chapters 3 (pp.38-56), 4

Optional additional reading:

Luce and Raiffa, Chapter 4

4. THE PRISONERS' DILEMMA

Topics:

Dominant strategy equilibrium in single play. Tacit cooperation in repeated play. Tit-for-tat and other strategies. Examples from business competition, international negotiations.

Reading:

Dixit and Nalebuff, Chapter 4

Optional additional reading:

Robert Axelrod, *The Evolution of Cooperation*, Basic Books, 1984
Ordeshook, Chapter 4, pp. 164-187

5. STRATEGIC MOVES

Topics:

Commitments, threats, promises and their credibility. First v. second-mover advantages. Examples from business competition, nuclear deterrence.

Reading:

Dixit and Nalebuff, Chapters 5, 6
Schelling, Chapters 2, 3, 5
Thomas Schelling, *Arms and Influence*, Chapters 1, 2
Thomas Schelling, *Choice and Consequence*, Chapters 3, 5

Optional additional reading:

Brams, Chapter 6

3

6. *BRINKMANSHIP*

Topics:

   Threats that leave something to chance. Nuclear deterrence. The Cuban missile crisis.

Reading:

   Dixit and Nalebuff, Chapter 8
   Schelling, Chapters 7, 8
   Thomas Schelling, *Arms and Influence*, Chapter 3
   Graham Allison, *Essence of Decision*, Little Brown, 1971

7. *EVOLUTIONARY STABILITY IN GAMES*

Topic:

   Dynamics of interaction when players follow fixed rules and success is rewarded. Examples from biology and from dilemma games.

Reading:

   Maynard Smith, Chapters 1, 2 (pp.10-23), 6, 7, 13.

8. *SOCIAL COORDINATION AND CONFLICT*

Topics:

   Multi-person dilemmas. Harmful external effects: congestion and pollution. Beneficial externalities, strategic complementarity: human capital and economic growth. Role of policy, social conventions etc.

Reading:

   Dixit and Nalebuff, Chapter 9
   Thomas Schelling, *Micromotives and Macrobehavior*, Chapters 4, 7

9. *INFORMATION*

Topics:

   Incentives to reveal and conceal private information, and strategies for doing so: signalling and screening. Design of contracts and incentives.

Reading:

   Dixit and Nalebuff, Chapter 12

Optional additional reading:

   Gibbons, pp. 152-168, 190-207; Ordeshook, Chapter 5

10. *BARGAINING*

Topics:

Cooperative and non-cooperative approaches. Value of patience. Role of focal points. Agreements and breakdowns - strikes.

Reading:

Dixit and Nalebuff, Chapter 11

Optional additional reading:

Howard Raiffa, *The Art and Science of Negotiation*, Harvard, 1982
Roger Fisher and William Ury, *Getting to Yes*, Penguin Books, 1991

11. *VOTING IN ELECTIONS AND LEGISLATURES*

Topics:

The median voter theorem and its limitations. Agenda manipulation.

Reading:

Dixit and Nalebuff, Chapter 10
Ordeshook, Chapter 3 section 3, Chapter 4
Brams, Chapters 2-5

BEYOND THIS COURSE

Game Theory has reached the point where several courses could follow this one and still not exhaust the subject. For those who want to sample this material (most of it highly mathematical), here is a short bibliography.

David Kreps, *Game Theory and Economic Modelling*, Oxford, 1990
Ken Binmore, *Fun and Games*, Heath, 1992
Drew Fudenberg and Jean Tirole, *Game Theory*, MIT Press, 1991
Roger Myerson, *Game Theory*, Harvard, 1991

5

Important: PRINT your name, and write and SIGN honor code pledge, on the cover of your answer-book.

QUESTION 1: (60 points, 30 minutes)

For each of the following three statements: [1] Say whether it is true or false. [2] In two or three brief sentences, state the reason for your answer. [3] Give an example of a game that illustrates your answer.

[a] In a sequential-move game, the player who moves first is sure to win.

[b] If a player has a dominant strategy in a simultaneous-move game, then he/she is sure to get his/her best outcome.

[c] If a game has several Nash equilibria, then the outcome of playing the game will be a random mixture between all these equilibria.

QUESTION 2: (40 points, 20 minutes)

EITHER:

Consider the following zero-sum game:

		Column	
		Left	Right
Row	Up	0	A
	Down	B	C

The entries are the Row player's payoffs, and the numbers A, B, and C are all positive. What other relations between these numbers (for example $A < B < C$) must be valid for each of the following cases to arise:

(1) At least one of the players has a dominant strategy.

(2) Neither player has a dominant strategy but there is a Nash equilibrium in pure strategies.

(3) There is a Nash equilibrium in mixed strategies.

If (3) is true, write down a formula for Row's probability of choosing Up, with A, B, and C on the right hand side.

OR:
Consider a game between a government and a terrorist group holding hostages. What threats or promises might each side make? Do you expect them to be credible? Why, or why not? (Warning: You have only 20 minutes. So be brief; think of the major points and focus on them.)

Princeton University
Department of Economics
Spring Term 1994
Economics 199 - Games of Strategy
FINAL EXAMINATION

READ THESE IMPORTANT INSTRUCTIONS CAREFULLY FIRST:

(1) This exam has 4 pages. Make sure you have them all.

(2) ANSWER EACH OF QUESTIONS 1-4 IN A **SEPARATE** BOOKLET.

(3) This is a closed-book exam; put away all your books, notes, notebook and palmtop computers, cellular phones etc NOW. A simple +-×+ calculator may be used for Question 4, but is not necessary.

(4) Each question carries 25 points. It is suggested that you spend 40 minutes answering each, reserving the first 20 minutes to read the exam carefully and plan your answers.

(5) Time will be called after three hours. After that, extra time can be "purchased" at the rate of TWO points per MINUTE or fraction thereof.

(6) Be brief and write legibly. We prefer you to use a ball-point pen or ink. Writing in pencil may get smudged or unclear; any such unclear answers will be interpreted as wrong. If you change your mind about an answer, make your erasures and corrections VERY CLEARLY and NOT IN PENCIL; any ambiguity will be interpreted as an incorrect answer.

(7) When answering one question, do not give cross-references to your answers on other questions - different booklets are graded separately.

(8) Write out and sign the honor pledge - "I pledge my honor that I have not violated the Honor Code during this examination" - on the cover of your answer booklet for Question 1.

QUESTION 1:

Define the following concepts, and BRIEFLY (under 100 words each) state their significance in game theory.

[i] Subgame perfectness
[ii] Polymorphic equilibrium
[iii] Tit-for-tat
[iv] Brinkmanship
[v] Separating equilibrium

QUESTION 2:

Answer [a] (4 points) AND any THREE of [b]-[f] below (7 points each). Your answers should be BRIEF (about 100 words each).

[a] A German property developer disappeared, leaving behind billions in debt. "He told me he was going on a trip to Tuscany," said an associate. "I assume that means he is definitely not in Tuscany." (New York Times, April 14, 1994.) Comment from a strategic perspective.

1

[b] Your parents phone to tell you that your long-lost great-uncle from Ruritania will visit Princeton this Saturday, and would like to meet you. His English is not very good, however, and they were unable to convey to him the fact that you are a student at Princeton University, nor were they able to convey any address more specific than Princeton, New Jersey. They could not find out what method of transport he will take, nor the time he will arrive. Of course, your parents expect you to do everything possible to meet him on Saturday: he is rumored to be very rich (but a bit stingy). Where will you look for him, and at what time? Explain the reasons for your choice.

[c] In a scene from the movie *Manhattan Murder Mystery*, Woody Allen and Diane Keaton are at a hockey game in Madison Square Garden. She is obviously not enjoying herself, but he tells her: "Remember our deal. You stay here with me for the entire hockey game, and next week I will come to the opera with you and stay until the end." Later we see them coming out of the Met into a deserted Lincoln Center square, while inside the music is still playing. Keaton is visibly upset: "What about our deal? I stayed to the end of the hockey game, and so you were supposed to stay till the end of the opera." Allen answers: "You know I can't listen to too much Wagner. At the end of the first act I already felt the urge to invade Poland." Comment from a strategic perspective.

[d] "To stop [the fighting in ex-Yugoslavia from spreading] a small UN force is symbolically stationed in Macedonia. It includes 300 Americans." (The Economist, April 23, 1994.) In strategic terms, what is the theory behind this troop deployment?

[e] "Mr. Robinson pretty much concludes that business schools are a sifting device - M.B.A. degrees are union cards for yuppies. But perhaps the most important fact about the Stanford business school is that all meaningful sifting occurs before the first class begins. No messy weeding is done within the walls. 'They don't want you to flunk. They want you to become a rich alum who'll give a lot of money to the school.' But one wonders: If corporations are abdicating to the Stanford admissions office the responsibility for selecting young managers, why don't they simply replace their personnel departments with Stanford admissions officers, and eliminate the spurious education? Does the very act of throwing away a lot of money and two years of one's life demonstrate a commitment to business that employers find appealing?" (From the review by Michael Lewis (Princeton '82) of Peter Robinson's *Snapshots from Hell: The Making of an MBA*, New York Times Book Review, May 8, 1994.) What answer to Lewis' question can you give based on our analysis of strategies in situations of asymmetric information?

[f] A house-painter has a regular contract to work for a builder. On these jobs, his cost estimates are generally right: sometimes a little high, sometimes a little low, but correct on the average. When the regular work is slack, he bids competitively for other jobs. "Those are different," he says. "They almost always end up costing more than I estimate." Assuming his estimating skills do not differ between the jobs, what can explain the difference?

2

QUESTION 3:

Based on your knowledge of strategic thinking, offer advice to ANY TWO of the following (not more than 250 words each):

(A) The Internal Revenue Service concerning its auditing strategy.

(B) The Clinton administration concerning the strategy to compel North Korea to permit international inspections of its nuclear facilities.

(C) An inventor or innovator (for example in computers or biotechnology) seeking finance from a bank or a venture capitalist, and needing to convince them of the potential profitability of his/her ideas.

(D) A Metropolitan Transport Authority, on how it should take congestion into account when setting the tolls for its tunnels and bridges, and fares for mass transit.

QUESTION 4:

Here you have a choice between a mathematical problem and an essay.

EITHER

Rosencrantz and Guildenstern pass the time on their voyage to England by playing the following game. Each makes an initial bet of 8 ducats. Then each separately tosses a fair coin (probability 1/2 each of Heads and Tails). Each sees the outcome of his own toss but not that of the other; Hamlet acts as the impartial referee and observes and records both outcomes to prevent cheating.

Then Rosencrantz decides whether to pass, or to bet an additional 4 ducats. If he chooses to pass, the two coin tosses are compared. If the outcomes are different, the one who has the Heads collects the whole pot. The pot has 16 ducats, of which he himself contributed 8, so his winnings are 8 ducats. If the outcomes are the same, the pot is split equally and each gets his 8 ducats back.

If Rosencrantz chooses to bet, then Guildenstern has to decide whether to concede, or match with his own additional 4 ducats. If Guildenstern concedes, then Rosencrantz collects the pot irrespective of the numbers tossed. If Guildenstern matches, then the coin tosses are compared. The procedure is the same as that in the previous paragraph, with Heads the winner, but the pot is now bigger.

When this game is written in the normal form, Rosencrantz has four strategies: pass always (PP), bet always (BB), bet if his own coin comes up Heads and pass if Tails (BP), and pass on Heads and bet on Tails (PB). Similarly, Guildenstern has four strategies: concede always (CC), match always (MM), match on Heads and concede on Tails (MC) and the other way round (CM).

3

You are told that the matrix of payoffs to Rosencrantz is as follows:

		Guildenstern			
		CC	MM	MC	CM
Rosen-crantz	PP	0	0	0	0
	BB	8	0	1	7
	BP	2	1	0	3
	PB	6	-1	1	4

For the strategy combinations (BB,MC) and (BP,CM), prove that the payoffs are as stated. [10 points] (In each case you will have to average over the consequences for each of the four possible combinations of the coin toss outcomes.)

Eliminate dominated strategies as far as possible. Find the mixed strategy equilibrium in the remaining matrix, and the expected payoff to Rosencrantz in the equilibrium. [10 points]

Explain intuitively why the equilibrium has mixed strategies. [5 points]

OR

Discuss the strategic moves that occurred in the movie Dr. Strangelove. Your focus should be on issues of credibility (observability and irreversibility) of commitments, and their vulnerability to errors. Your answer should be about 500 words long.

4

Princeton University
Department of Economics
Spring Term 1994
ECONOMICS 199 (U) - GAMES OF STRATEGY
Problem Set 1

Note: [1] Read and remember the procedures concerning deadlines, penalties etc. that were handed out in the first class. [2] You are allowed to discuss the problems with your fellow students, but your submission should be based on your own understanding and not be copied from someone else's work.

QUESTION 1: 70 POINTS

The following is a simplified version of the upcoming health care debate and legislation in the Congress.

There are three bills: [1] the one submitted by the Clinton administration, [2] the alternative proposed by Congressman Cooper, and [3] some minor tinkering with the existing system.

There are three groups of legislators, the liberal Democrats (LD), the conservative Democrats (CD), and the Republicans (R).

The liberal Democrats like [1] best, but may compromise on [2]. The conservative Democrats like [2] best, but may compromise on [1] or [3]. The Republicans like [3] best, but may compromise on [2].

If two of the three groups choose the same position, that bill will be passed. If all three choose different positions, there will be no bill.

There are twelve possible strategy combinations yielding different outcomes. The table on the following page describes these, and also shows how the three groups rate these alternatives, in each case 12 being best and 1 worst.

You are asked to consider this as a three-player game.

(1) First suppose it is a simultaneous-move game. Show the (3-dimensional) payoff matrix, either as three 2-by-2 or two 2-by-3 matrices (15 points). Find all the Nash equilibria in pure strategies (15 points).

(2) Next suppose it is a sequential move game. How many different orders of moves are logically possible? (5 points). Choose any three of them, with the liberal Democrats moving first in one, second in another, and third in the third. For each of the three you choose, draw the game tree and find the subgame perfect (backward induction) equilibrium (10 points each).

(3) What, if anything, can the liberal Democrats do to achieve an outcome that is better for them? Briefly state any ideas you have; we will develop some systematic theory of such strategies later in the course. (5 points)

Choices			Outcomes	Payoffs		
LD	CD	R		LD	CD	R
1	1	2	Clinton bill passes along party lines, R look moderate in opposition	11	7	4
1	1	3	Clinton bill passes along party lines, R look extreme in opposition	12	6	5
1	2	2	Cooper bill passes, R take credit for compromise	6	10	9
1	2	3	No bill, gridlock, Congress as a whole is criticized	3	3	1
1	3	2	No bill, CD look extreme, R look moderate	2	2	2
1	3	3	Tinkering reform, CD and R claim credit for saving country from socialism	4	5	12
2	1	2	Cooper bill passes, R claim credit, CD get their wish, but look foolish	8	9	10
2	1	3	No bill. R claim credit for saving country from socialism, CD look foolish	1	1	3
2	2	2	Cooper bill passes unanimously, Congress as a whole claims credit	9	11	8
2	2	3	Cooper bill passes along party lines, LD and CD claim credit	10	12	7
2	3	2	Cooper bill passes, CD look foolish	7	8	6
2	3	3	Tinkering reform, CD and R claim credit for saving country from socialism, but not very successfully because LD were compromising	5	4	11

2

QUESTION 2: 30 POINTS

The labor union and the management of a company are submitting a wage dispute to arbitration. The board is to consist of one representative of each side, and an impartial chair. The outcome will be the resulting wage increase, measured in dollars per week.

The game is between the union and the management, and the strategy for each is to choose its nominee. Each side has four candidates, with different degrees of commitment to their side and different degrees of vehemence in pursuing their side's case. We will label each side's candidates as unbiased (U), biased (B), soft-spoken (S) and hard-line (H). We will also label the sides as labor (L) and management (M); thus labor choosing a hard-line nominee will be strategy LH, and so on.

This is a zero-sum game: the union wants large wage increases and the management wants small ones.

The payoff matrix is known to both players, and is as follows:

		Management			
		MU	MB	MS	MH
Labor	LU	15	5	10	10
	LB	45	40	20	25
	LS	20	10	30	30
	LH	15	20	15	15

(Note that a hard-line or biased nominee is not always an advantage; for example that may alienate the chair.)

(1) For Labor, which strategies are dominated by which other strategies? (5 points)

(2) After eliminating Labor's dominated strategies, which strategies for the Management are dominated by which other strategies? (5 points)

(3) Successively eliminating the dominated strategies identified above should leave a 2-by-2 matrix. Find the mixed strategy equilibrium for this. Find each side's mixture (15 points) and the expected wage increase in the equilibrium (5 points).

3

QUESTION 1 - 80 POINTS

Boeing and Airbus are rival aircraft manufacturers deciding whether to develop of a new type of commercial jet airplane. The US government can help our national firm Boeing, and the European governments can help their national firm Airbus, by subsidizing the development costs, or by closing the national market to the rival firm. This problem will examine the desirability of doing so.

It will cost each firm $7.2 billion to develop the plane, and $20 million to manufacture each plane. The total sales of such an aircraft will be 200 to US airlines, 200 to European airlines, and 200 to other countries' airlines. In any of these three markets, the price of each plane will be $50 million if one firm has a monopoly in that market (either because the other chooses not to develop the plane at all, or because the US and/or European market is closed to the other firm), and $40 million if the two firms compete in that market. In the latter case, they will split the total sales in that market equally.

We will consider various games involving the two firms, and the US and European governments. We begin by defining the payoff.

Each firm's payoff equals 0 if it does not develop the plane. If it does, the payoff (profit) equals the sum of its revenues from sales in all the markets that are open to the firm, minus the costs of manufacture of the planes it sells, minus the development costs.

Each government's payoff is defined as the sum of the following THREE items: [1] Its national firm's profit; this enters positively in the government's payoff. [2] Any tax dollars given in government support to its national firm; this enters negatively. [3] Its national consumers' benefit (which enters positively) when a competitively priced new aircraft is available. This is equal to the difference between the prices under monopoly and competition, $50-40 = 10$ million, times the number of the new aircraft sold in that country's market, 200, so it comes to $2 billion.

NO POLICY

[a] First suppose that neither government offers any subsidy, and all three markets (US, European and rest of the world's airlines) are open to both firms. Calculate the payoff matrix of the simultaneous-move game where each firm decides whether to develop the plane. Show that the game is one of Chicken.

[b] Suppose the outcome of this game is the mixed strategy equilibrium. In it: [i] Show that each firm will develop the aircraft with probability 0.9; [ii] Find the expected payoff to each firm. [iii] Show that the expected benefit to consumers in each country is $1.62 billion. [iv] Calculate the resulting expected payoff to the US and European governments (even though they are not players in the game at this point).

SUBSIDIES

[c] Next suppose the European government makes a strategic move and promise to pay the development costs of Airbus if it goes ahead with the project, while the US government remains passive. How does this alter the game between Boeing and Airbus? Calculate the resulting payoff to the European government, and compare it to that you calculated in [b] above. Does the European government increase its payoff by making this strategic move?

[d] Next suppose both governments have such a subsidy policy in place. What happens to the game between Boeing and Airbus? What are the resulting payoffs to the two governments?

[e] Finally, consider a two-stage game with simultaneous moves within each stage. At the first stage the US and European governments decide whether to promise to pay the development costs of Boeing and Airbus respectively, and at the second stage the firms decide whether to develop the new plane. Calculate the payoff matrix of the first stage, using the results from parts [b]-[d] above to get some relevant information about the second stage. Find the subgame perfect equilibrium of the full game.

PROTECTED MARKETS

[f] Now suppose the European government, instead of subsidies, uses the "buy national" policy, where it decrees that if Airbus develops the plane, European airlines must buy from it. (If Airbus does not develop the plane, they are free to buy from Boeing.) Then Airbus can get a monopoly of the European market, and can also competes with Boeing in US and rest of the world. The US government is inactive in policy. What now is the result of the game between Boeing and Airbus? Is the strategic move in the European government's interest, again when compared to having no policy at all as in case [b] above?

[g] Next suppose the US government also enacts a similar "buy national" policy. Thus, if both firms develop the plane, each will have a monopoly in its home market while they compete in the rest of the world. What is the equilibrium of the firms' game? What is the payoff to each government?

[h] Finally consider a two-stage game, with simultaneous moves within each stage. The governments act in the first stage, and decide whether to enact a "buy national" policy. The firms act in the second stage, and choose whether to proceed with the development. Find the subgame perfect equilibrium. Hint: use the payoff information from [b], [f] and [g] above.

OVERALL EVALUATION

[i] In parts [e] and [h] above, you should have noticed that the first stage is a Prisoners' Dilemma for the governments. In a brief paragraph, suggest one way for them to achieve the cooperative outcome, and discuss its credibility.

PROBLEM SET CONTINUES WITH QUESTION 2 ON PAGE 3

You are one of 12 jurors contemplating your verdict on a case. The jurors will vote by secret ballot; unanimity is required for conviction. Based on all the evidence you have heard, you estimate the probability of the accused being guilty at 80%. Your valuation of the four possible outcomes (conviction or acquittal of an actually guilty or an actually innocent person) is as follows:

		Outcome of trial	
		Convicted	Acquitted
Reality	Guilty	1	-1
	Innocent	-97	1

(Caution: This is not the game payoff matrix; that will be 12-dimensional since there are 12 "players." Do not try to write the full matrix; a minute's thought about the possible combinations of strategies is worth more than an hour's matrix-writing for this problem.) **Prove** that your dominant strategy is to vote for acquittal. How high must your estimate of the probability of guilt be before your dominant strategy will become voting for conviction?

3

QUESTION 1 - 35 POINTS

When in a football game, the offense needs to gain 20 yards and has two plays to do it, commentators often discuss whether it is better to try for the whole lot in one play, or go for half the distance each time. This problem should teach you how to think through this, and startle your friends with your insight next fall.

Suppose the offense has to get 20 yards in two downs, labelled third and fourth, to win, else it loses. The offense's coach has two plays for this situation, one that if successful will cover 10 yards, the other, 20. The opposing coach, knowing this, can set his defense to cover either. The offense's probabilities of success for the possible combinations of the two sides' choices in any one down are as follows:

		Defense	
		10	20
Offense	10	4/5	1
	20	1	1/2

The payoffs for the ultimate outcomes are as follows: if the offense wins it gets 1, if it loses it gets 0. This is a zero-sum game.

Solve this game backward. Begin by considering the fourth down, which may occur with either 10 or 20 yards to go depending on what happened on the earlier third down. In each of these two cases, find the fourth-down equilibrium (possibly in mixed strategies), and the resulting payoff for the offense. Note that the offense wins if it completes the 20 yard play when it needs only 10 yards, but not vice versa. (Note: if mixture probabilities or payoffs are fractions, simplify them as fractions, but DO NOT try to divide and express them in decimals.)

Now consider the third down. You must derive the payoff matrix for the possible strategy combinations here. In each case, carefully calculate all the possible eventual outcomes and their probabilities. Show that in the equilibrium of the third down, the offense will use the 10-yard play with probability 7/9.

Briefly (100 words or less) indicate how this numerical example helps you think about the general question stated at the beginning. No actual calculations of the more general analysis are required.

QUESTION 2 - 35 POINTS

A single play of a Prisoners' Dilemma has the following payoffs:

		Player 2	
		Cooperate	Defect
Player 1	Cooperate	3, 3	1, 4
	Defect	4, 1	2, 2

There is a large population of individuals, the behavior of each of whom is genetically determined. Each is either a defector (always defects in any play of a Prisoners' Dilemma) or a tit-for-tat player (in any sequence of Prisoners' Dilemmas, cooperates on the first play, and on any subsequent play does what his opponent did on the previous play).

Pairs of randomly chosen players from this population play "sets" of n single plays of this dilemma. The payoff of each player over one whole set is the sum of his payoffs over the n plays. Show in a two-by-two table the payoffs over one set when each of the two types meets an opponent of each of the two types.

The population has a proportion p of defectors and (1-p) of tit-for-tat players. Each plays such sets repeatedly, matched against a new randomly chosen opponent for each set. A tit-for-tat player always begins each new set by cooperating on its first play. Find the fitness (average payoff over one set against a randomly chosen opponent) for a defector. Do the same for a tit-for-tat player. Show that when $p > (n-2)/(n-1)$, the defector type has the greater fitness, and when $p < (n-2)/(n-1)$ the tit-for-tat type has the greater fitness.

If evolution leads to a gradual increase in the proportion of the fitter type in the population, what are the possible eventual outcomes of this process (the evolutionary stable strategies)?

In what sense does longer repetition (larger n) facilitate the evolution of cooperation?

QUESTION 3 - 30 POINTS

Write a BRIEF account of a game of strategy in which you have been personally involved (not board games or video or computer games, but real-life strategic interactions; sports are OK so long as the focus is on strategy).

You will be graded for the following: [1] The intrinsic strategic subtlety and interest of the situation you describe. [2] Your strategic insights on the game: your judgment as to who played well or badly and why. [3] Novelty: choosing a situation different from one chosen by several of your classmates. [4] Brevity: THE TARGET LENGTH IS TWO DOUBLE-SPACED TYPED OR PRINTED PAGES IN A 12-CHARACTER-FONT AND 1" MARGINS ON ALL FOUR SIDES (LIKE THIS PAGE BUT DOUBLE-SPACED). Keeping the length below this target will be rewarded a little, and exceeding the target will be penalized VERY heavily.

Mr. Frech   UNIVERSITY OF CALIFORNIA   Fall 1994
                        SANTA BARBARA

Economics 210A
Microeconomic Theory

OBJECTIVE. This course is designed to educate the student
in the results, and more importantly, the methods of
economic reasoning. As an introduction to the theory
sequence, this course will stress economic concepts and
their application, rather than formal technique.

PROCEDURES. Classes will be a mixture of lecture and
discussion. Questions and comments are welcome.
Examinations will test the student's ability to use economic
reasoning on new problems as well as the retention of
specific material.

READINGS. Some required readings will be in a packet
available from Kinko's in Isla Vista (K). Some books will
be on reserve at the library. The required textbooks are:

Hirshleifer, Jack and Amihai Glazer. Price Theory and
Applications, 5th ed. Engelwood Cliffs, N.J.: Prentice-
Hall, 1992, (HG). (This is an interesting and thoughtful
intermediate theory book, with rich examples and problems,
but little mathematics.)

Silberberg, Eugene. The Structure of Economics, 2nd ed.
New York: McGraw-Hill, 1990 (S).

Varian, Hal R. Microeconomic Analysis, 3rd ed. New York:
Norton, 1992, (V). (V and S will not be used heavily in
this class, but they will be used in other theory classes.)

Other useful books, some on reserve at the library are:

Alchian, Armen A. Economic Forces at Work. Indianapolis,
Ind.: Liberty Press, 1977.

Becker, Gary S. Economic Theory. New York: Alfred A.
Knopf, 1971.

Becker, Gary S. A Treatise on the Family. Cambridge,
Mass.: Harvard Univ. Press, 1981.

Breit, William and Harold M. Hochman. Readings in
Microeconomics, 2nd ed. New York: Holt, Rinhart and
Winston, 1988.

Carlton, Dennis W. and Jeffrey M. Perloff. <u>Modern Industrial Organization</u>. Glenville, Ill.: Scott, Foresman/Little, Brown, 1990.

Coase, Ronald H. <u>The Firm, The Market and The Law</u>. Univ. of Chicago Press, 1988.

Friedman, Milton. <u>Price Theory</u>. Chicago: Aldine, 1976.

Hirshleifer, Jack. <u>Investment, Interest and Capital</u>. Englewood Cliffs, N.J.: Prentice-Hall, 1970.

Hirshleifer, Jack and John G. Riley. <u>The Analytics of Uncertainty and Information</u>. Cambridge: Cambridge Univ. Press, 1992.

Krouse, Clement G. <u>Theory of Industrial Economics</u>. Cambridge, Mass.: Basil Blackwell, 1990.

Milgrom, Paul and John Roberts. <u>Economics, Organization & Management</u>. Englewood Cliffs, N.J.: Prentice-Hall, 1992.

Nicholson, Walter. <u>Microeconomic Theory: Basic Principles and Extensions</u>, 4th ed. Chicago: Dryden, 1989. (This is another excellent intermediate theory book, but more formal and with fewer applications and problems than HG.)

Scherer, F.M. and David Ross. <u>Industrial Market Structure and Economic Performance</u>, 3rd ed. Boston: Houghton Mifflin, 1990.

Stigler, George. <u>The Theory of Price</u>, 3rd ed. New York: Macmillian, 1966.

Stigler, George J. <u>The Organization of Industry</u>. Chicago: Univ. of Chicago Press, 1968.

Tirole, Jean. <u>The Theory of Industrial Organization</u>. Cambridge, Mass." MIT Press, 1988.

Many intermediate theory books are excellent for review. Some recent examples with particularly rich applications and problems are:

Friedman, David D. <u>Price Theory: An Intermediate Text</u>, 2nd ed. Cincinnati, Ohio: South-Western, 1990.

Landsberg, Steven E. <u>Price Theory and Applications</u>. Chicago: Dryden, 1989.

Pindyck, Robert S. and Daniel L. Rubinfeld. <u>Microeconomics</u>. New York: Macmillian, 1989.

A direct competitor to Varian, but with a completely different approach (dominated by game theory) is:

Kreps, David M. <u>A Course in Microeconomic Theory</u>. Princeton Univ. Press, 1990.

<u>Reading Priority</u>. Readings marked with ** are especially important, those marked * are of intermediate importance. Unmarked readings are optional.

I.   <u>Methodology</u>

**   HG, ch. 1

**   Hayek, F.A. <u>Studies in Philosophy, Politics and Economics</u>. New York: Simon and Schuster, 1967, chs. 1**, 2*

*   Nicholson, ch. 1.

*   Stigler 1966, chs. 1, 2

*   Hayek, F.A. <u>The Counter Revolution of Science</u>. New York: Free Press, 1955, pp. 25-36

*   Friedman, Milton. "The Methodology of Positive Economics." In <u>Essays in Positive Economics</u>, ed. by Milton Friedman, 1953: 3-47. Repr. in BH, ch. 2.

*   Mayer, Thomas. "Friedman's Methodology of Positive Economics: A Soft Reading." <u>EI</u> 31 (1) (April 1993): 213-223. (Comment on Friedman, above.)

     Nagel, Ernest. "Assumptions in Economic Theory," <u>AER</u> LIII (2) (May 1963): 211-219. Repr. in Breit & Hochman, ch. 3. (Comment on Friedman, above.)

*   "Artificial Intelligence: A Debate." <u>Scientific American</u> 262 (1) (Jan. 1990): 25-39.

     Caldwell, Bruce J. "Clarifying Popper." <u>JEL</u> XXIX (1) (Mar. 1991): 1-33.

     Kuhn, <u>The Structure of Scientific Revolution</u>, 2nd ed. Univ. of Chicago Press, 1970.

     Klamer, Arjo and David Colander. <u>The Making of an Economist.</u> Boulder Colo.: Westview Press, 1990.

Penzias, Arno. _Ideas and Information_. New York: Touchstone, Simon and Schuster, 1989.

Buchanan, James M. _What Should Economists Do_? Indianapolis: Liberty Press, 1979.

McCloskey, Donald N. _If You're So Smart: The Narrative of Economic Expertise_. Chicago: Univ. of Chicago Press, 1990.

Hirshleifer, Jack. "Economics From a Biological Viewpoint," _JLE_ XXI (1) (April 1977): 1-52.

Baumol, William J. and Jess Benhabib. "Chaos: Significance, Mechanism, and Economic Applications." _Journal of Economic Perspectives_ 3 (1) (Winter 1989): 7-106

Gleick, James. _Chaos: Making a New Science_. New York: Penguin, 1987.

II. _The Standard Competitive Framework: Exchange and Equilibrium_

** HG, chs. 2, 13

** Hirshleifer, ch. 1

* Nicholson, ch. 8

V, ch. 17

S, chs. 15-17, 19

III. _Consumption, Demand and Rationality_

** HG, chs. 3-5.

** Becker, 1971, chs. 2, 3, p. 162-169

** Becker, Gary S. "A Theory of the Allocation of Time." _Economic Journal_ LXXV (299) (Sept. 1965): 493-517

* Johnson, M. Bruce. "Travel Time and the Price of Leisure." _Western Economic Journal_ 4 (2) (Spring 1966): 135-145

* Becker, 1981, ch. 1

** Becker, Gary S. "Irrational Behavior and Economic Theory." <u>JPE</u> 70 (1) (Feb. 1962): 1-13

* Kirzner, Israel M. "Rational Action and Economic Theory." <u>JPE</u> 70 (4) (Aug. 1962): 38-385

* Becker. "A Reply to I. Kirzner." <u>JPE</u> 71 (1) (Feb. 1963): 82-83

* Kirzner. "Rejoinder." <u>JPE</u> 71 (1) (Feb. 1963): 84-85

Friedman, ch. 2

Stigler 1966, chs. 3-4

Nicholson, chs. 3-7.

V, chs. 7-10

S, chs. 10-11

Stigler, George and Gary S. Becker. "De Gustibus Non Est Disputandum." <u>AER</u> 67 (2) (Mar. 1977): 76-90

Kagel, Battalio, et al. "Experimental Studies of Consumer Demand Behavior Using Laboratory Animals." <u>Economic Inquiry</u> 13 (1) (Mar. 1975): 22-38

Tullock, Gordon. "The Coal Tit as a Careful Shopper." <u>The American Naturalist</u> 105 (941) (Jan.-Feb. 1971): 77-80

IV. <u>The Firm and Production: The Standard Approach</u>

** HG, chs. 6-7, 11-12

* Stigler, 1966, chs. 5-6

* Nicholson, chs. 10-12, 21-22

Becker, 1971, chs. 5-8

* Friedman, chs. 5, 6*, 9-10

V, chs. 1-6

S, chs. 4, 6, 7, 8-9

Hirshleifer, Jack. "Exposition of the Equilibrium of the Firm: Symmetry Between Product and Factor Analysis." <u>Economica</u> 29 (115) (Aug. 1962): 263-268

V.   The Firm and Production: Extensions

A.   Costs and Outputs

**   Alchian, Armen A. "Costs and Outputs." in The
       Allocation of Economic Resources, Moses Abramowitz
       et al. Stanford Univ. Press, 1959:   23-40.
       Repr. in Breit & Hochman, ch. 12 and in A, ch. 11.

**   Hirshleifer, Jack. "The Firm's Cost Function: A
       Successful Reconstruction?" Journal of Business 35 (3)
       (July 1962):   235-255

*   De Alessi, Louis. "The Short Run Revisited." AER
       57 (3) (June 1967):   450-461. Repr. in Breit &
       Hochman, ch. 11.

*   Buchanan, James M. Cost and Choice. Chicago:
       Markham, 1969, chs. 1, 2.

       Stigler, 1966, ch. 15

       Buchanan, James M. and G.F. Thirlby. L.S.E. Essays on
       Costs. New York Univ. Press, 1981.

       Alchian, Armen A. "Cost." International Encyclopedia
       of the Social Sciences, vol. 3. Crowell Collier and
       Macmillian, 1968:   404-415. Repr. in Alchian, ch. 12.

B.   The Nature of the Firm

**   Alchian, Armen A. "The Basis of Some Recent Advances
       in the Theory of the Management of the Firm." Journal
       of Industrial Economics 14 (1) (Nov. 1965):   30-41.
       Repr. in Breit & Hochman, ch. 9.

*   Williamson, Oliver E. The Economic Institutions
       of Capitalism. New York: The Free Press, 1985:
       chs. 1, 2, 6.

*   Alchian, Armen A. and Susan Woodward. "The Firm is
       Dead; Long Live the Firm: A Review of Oliver E.
       Williamson's The Economic Institutions of Capitalism."
       JEL XXVI (1) (Mar. 1988):   65-79.

*   Coase, Ronald H. "The Nature of the Firm." Economica
       new series, 4 (16) (Nov. 1937): 386-405. Repr. in
       Coase, ch. 2.

**   Frech, H.E. III "The Property Rights Theory of the Firm: Empirical Results from a Natural Experiment." <u>JPE</u> 84 (1) (Jan. 1976): 143-152.

*   Frech, H.E. III. "The Property Rights Theory of the Firm and Competitive Markets for Top Decision-Makers." <u>Research in Law and Economics</u> 2 (1980): 49-63.

Milgrom and Roberts, chs. 1, 2, 9, 15.

Comanor, William S. "Review of <u>Studies in Economic Rationality: X-Efficiency Examined and Extolled</u>." <u>JEL</u> XXX (1) (Mar. 1992): 191-192.

Nicholson, ch. 13

Coase, Ronald H. "The Institutional Structure of Production." <u>AER</u> 82 (4) (Sept. 1992): 713-719.

Alchian, chs. 5, 9.

Alchian, Armen A. "Uncertainty, Evolution and Economic Theory." <u>JPE</u> 58 (3) (June 1950): 211-221. Repr. in Alchian, ch. 1.

Alchian, Armen A. and Harold Demsetz. "Production, Information Costs and Economic Organization." <u>AER</u> 62 (5) (Dec. 1972): 777-795. Repr. in Alchian, ch. 3.

Williamson, Oliver E. and Sidney G. Winter, eds. (Special Conference Issue on Coase and the Theory of the Firm). <u>Journal of Law, Economics and Organization</u> 4 (1) (Spring 1988).

Frech, H.E. III. "The Property Rights Theory of the Firm: Some Evidence from the U.S. Nursing Home Industry." <u>Journal of Institutional and Theoretical Economics</u> 141 (1) (Mar. 1985): 146-166.

Jensen, Michael C. and William H. Meckling. "Theory of the Firm: Managerial Behavior, Agency Costs and Ownership Structure." <u>Journal of Financial Economics</u> 3 (4) (Oct. 1976): 305-360.

Stigler, George. "The Division of Labor is Limited by the Extent of the Market." <u>JPE</u> 59 (3) (June 1951): 185-193. Repr. by Breit & Hochman, ch. 10.

De Alessi, Louis. "Property Rights, Transactions Costs, and X-Efficiency: An Essay in Economic Theory." <u>AER</u> 73 (1) (Mar. 1983): 64-81.

Boardman, Anthony E. and Aidan R. Vining. "Ownership Performance in Competitive Environments: A Comparison of the Performance of Private, Mixed and State-owned Enterprises." <u>JLE</u> XXXII (1) (April 1989): 1-34.

Nelson, Richard R. and Sidney G. Winter. <u>An Evolutionary Theory of Economic Change</u>. Harvard Univ. Press, 1982.

Weisbrod, Burton A. <u>The Nonprofit Economy</u>. Harvard Univ. Press, 1988.

Kirzner, Israel M. <u>Perception, Opportunity and Profit</u>: <u>Studies in the Theory of Entrepreneurship</u>. Univ. of Chicago Press, 1979.

VI. Imperfect Competition

A. Monopoly and Price Discrimination

** HG, ch. 8

* Nicholson, ch. 18

   V, chs. 14

   Krouse, ch. 7

   Scherer, ch. 13

   Stigler 1988, ch. 15

   Tirole, ch. 3

   Carlton & Perloff, chs. 5, 14, 15

   Stigler, 1966, chs. 11-13, 15

B. Oligopoly

** HG, ch. 10

* Nicholson, ch. 20

* Stigler, 1968, ch. 5

   Krouse, chs. 3, 9

   Carlton & Perloff, chs. 9, 10

   Thompson, Earl A. and Roger Faith. "A Pure Theory of

Strategic Behavior and Social Organization." <u>AER</u> 71 (3) (June 1981): 366-380.

C.   <u>Monopolistic Competition</u>

**   HG, ch. 9

Nicholson, ch. 19

Krouse, chs. 4-6, 14, 14

Tirole, ch. 7

Scherer & Ross, ch. 16

Carlton & Perloff, chs.. 12, 17, 18

VII. <u>Information: Moral Hazard & Adverse Selection</u>

**   Hirshleifer, ch. 8

*   Nicholson, ch . 9

Hirshleifer & Riley, chs. 1-4, 8

Marshall, John M. "Insurance Theory: Reserves versus Mutuality." <u>EI</u> 12 (4) (Dec. 1974): 476-492.

**   Pauly, Mark V. "The Economics of Moral Hazard: Comment." <u>AER</u> 58 (3) (June 1968): 531-537.

Frech, H.E. III, "Market Power in Health Insurance, Effects on Insurance and Medical Markets," <u>Journal of Industrial Economics</u> 27 (1) (Sept. 1979): 55-72.

Marshall, John M. "Moral Hazard." <u>AER</u> 66 (5) (Dec. 1976): 880-890.

*   Akerloff, George A. "The Market for Lemons: Qualitative Uncertainty and the Market Mechanism." <u>QJE</u> 84 (3) (August 1970): 488-500.

Heal, Geoffrey. "Do Bad Products Drive out Good?" <u>QJE</u> 85 (1) (Feb. 1977): 499-502. (Comment on above.)

**   Rothschild, Michael and Joseph Stiglitz. "Equilibrium in Competitive Insurance Markets." <u>QJE</u> 90 (4) (Nov. 1976): 629-649.

Milgrom & Roberts, chs. 6, 7.

VIII.   Public Goods, Externalities and the Environment

A.   Public Goods

**   HG, pp. 461-471.

**   Samuelson, Paul A.   "Diagramatic Exposition of a
     Theory of Public Expenditure." Review of Economics
     and Statistics 27 (4) (Nov. 1955):   350-356. Repr. in
     Breit & Hochman, ch. 35.

     Nicholson, pp. 726-735.

     V, ch. 23

B.   Externalities

**   HG, pp. 457-461.

*   Coase, Ronald H.   "The Problem of Social Cost." JLE 3
     (1960):   1-44. Repr in Breit & Hochman, ch. 33 and
     Coase, ch. 5.

     Coase.   "Notes on the Problem of Social Cost."
     Coase, ch. 6.

**   Frech, H.E III.   "The Extended Coase Theorem and Long
     Run Equilibrium: The Nonequivalence of Liability Rules
     and Property Rights." EI XVII (1) (April 1979):
     254-268.

     Nicholson, pp. 717-726

     V, ch. 24

     Baumol, William J.   "On Taxation and the Control of
     Externalities." AER 62 (3) (June 1972):   307-322

     Baumol, William J. and Wallace E. Oates.   The Theory of
     Environmental Policy. Englewood Cliffs, N.J.:
     Prentice-Hall, 1975.

     Dales, J.H.   Pollution, Property and Prices. Univ.
     of Toronto Press, 1968.

     Meade, James E.   "External Economies and Diseconomies
     in a Competitive Situation." EJ 62 (245) (Mar. 1952):
     Cheung, Stephen N.S.   "The Fable of the Bees: An
     Economic Investigation." JLE 16 (1) (April 1973):
     35-52.
     100

Mid-Term Examination Economics 210A Mr. Frech
TIME: 1.25 hours (100 points possible) Fall 1993

GENERAL INSTRUCTIONS: Read each question carefully. Plan
your answers; excessive wordiness, poor organization and
illegible writing will be penalized. Explain all answers.
Note carefully the point value of all questions.

1. Housing Prices (20 points)
Suppose that land use controls raise the price of housing.
Who do you suppose would have the larger reduction in
quantity demanded: people under 25 or over 60?

2. Labor Supply (20 points)
Since the War (WW II), famale labor supply has greatly
expended. How would you explain this?

3. Demand Curves (20 points)
Show the difference, if any, between Slutsky, Hicks, and
Marshallian demand curves for an inferior good.

4. Falsification versus Confirmation (20 points)
Why is falsification of a theory considered more decisive
than confirmation of a theory?

5. Costs and Outputs (20 points)
Volume of production does not appears in standard theory.
What are Hirshleifer's two interpretation of volume? How do
they relate to the short run/long run distinction?

Economics 210A   Mr. Frech
(100 points possible)   Fall 1993

GENERAL INSTRUCTIONS: Read each question carefully. Plan
your answers; excessive wordiness, poor organization and
unreadable writing will be penalized. Explain all answers.
Note carefully the point value of all questions.

1.   Rationality (10 points)
According to Gary Becker, the important theorems of modern
economics do not depend on rationality. Is this correct?

2.   Monopolistic Competition (15 points)
Consider a monopolistically competitive model. What effect
does a tax of a fixed amount per unit of output have on the
equilibrium?

3.   Entry (15 points)
Consider a monopoly. If a potential entrant made the
Bertrand assumption about the behavior of the original
monopolist, would it enter? Suppose instead it made a
Cournot assumption, would it enter?

4.   Insurance (12 points)
We observe private insurance markets for some bad events,
but not for others. How would you explain why we observe
little or no private insurance against the following:
     A.   Unemployment,
     B.   Worldwide famine,
     C.   Damage to machines due to wear,
     D.   Crop failure.

5.   Dentists (15 points)
Recently, a student went to the dentist. After telling the
dentist that he had low income, the dentist reduced the
price to him. Is this price discrimination? How do you
reconcile this with the observation that there are many
dentists in Santa Barbara?

6.   Adverse Selection (15 points)
Suppose that the price and (Rothschild/Stiglitz) definition
of an insurance policy is fixed by regulation. Does that,
in itself, eliminate adverse selection.

7.   The Course (5 points)
What is the most striking idea you have come across in your
reading or lectures in this course? How has it affected
your thinking?

8.   Trade and Equlibrium (13 points)
Would the introduction of trade lead a consumer to
specialize more or less than if there were no trade?

Mid-Term Examination   Economics 210A   Mr. Frech
TIME: 1.25 hours   (100 points possible)   Fall 1994

GENERAL INSTRUCTIONS: Read each question carefully. Plan
your answers; excessive wordiness, poor organization and
illegible writing will be penalized. Explain all answers.
Note carefully the point value of all questions.

1.   Cost Theory (20 points)
If there are several opportunities lost by taking a
particular action, which one is the cost of the choice
actually taken?   What assumptions are necessary to
interpret objectively measurable costs as the true cost?

2.   Taxes and Work Effort (20 points)
Between 1950 and 1990, the marginal tax rate facing the
average American worker increased a great deal. Yet, work
effort changed little. Does this mean that there is no
inefficiency or deadweight loss resulting from taxes on
labor?

3.   Demand Estimation (25 points)
It common to estimate demand for a good as a function of its
own price and aggregate income. In principle, what are the
problems with this specification? When is this
specification to be a relatively good approximation?

4.   Exact Models (10 points)
Why are exact models rare in economics, while they are
common in classical physics? Does that imply that economics
is unscientific or backward?

5.   Gains To Trade (25 points)
Suppose that there is a wino whose preferences can be
characterized as lexicographic between wine and bread.
Another individual has preferences for bread and wine can be
characterized as perfect substitutes. Are gains to trade
possible? Describe the equilibrium allocation of bread and
wine. What is the equilibrium price ratio?

Final Examination   Economics 210A   Mr. Frech
TIME: 2.5 hours   (100 points possible)   Fall 1994

GENERAL INSTRUCTIONS: Read each question carefully. Plan
your answers; excessive wordiness, poor organization and
unreadable writing will be penalized. Explain all answers.
Note carefully the point value of all questions.

1   Income Inequality (10 points)
Evaluate the following: "Much observed income inequality is
the result of individual choice."

2.   Monopolistic Competition and Gaps (15 points)
Consider an address model of monopolistic competition.
Suppose there were a short run equilibrium where there were
gaps in product space surrounding one particular firm.
(That is, where consumers with preferences for similar
products choose to consumer no products.) How would you
characterize the short run equilibrium of that particular
firm?

3.   Firm Size and Replication (10 points)
If experiments can be replicated, what keeps firms from
growing arbitrarily large?

4.   Property Rights and the Corporation (15 points)
How do you reconcile the following arguments:
     a.   Control is separated from control in the modern
corporation.
     b.   The owners of the modern corporation have complete
private property rights.

5.   Adverse Selection (15 points)
Consider an equilibrium of the Rothschild-Stiglitz model.
Suppose that most of the consumers are of the high risk
type. Is a costless government program of forced pooling
likely to lead to a Pareto improvement (make both high and
low risks better off)? Would your answer change if most of
the consumers are of the low risk type?

6.   The Course (5 points)
What is the most striking idea you have come across in your
reading or lectures in this course? How has it affected
your thinking?

7.   Oligopoly (20 points)
Suppose that duopolists agree to share the market equally.
What does their agreement implies in terms of effective
conjectural variation?

8.   Negative Supply (10 points)
Can the quantity supplied by an individual be negative in
exchange models? Can it be negative in models with
production?

104

Fall 1994   Professor Henry Grabowski

This is an honors seminar course. There will be no lectures or exams. There will be weekly readings and student-led presentations designed to promote discussion and debate. We will consider a broad range of topics that eventually could lead to an honors thesis in subsequent semesters.

After an initial session on the sources of market and government failure, the seminar will consider various topics based on symposia which have appeared in *The Journal of Economic Perspectives* as well as other publications. We will typically spend one session per topic. All members of the class will read the symposia material each week so as to be generally familiar with the key questions and issues.

For each topic, three or four student presenters will be selected. Two weeks prior to the scheduled class, these students will meet to organize the topic material. Each of them will also prepare a three-page single-spaced typed paper on a relevant aspect of the topic. These papers will be due in my office (314 Social Sciences) by noon on the Monday preceding our Tuesday afternoon seminar on that topic. My secretary will have copies made up of these papers for all class members by Monday afternoon at 3:00 P.M.

In the Tuesday seminar, each of the student presenters will briefly summarize their papers and also will be responsible for leading the discussion on the relevant economic issues posed by the topic. All class members are expected to participate in these discussions every week. Class participation will be an important component of the final grade.

In addition, a short term paper (approximately 10 double-spaced pages) is due at the end of the course. This can be a more extended analysis of a public policy issue discussed in class or a proposal for an honors thesis project. The actual research for the honors thesis is typically done in conjunction with an independent study or an advanced economics course.

Grades in Economics 201 will be based on the class papers and presentations, the term paper, and overall class participation.

My office is 314 Social Sciences Building. My office hours are by appointment. My telephone number is 660-1839.

Schedule--First Two Weeks

August 30   Organizational Session
September 6   Readings: Henry Grabowski, "Market Failure: The
                 Normative Basis for Government in a Market Economy"
                 and "Sources of Non-market Failure"

Airline Deregulation

Readings

1.   Steven Borenstein, "The Evolution of U.S. Airline Competition," Journal of Economic Perspectives, Vol. 6, No. 2, Spring 1992, pp. 45-73.

2.   Nancy L. Rose, "Fear of Flying? Economic Analysis of Airline Safety," Journal of Economic Perspectives, Vol. 6, Spring 1992, pp. 75-94.

3. Andrew N. Kleit, "Competition Without Apology: Market Power and Entry in the Deregulated Airline Industry," Regulation: The Cato Review of Business and Government, Cato Institute, Washington, Summer 1991, pp. 68-74.

Alcohol

Readings

1. Phillip Cook, "The Social Costs of Drinking," July 1990.

2. Phillip Cook and Michael Moore, "This Tax's for You: The Case for Higher Beer Taxes," June 1994. Phillip Cook, "Increasing the Federal Excise Tax on Alcoholic Beverages," Editorial, Journal of Health Economics, Vol. 7, 1988, pp. 89-91.

3. Phillip Cook and Michael Moore, "Drinking and Schooling," Journal of Health Economics, Vol. 12, 1993, pp. 411-429.

Tobacco

Readings

1. Michael Grossman et al., "Alcohol and Cigarette Taxes," Journal of Economic Perspectives, Vol. 7, Fall 1993, pp. 211-222.

2. Kenneth Warner, "Health and Economic Implications of a Tobacco-Free Society," JAMA, October 16, 1987, Vol. 285, pp. 2080-2086.

3. W. Kip Viscusi, Making the Risky Decision, Oxford University Press, 1992, pp. 3-15; 144-152.

4. Michael Schudson, "Symbols and Smokers: Advertising, Health Messages and Public Policy," in Smoking Policy: Law, Politics and Culture, pp. 208-228.

Liability

Readings

1. Carl Shapiro, "Symposium on the Economics of Liability," Journal of Economic Perspectives, Vol. 5, No. 3, Summer 1991, pp. 3-10.

2. George L. Priest, "The Modern Expansion of Tort Liability: Its Sources, Its Effects and Its Reform," ibid., pp. 31-50.

3. Patricia M. Danzon, "Liability for Medical Malpractice," ibid., pp. 51-69.

4. W. Kip Viscusi, "Product and Occupational Liability," <u>ibid.</u>, pp. 71-91.

5. Robert E. Litan and Clifford Winston, eds., <u>Liability: Perspectives and Policy</u>, The Brookings Institution: Washington, D.C., 1988, Chapter 8, "Policy Options," pp. 227-241.

Professional Sports

<u>Readings</u>

1. James Quirk and Rodney D. Fort, <u>Pay Dirt: The Business of Professional Team Sports</u>, Princeton University Press, 1992, Chapter 1, pp. 1-22.

2. Edward Gramlich, "A National Experiment in Styles of Capitalism: Professional Sports," <u>Quarterly Review of Economics and Finance</u>, volume 34, Summer 1994, No. 2, pp. 121-130.

3. Edward Gramlich et al., <u>Major League Baseball Economic Study Committee: Staff Analysis</u>, December 1992. (Not copyrighted.)

4. Roger Noll, "Professional Basketball: Economic and Business Perspectives," Paul D. Staudohar and James A. Mangan, eds., <u>The Economics of Professional Sports</u>, 1991, pp. 18-47.

Higher Education

<u>Readings</u>

1. Charles Clotfelter and Michael Rothchild, <u>Studies of Supply and Demand in Higher Education</u>, pp. 20-37.

2. Phil Cook and Robert Frank, "The Growing Concentration of Top Students at Elite Schools," in Clotfelter and Rothchild, pp. 121-140.

3. Estelle James et al., "College Quality and Future Earnings: Where Should You Send Your Child to College," <u>American Economic Review</u>, May 1989, pp. 247-252.

4. Allen Krueger and William Bowen, "Income-Contingent College Loans," <u>Journal of Economic Perspectives</u>, Summer 1993, pp. 193-201.

5. Charles Clotfelter, <u>Buying the Best</u>, 1994, Chapter 9.

Electric Utilities

Readings

1. Viscusi, Vernon and Harrington, "Natural Monopoly Regulation," Economics of Regulation and Antitrust, Chapter 12.

2. Matthew C. Hoffman, "The Future of Electricity Provision," Regulation, 1994, No. 3, pp. 55-62.

3. Graham H. Hadley, "A Competitive Electricity Market: Lessons from the U.K.?" Chapter 4 in The Electric Industry in Transition, pp. 39-49.

Telecommunications

Readings

1. Robert W. Crandall, "Relaxing the Regulatory Stranglehold on Communications," Regulation, Summer 1992, pp. 26-35.

2. W. Kip Viscusi, John M. Vernon, and Joseph S. Harrington, Jr., "Dynamic Issues in Natural Monopoly Regulation: Telecommunications," Chapter 15.

3. Symposium on the Future of Telecommunications in Regulation, Summer 1993, No. 3, Articles by Gilder, Noam, Huber, Hazlett, and Kwerel and Williams.

Global Warming

Readings

1. Stephen H. Schneider, "The Greenhouse Effect: Science and Policy," Science, Feb. 1989, pp. 771-781.

2. William D. Nordhaus, "Economic Approaches to Greenhouse Warming," in R. Dornbusch and J. M. Poterba, eds., Global Warming: Economic Policy Responses (Cambridge: MIT Press, 1991), pp. 33-66.

3. Richard Schmalensee, "Symposium on Global Climate Change," Journal of Economic Perspectives, Vol. 7, Fall 1993, pp. 3-10.

4. James Poterba, "Global Warming Policy, "A Public Finance Perspective," Journal of Economic Perspectives, Vol. 7, Fall 1993, pp. 47-63.

Pharmaceuticals

Readings

1. Larry L. Duetsch, "Pharmaceuticals: The Critical Role of Innovation," in L. Duetsch, ed., Industry Studies, pp. 116-137.

2. Congressional Budget Office, "Industry and Market Background," in How Health Care Reform Affects Pharmaceutical Research and Development, June 1994.

3. F. M. Scherer, "Pricing, Profits and Technological Progress in the Pharmaceutical Industry," Journal of Economic Perspectives, Volume 7, No. 3, Summer 1993, pp. 97-115.

4. Shawn Tully, "The Plots to Keep Drug Prices High," Fortune, December 27, 1993, pp. 120-124.

Financial Market Regulation

Readings

1. Damodar Gujarati, "The SEC and Regulation of Securities Markets," in Government and Business pp. 354-364, 386-387.

2. Dean Furbush, "Program Trading in Context: The Changing Structure of World Equity Markets," Regulation, Spring 1991, pp. 71-77.

3. Financial Services Regulation Symposium, Regulation, 1994, No. 4, pp. 38-75. (Papers are Derivatives, Market Manipulation, and Running the CFTC.)

4. Douglas H. Ginsburg and John F. Robinson, "The Case Against Federal Intervention in the Market for Corporate Control," and F. M. Scherer, "Takeovers: Present and Future Dangers," The Brookings Review, Winter/Spring 1986, pp. 9-21.

China

Readings

1. The Economist, A Survey of China, November 28, 1992.

2. Symposia on China, Journal of Economic Perspectives, Spring 1994, Vol. 8, No. 2, pp. 23-82.

3. Bruce Reynolds, "Exploring East Asia Growth: Is Culture the Key?" Cornell University, September 1994.

Welfare

Readings

1. Gary Burtless, "The Economist's Lament: Public Assistance in America"; Judith Gueron, "Work and Welfare: Lessons on Employment Problems," <u>JEP</u>, Winter 1990, pp. 57-98.

2. Robert Haveman and Barbara Wolf, "Children's Prospects and Children's Policy," <u>JEP</u>, Fall 1993, pp. 153-74.

3. C. Eugene Steurle, "Tax Credits for Low-Income Workers with Children," <u>JEP</u>, Summer 1990, pp. 201-12.

4. Robert Lerman, "Child Support Policies," <u>JEP</u>, Winter 1993, pp. 171-82.

Health Reform

Readings

1. Charles Phelps, "Health Insurance in the Marketplace," <u>Health Economics</u>, Ch. 11, pp. 307-329.

2. David Cutler, "A Guide to Health Care Reform," <u>JEP</u>, Summer 1994, pp. 13-29.

3. Victor Fuchs, "The Clinton Plan: A Researcher Examines Reform," <u>Health Affairs</u>, Spring 1994, pp. 103-13.

4. Mark Pauly et al., "A Plan for Responsible National Health Insurance," <u>Health Affairs</u>, Spring 1991, pp. 5-26.

5. Vincente Navarro, "A National Health Program is Necessary," <u>Challenge</u>, May-June 1989, pp. 36-40.

G

Harvard School of Public Health
HPE 284a--Decision Theory (2.5 credits)

Professors James K. Hammitt and A. David Paltiel

This is a doctoral level course in the theory of choice, with applications to cost-benefit analysis. It is intended for students who plan to pursue health-related, decision analytical research. The objectives of the course are to introduce the axiomatic method of economic reasoning, to present the standard model of individual decision making under uncertainty, challenges and alternatives to it, and to explore methodological issues arising from the application of these techniques to health issues.

Topics will include the theory of choice, traditional models of expected utility, multi-attribute utility theory, subjective probability, Bayesian statistical decision theory, judgment under uncertainty, elicitation and calibration of expert opinion, alternative representations of uncertainty (Dempster-Shafer theory, generalized probability), and alternative models of decision making (regret theory, prospect theory).

Prerequisites for the course are a knowledge of calculus and linear algebra at the level of Mathematics 20, completion of at least one probability course that employs calculus, and a course in the methods of decision analysis. Students should be familiar with material at the level of HPB280b (Decision Analysis for Health and Medical Practices), HPB281c (Seminar on Clinical Decision Analysis), or a course in Analytic Methods or Operations Research.

The class will meet Tuesdays and Thursdays, 10:30-12:20, in Kresge 202. There will be two problem sets (worth 30% of the grade) and a final exam (the other 70%). While students are welcome to work together on the homework assignments, each will be expected to submit a separate write-up.

Professor Hammitt's office is at the Center for Risk Analysis, 718 Huntington Ave. You may contact him via e-mail at jkh@hsph.harvard.edu or by telephone at 432-4030. The most reliable means of reaching Professor Paltiel is via electronic mail at paltiel@hsph.harvard.edu. He can also be reached at 432-3111 or in Kresge 416A at the School of Public Health.

Primary Texts:

David M. Kreps, *Notes on the Theory of Choice*, Westview (1988).
Ralph J. Keeney and Howard Raiffa, *Decisions with Multiple Objectives: Preferences and Value Tradeoffs*, Cambridge (1976).

Secondary Texts:

Roger M. Cooke, *Experts in Uncertainty: Opinion and Subjective Probability in Science*, Oxford (1991).
Morris H. DeGroot, *Optimal Statistical Decisions*, McGraw-Hill (1970).
Gudman R. Iverson, *Bayesian Statistical Inference*, Sage University Papers No. 43, Newbury Park, CA (1984).
Daniel Kahneman, Paul Slovic, and Amos Tverskey (eds.), *Judgment Under Uncertainty: Heuristics and Biases*, Cambridge (1982).
Paul R. Kleindorfer, Howard C. Kunreuther, and Paul J.H. Schoemaker, *Decision Sciences: An Integrative Perspective*, Cambridge (1993).
M. Granger Morgan and Max Henrion, *Uncertainty: A Guide to Dealing with Uncertainty in Quantitative Risk and Policy Analysis*, Cambridge (1990).
John Pratt, Howard Raiffa, and Robert Schlaifer, *Introduction to Statistical Decision Theory*, McGraw Hill, 1965.

Textbook readings will be supplemented by selected articles.

Course Outline

I. UTILITY AND CHOICE UNDER OBJECTIVE UNCERTAINTY

1) Introduction / Preference Relations

Motivation
Descriptive / normative / prescriptive
Binary relations
Preference relations

Readings:
Kreps, Chapters 1 and 2
Kleindorfer, Chapter 4

2) Ordinal Utility

Readings:
Kreps, Chapter 3

3) Von Neumann-Morgenstern Expected Utility

Choice under uncertainty
An intuitive introduction
The VNM axioms
Cardinal utility
The "Sure thing" principle

Readings:
Kreps, Chapters 4 and 5
Keeney and Raiffa, Chapter 4

4) Risk Aversion / Dominance

Measures of risk aversion
Stochastic dominance

Readings:
Kreps, Chapter 6
J.W. Pratt, "Risk Aversion in the Small and in the Large", *Econometrica* 32: 122-136, (1964).
Chi-fu Huang, *Foundations for Financial Economics*, North Holland, New York (1988),
    Chapters 1 and 2
Michael Rothschild and Joseph E. Stiglitz, "Increasing Risk: 1. A Definition. "*Journal of
    Economic Theory* 2: 225-243 (1970).

5) Multiattribute Utility

Tradeoffs under certainty and uncertainty
Preference independence
Utility independence
Additive separability

Readings:
Keeney & Raiffa, Chapter 3, 5, 6

6) Social Preferences and Cost-Benefit Analysis

Arrow's impossibility theorem
WTP and WTA

Readings:
Keeney & Raiffa, Chapter 10
Hanemann, Michael W., "Willingness to Pay and Willingness to Accept: How Much Can
    They Differ?" *American Economic Review* 81: 635-647 (1991).
Foster, William, and Richard E. Just, "Measuring Welfare Effects of Product Contamination
    with Consumer Uncertainty," *Journal of Environmental Economics and Management* 17:
    266-283 (1989).
Viscusi and Evans, "Utility Functions that Depend on Health Status: Estimates and Economic
    Implications," *American Economic Review* 80: 353-374 (1990).

7) Inter-temporal Preferences

Exponential and hyperbolic discounting
Dynamic consistency

Readings:

Keeney & Raiffa, Chapters 9 and 10

Goodin, Robert E., "Discounting Discounting," *Journal of Public Policy* 2: 53-72 (1982).

Keeler, Emmett B., and Shan Cretin, "Discounting of Life-Saving and Other Nonmonetary Effects," Management Science 29: 300-306, 1983.

Lowenstein, George, and Richard Thaler, "Anomalies: Intertemporal Choice," *Journal of Economic Perspectives* 3: 181-193 (1989).

Gately, Dermot, "Individual Discount Rates and the Purchae and Utilization of Energy-Using Durables," *Bell Journal of Economics* 11: 373-374 (1980).

Harvey, Charles M., "The Reasonableness of Non-Constant Discounting," *Journal of Public Economics* 53: 31-51 (1994).

Hammitt, J.K. "Discounting Health Increments," *Journal of Health Economics* 12: 117-120 (1993).

Feldstein, Martin, "Financing in the Evaluation of Public Expenditure," in Warren L. Smith and John M. Culbertson. (eds.), *Public Finance and Stabilization Policy: Essays in Honor of Richard A. Musgrave,* North Holland, Amsterdam, 1974.

Lind, Robert, et al., *Discounting for Time and Risk in Energy Policy*, Resources for the Future (1982). (Selections, Handout)

8) Health Applications

QALYs and HYEs
Value of life

Readings:

Torrance, George, "Measurement of Health State Utilities for Economic Appraisal: A Review," *Journal of Health Economics* 5: 1-30 (1986).

Pliskin, Joseph S., Donald S. Shepard, and Milton C. Weinstein, "Utility Functions for Life Years and Health Status," *Operations Research* 28: 206-224 (1980).

Mehrez, Abraham, and Amiram Gafni, "Quality Adjusted Life Years, Utility Theory, and Healthy-year Equivalents, " *Medical Decision Making* 91: 142-149 (1989).

Johanneson, Magnus, Joseph S. Pliskin, and Milton C. Weinstein, "Are Healthy-years Equivalents an Improvement Over Quality-Adjusted Life Years?" *Medical Decision Making* 13: 281-286 (1993).

Broome, John, "The Economic Value of Life," *Economica* 52: 281-294 (1985).

Rosen, Sherwin, "The Value of Changes in Life Expectancy," *Journal of Risk and Uncertainty* 1: 285-304 (1988).

Shepard, Donald S., and Richard J. Zeckhauser, "Survival versus Consumption," Management Science 30: 423-439 (1984).

II. SUBJECTIVE UNCERTAINTY / BAYESIAN STATISTICAL INFERENCE

9) Subjective Probability I

Foundations

Readings:
Kreps, Chapters 11 and 8
Kleindorfer, Chapter 3

10) Subjective Probability II

The Savage Axioms

Readings:
Kreps, Chapter 9
Cooke, Chapters 6 and 7
Morgan and Henrion, Chapters 4 and 5.1-5.3

11) Value of Information

Bayes' theorem
Probability revision
Conjugate probability distributions
The value of information

Readings:
DeGroot, Chapters 4 (skim), 9
Morgan and Henrion, Chapter 12
Hammitt and Cave, *Research Planning for Food Safety*, RAND R-3946-ASPE/NCTR,
    Chapters 1, 3, 4, 6
Hammitt "Can More Information Increase Uncertainty?"

12) Dynamic Choice

Sequential testing
N-armed bandit
Dynamic programming

Readings:
Kreps, Chapter 13
Spence, Michael, and Richard Zeckhauser, "The Effect of the Timing of Consumption Decision and the Resolution of Lotteries on the Choice of Lotteries," Econometrica 40: 401-403 (1972).
Pindyck, Robert S., "Irreversibility, Uncertainty, and Investment," *Journal of Economic Literature* 29: 1110-1148 (1991).

13) Alternative Representations of Uncertainty

Generalized Probability
Dempster-Shafer Theory of Evidence
Fuzzy Sets

Readings:
Leamer, Edward E., *Specification Searches*, Wiley (1978). Chapters 1 and 2.
Spiegelhalter, David J., "A Statistical View of Uncertainty in Expert Systems," *Artificial Intelligence and Satistics,* William A. Gale (ed.), Addison-Wesley (1986).
Buchanan, Bruce G., and Edward H. Shortliffe, *Rule-Based Expert Systems: The MYCIN Experiments of the Stanford Heuristic Programming Project*, Addison-Wesley, (1985). Chapters 11-13.
Wagner, Carl G., "Imprecise Probabilities and Integrated Resource Planning," University of Tennessee.

14) Elicitation / Calibration

Expert opinion
Heuristics and biases
Elicitation
Calibration methods

Readings:
Tverskey, Amos and Daniel Kahneman, "Heuristics and Biases," *Science* 185: 1124-1131, 1974.
Selections from Cooke
Morgan and Henrion, Chapters 6 and 7

III. PARADOXES AND ALTERNATIVE THEORIES

15) Judgment Under Uncertainty

Experimental evidence
Prospect theory

Readings:
Kahneman, Daniel, and Amos Tverskey, "Prospect Theory: An Analysis of Decision Under Risk," *Econometrica* 47: 263-291 (1979).
Tverskey and Kahneman, "Advances in Prospect Theory: Cumulative Representation of Uncertainty," *Journal of Risk and Uncertainty* 5: 297-323 (1992).
Selections from Wright
P.J.H. Schoemaker "The Expected Utility Model: Its Variants, Purposes, Evidence, and Limitations," *Journal of Economic Literature* 20: 529-563 (1982).

16) Regret Theory

Readings:
D.E. Bell "Regret in Decision Making Under Uncertainty," *Operations Research* 30: 961-981 (1982).

17) Non-Expected Utility

Readings:
Machina, Mark J., "Dynamic consistency and non-expected utility models of choice under uncertainty," *Journal of Economic Literature* 27: 1622-1668 (1989).
Machina, Mark J., "Choice under uncertainty: problems solved and unsolved," *Journal of Economic Perspectives* 1: 121-154 (1987).

Economics 511/779B: Experimental Economics
University of South Carolina
G

Instructor: Professor Glenn W. Harrison

Class: 511: Tuesday & Thursday, 2.00-3.15 (BA 435).
779B: Tuesday & Thursday, 2.00-3.15 (BA 435) *and* 3.30-4.30 (BA 435).

Objective

This course is an introduction to the use of experimental methods in economics. It is intended to introduce students to the motivation, design, conduct, analysis and policy implications of this methodology.

Required Text

Davis, Douglas D., and Holt, Charles A., *Experimental Economics* (Princeton, NJ: Princeton University Press, 1993). All students should be armed with a good intermediate micro text or graduate text. We can discuss appropriate texts in the first class. All graduate students taking 779B will be required to purchase a packet of additional readings.

Outline

The course will be conducted in two sessions on each of Tuesday and Thursday. The first session will be aimed at the undergraduate students in Economics 511, and will involve extensive use of the main textbook and some participation in actual experiments. The second session will cover the same topic as the first session, but at a more advanced level for graduate students in Economics 779. The second session will focus on one or more of the primary sources, reflected in the journal articles listed below. Graduate students will be expected to attend *both* sessions; undergraduates are welcome to attend both at their discretion, but are not expected to attend the second session.

There will also be a series of brownbags and seminars dealing with experimental economics, and these are also listed below. They should be considered as regular class times for all students. The references in curly brackets indicate readings appropriate for each class, and sections of the text that will only be covered in the Economics 779 session.

Tuesday, January 18. History and overview. DH, ch. 1. {DH, ch.9; Smith [1982][1992]}
Thursday, January 20. Expected utility theory and risk aversion. DH, § 2.2, 2.4. {Harrison [1986]}.
Tuesday, January 25. Normal-form games. DH, § 2.5. {Andreoni and Miller [1993]; Cooper et al. [1989][1990]; Mehta, Starmer and Sugden [1992]}.
Thursday, January 27. Extensive-form games. DH, § 2.6. {McKelvey and Palfrey [1992]}
Tuesday, February 1. The double auction. DH, § 3.2-3.7. {Smith [1962]; Gode and Sunder [1993]}.
Thursday, February 3. Experimental asset markets. DH, § 7.5, 7.6. {Forsythe, Palfrey and Plott [1982]; Plott and Sunder [1982]; Friedman, Harrison and Salmon [1984]}.
Tuesday, February 8. The Iowa Presidential Stock Market. DH, § 7.7 {Forsythe, Nelson, Neumann and Wright [1992]}.
Thursday, Febraury 10. Bubbles and crashes in stock markets. DH, § 3.7. {Smith, Suchanek and Williams [1988]; Harrison [1991]}.

120

Tuesday, February 15. Posted-offer markets. DH, § 4.2, 4.3. {Davis, Harrison and Williams [1993]}.

Thursday, February 17. Monopoly behavior, decentralized regulation, and contestable markets. DH, § 4.4, 4.6. {Coursey, Isaac and Smith [1984]; Harrison and McKee [1985a]; Harrison [1987]}.

Tuesday, February 22. Different types of auctions. DH, § 5.6. {Cox, Roberson and Smith [1984]}.

Wednesday, February 23 (Seminar). Jay Shogren (Iowa State University) on "Herding Behavior in the Vickrey Auction."

Thursday, February 24. First-price auctions. DH, § 5.7. {Harrison [1989][1990]}.

Tuesday, March 1. Second-price auctions. DH, § 5.6. {Coursey, Schulze and Hovis [1987]; Neill et al. [1994]; Rutström [1993]; Shogren et al. [1994]}.

Thursday, March 3. The winners curse. DH, § 5.8. {Kagel and Levin [1986]; Hansen and Lott [1991]}.

Tuesday, March 8. Spring Break.

Thursday, March 10. Spring Break.

Tuesday, March 15. Mid-term exam.

Thursday, March 17. Designer auctions. DH, § 5.9. {Rassenti, Smith and Bulfin [1982]; McCabe, Rassenti and Smith [1992]}.

Tuesday, March 22. The Nash Solution to bargaining games. DH, § 5.2. {Roth and Malouf [1979], Roth and Schoumaker [1983]}.

Thursday, March 24. Coasian bargaining. DH, § 5.3. {Harrison and McKee [1985b]}.

Tuesday, March 29. Ultimatum bargaining. DH, § 5.4. {Harrison and McCabe [1992b]}.

Thursday, March 31. Alternating-offer bargaining. DH, § 5.5. {Harrison and McCabe [1992a], Harrison, Harstad, Rausser and Simon [1993]}.

Tuesday, April 5. The Allais Paradox and preference reversals. DH, § 8.2, 8.3, 8.6. {Grether and Plott [1979], Harrison [1994]}.

Thursday, April 7. Preference elicitation and hypothetical surveys. DH, § 8.5. {Cummings, Harrison and Rutström [1992]; Blackburn, Harrison and Rutström [1993]; Harrison et al. [1993]}.

Tuesday, April 12. Bayes rule. DH, § 8.8. {Grether [1980]; Harrison [1994]}.

Thursday, April 14. Search Behavior. DH, § 2.3. {Harrison and Morgan [1990]}.

Tuesday, April 19. Free-riding in the provision of public goods. DH, § 6.1-6.4. {Cummings and Harrison [1994]; Harrison and Hirshleifer [1989]}.

Thursday, April 21. Incentive compatible institutions for public goods. DH, § 6.5. {Bohm [1972][1979]; Smith [1979]; Harstad and Marrese [1982]; Brookshire and Coursey [1987]; Cummings and Harrison [1993]}.

Tuesday, April 26. Voting. DH, § 6.7. {Fiorina and Plott [1978]}.

Thursday, April 29. The payoff dominance controversy. {Harrison [1989][1992][1994]; Harrison and Morgan [1990]}.

Assessment

Economics 511: Quiz sessions at the beginning of all classes, one mid-term exam, and a final exam. Each will be worth ⅓ of the overall grade.

Economics 779: Quiz sessions at the beginning of all classes, one mid-term exam, and a research essay or final exam. Each will be worth ⅓ of the overall grade.

The quiz sesssions are designed to provide incentives for everybody to read the text before class. They will consist of two or three questions which should be trivial if you have simply read the text. The class covers so many topics that it might be tempting not to get the *basic* reading done before class, and that will inevitably cause cascading despair and depression as we move on to newer material. Each student will be allowed to "miss" two such quizzes; all other unexcused "misses" will be graded as a zero for that quiz.

References

Andreoni, James, and Miller, John H., "Rational Cooperation in the Finitely Repeated Prisoner's Dilemma: Experimental Evidence", *Economic Journal*, 103, May 1993, 570-585.

Blackburn, McKinley; Harrison, Glenn W., and Rutström, E.E., "Statistical Bias Functions and Informative Hypothetical Surveys", *Economics Working Paper B-93-02*, Department of Economics, College of Business Administration, University of South Carolina, 1993; forthcoming, *American Journal of Agricultural Economics*, December 1994.

Bohm, Peter, "Estimating the Demand for Public Goods: An Experiment", *European Economic Review*, 3, June 1972, 111-130.

Bohm, Peter, "Estimating Willingness to Pay: Why and How?", *Scandinavian Journal of Economics*, LXXXI, 1979, 142-153.

Brookshire, David S., and Coursey, Don L., "Measuring the Value of a Public Good: An Empirical Comparison of Elicitation Procedures", *American Economic Review*, 77(4), September 1987, 554-566.

Cooper, Russell; DeJong, Douglas V.; Forsythe, Robert, and Ross, Thomas W., "Communication in the Battle of the Sexes Game: Some Experimental Results", *Rand Journal of Economics*, 20, Winter 1989, pp. 568-587.

Cooper, Russell; DeJong, Douglas V.; Forsythe, Robert, and Ross, Thomas W., "Selection Criteria in Coordination Games: Some Experimental Results", *American Economic Review*, 80, March 1990, pp. 218-233.

Coursey, Don; Isaac, R. Mark, and Smith, Vernon L., "Natural Monopoly and the Contested Markets: Some Experimental Results," *Journal of Law and Economics*, 27, 1984, 91-113.

Coursey, Don L.; Schulze, William D., and Hovis, J. J., "On the Supposed Disparity Between Willingness to Accept and Willingness to Pay Measures of Value", *Quarterly Journal of Economics*, 102, August 1987, 679-690.

Cox, James C.; Roberson, Bruce, and Smith, Vernon L., "Theory and Behavior of Single Object Auctions," in V. L. Smith (ed.), *Research in Experimental Economics*, vol. 2 (Greenwich, CT: JAI Press, 1982).

Cummings, Ronald G., and Harrison, Glenn W., "A New Approach to Eliciting Incentive-Compatible Values for Public Goods: The Inference Game", *Unpublished Draft Manuscript*, Department of Economics, University of South Carolina, 1993.

Cummings, Ronald G., and Harrison, Glenn W., "Was the *Ohio* Court Well Informed in Their Assessment of the Accuracy of the Contingent Valuation Method?", *Natural Resources Journal*, 34, Winter 1994, 1-36.

122

Cummings, Ronald G.; Harrison, Glenn W., and Rutström, E.E., "Homegrown Values and Hypothetical Surveys: Is the Dichotomous Choice Approach Incentive Compatible?", *Economics Working Paper B-92-12*, Department of Economics, College of Business Administration, University of South Carolina, 1992; forthcoming, *American Economic Review*, March 1995.

Davis, Douglas D.; Harrison, Glenn W., and Williams, Arlington W., "Convergence to Nonstationary Competitive Equilibria: An Experimental Analysis", *Journal of Economic Behavior and Organization*, 14, 1993, forthcoming.

Fiorina, Morris P., and Plott, Charles R., "Committee Decisions under Majority Rule: An Experimental Study," *American Political Science Review*, 72, 1978, 575-598.

Forsythe, Robert; Nelson, Forrest; Neumann, George R., and Wright, Jack, "Anatomy of an Experimental Political Stock Market", *American Economic Review*, 82, December 1992, 1142-1161.

Forsythe, Robert; Palfrey, Thomas R., and Plott, Charles R., "Asset Valuation in an Experimental Market", *Econometrica*, 50, 1982, 537-582.

Friedman, Daniel; Harrison, Glenn W., and Salmon Jon W., "The Informational Efficiency of Experimental Asset Markets", *Journal of Political Economy*, 92, June 1984, 349-408.

Gode, Dhananjay K., and Sunder, Shyam, "Allocative Efficiency of Markets with Zero-Intelligence Traders: Market as a Partial Substitute for Individual Rationality", *Journal of Political Economy*, 101(1), February 1993, 119-137.

Grether, David M., "Bayes' Rule as a Descriptive Model: The Representativeness Heuristic," *Quarterly Journal of Economics*, 95, 1980, 537-557.

Grether, David M., and Plott, Charles R., "Economic Theory of Choice and the Preference Reversal Phenomenon," *American Economic Review*, 69, September 1979, 623-638.

Hansen, Robert G., and Lott, John R., "The Winner's Curse and Public Information in Common Value Auctions: Comment," *American Economic Review*, 81, 1991, 347-361.

Harrison, Glenn W., "An Experimental Test for Risk Aversion," *Economics Letters*, 21, No.1, 1986, 7-11.

Harrison, Glenn W., "Experimental Evaluation of the Contestable Markets Hypothesis," in E. E. Bailey (ed.), *Public Regulation: New Perspectives on Institutions and Policies* (Cambridge: MIT Press, 1987).

Harrison, Glenn W., "Theory and Misbehavior of First-Price Auctions," *American Economic Review*, 79, September 1989, 749-762.

Harrison, Glenn W., "Risk Attitudes in First-Price Auction Experiments: A Bayesian Analysis," *The Review of Economics & Statistics*, 72, August 1990, 541-546.

Harrison, Glenn W., "Rational Expectations and Experimental Methods," in B.A. Goss (ed.), *Rational Expectations and Efficiency in Futures Markets* (London: Routledge, 1991).

123

Harrison, Glenn W., "Theory and Misbehavior of First-Price Auctions: Reply", *American Economic Review*, 82, December 1992, 1426-1443.

Harrison, Glenn W., "Expected Utility Theory and The Experimentalists", *Empirical Economics*, 1994, forthcoming.

Harrison, Glenn W.; Beekman, Robert L.; Brown, Lloyd B.; Clements, Leianne A.; McDaniel, T.M.; Odom, Sherry L. and Williams, M.B., "Environmental Damage Assessment With Hypothetical Surveys: The Calibration Approach", *Economics Working Paper B-93-18*, Department of Economics, College of Business Administration, University of South Carolina, 1993.

Harrison, Glenn W.; Harstad, Ronald M.; Rausser, Gordon C., and Simon, Leo K., "Multilateral Bargaining in a Spatial Environment", *Unpublished Draft Manuscript*, Department of Economics, University of South Carolina, 1993.

Harrison, Glenn W., and Hirshleifer, Jack, "An Experimental Evaluation of Weakest-Link/Best-Shot Models of Public Goods", *Journal of Political Economy*, 97, February 1989, 201-225.

Harrison, Glenn W., and McCabe, Kevin, "Testing Noncooperative Bargaining Theory in Experiments", in R.M. Isaac (ed.), *Research in Experimental Economics* (Greenwich: JAI Press, Volume 5, 1992a).

Harrison, Glenn W., and McCabe, Kevin A., "Expectations and Fairness in a Simple Bargaining Experiment", *Economics Working Paper B-92-10*, Division of Research, College of Business Administration, University of South Carolina, September 1992b; forthcoming, *International Journal of Game Theory*.

Harrison, Glenn W., and McKee, Michael J., "Monopoly Behavior, Decentralized Regulation, and Contestable Markets: An Experimental Evaluation", *The Rand Journal of Economics*, 16, Spring 1985a, 51-69.

Harrison, Glenn W., and McKee, Michael J., "Experimental Evaluation of the Coase Theorem", *Journal of Law and Economics*, 28, October 1985b, 653-670.

Harrison, Glenn W., and Morgan, Peter, "Search Intensity in Experiments", *The Economic Journal*, 100, June 1990, 478-486.

Harstad, Ronald M., and Marrese, Michael, "Behavioral Explanations of Efficient Public Good Allocations," *Journal of Public Economics*, 19, 1982, 367-383.

Kagel, John H., and Levin, Dan, "The Winner's Curse and Public Information in Common Value Auctions," *American Economic Review*, 76, December 1986, 894-920.

McCabe, Kevin A.; Rassenti, Stephen J., and Smith, Vernon L., "Designing 'Smart' Computer-Assisted Markets" *European Journal of Political Economy*, 5, 1989.

McCabe, Kevin A.; Rassenti, Stephen J., and Smith, Vernon L., "Designing Auction Institutions: Is Double Dutch the Best?" *Economic Journal*, 102, January 1992, 9-23.

McKelvey, Richard D., and Palfrey, Thomas R., "An Experimental Study of the Centipede Game", *Econometrica*, 60(4), July 1992, 803-836.

124

Mehta, Judith; Starmer, Chris; and Sugden, Robert, "The Nature of Salience: An Experimental Investigation of Pure Coordination Games," *Unpublished Manuscript*, School of Economic and Social Studies, University of East Anglia, 1992.

Neill, Helen R.; Cummings, Ronald G.; Ganderton, Philip T.; Harrison, Glenn W.; and McGuckin, Thomas, "Hypothetical Surveys and Real Economic Commitments", *Economics Working Paper B-93-01*, Department of Economics, College of Business Administration, University of South Carolina, January 1993; forthcoming, *Land Economics*, 70, May 1994.

Plott, Charles R., and Sunder, Shyam, "Efficiency of Experimental Security Markets with Insider Information: An Application of Rational-Expectations Models", *Journal of Political Economy*, 90, 1982, 663-698.

Rassenti, Stephen J.; Smith, Vernon L., and Bulfin, R.L. "A Combinatorial Auction Mechanism for Airport Time Slot Allocation," *Bell Journal of Economics*, 13(2), Autumn 1982, 402-417.

Roth, Alvin E., and Malouf, Michael W. K., "Game-Theoretic Models and the Role of Information in Bargaining," *Psychological Review*, 86, 1979, 574-594.

Roth, Alvin E., and Schoumaker, Francoise, "Expectations and Reputations in Bargaining: An Experimental Study", *American Economic Review*, 73(3), June 1983, 362-372.

Rutström, E.E., "Home-Grown Values and Incentive Compatible Auction Design", *Unpublished Manuscript*, Department of Economics, College of Business Administration, University of South Carolina, 1993; forthcoming, *International Journal of Game Theory*.

Shogren, Jason F.; Shin, Seung Y.; Hayes, Dermot J., and Kliebenstein, James B., "Resolving Differences in Willingness to Pay and Willingness to Accept," *American Economic Review*, 84, 1994, forthcoming.

Smith, Vernon L., "An Experimental Study of Competitive Market Behavior", *Journal of Political Economy*, 70, 1962, 111-137.

Smith, Vernon L., "Incentive Compatible Experimental Processes for the Provision of Public Goods," in V. L. Smith (ed.), *Research in Experimental Economics*, vol. 1 (Greenwich, CT: JAI Press, 1979).

Smith, Vernon L., "Microeconomic Systems as an Experimental Science", *American Economic Review*, 72(5), December 1982, 923-955.

Smith, Vernon L., "Game Theory and Experimental Economics: Beginnings and Early Influences", *History of Political Economy*, 24, Special Issue 1992, 241-282.

Smith, Vernon L.; Suchanek, Gerry L., and Williams, Arlington W., "Bubbles, Crashes, and Endogenous Expectations in Experimental Spot Asset Markets", *Econometrica*, 56, 1988, 1119-1151.51., *Eonometrica*, 56, 1988.

125

University of Warwick

Prof. M. Hviid & Prof. M. Waterson

EC 208 Economics of the Firm and Industry   U

This course aims at analysing explanations of why firms exist, why they are organised internally in the ways they are, why they are grouped together in industries in particular ways, why they interact as they do in markets, and how the nature of these interactions influences economic performance in terms of efficiency, profits, technical progress and welfare.

The **objective** of the course is to develop an appreciation of these and similar issues through a mixture of theoretical and empirical analyses. The theory is seen not as an end in itself but as a vehicle by which insights may be obtained. Empirics are also used in this way.

Term one concentrates on topics in economics of the firm. **Term two** considers the economics of industry.

Lecture and Class Arrangements

Lectures will take place twice weekly on Tuesday, 2-3 pm in S0.21 and Thursday, 2-3 pm in S0.13.

Details of fortnightly tutorial classes will be placed on the 2nd year economics notice board. Exercises, questions and topics for discussion in these will be handed out in the lectures at least one week before the class. The classes are deliberately designed to provide a counterpoint to the lectures rather than covering the material again.

Examination method

3-Hour final exam (70%).

Three essays (10% each) not exceeding 1500 words. Topics will normally be announced at least four weeks before submission dates and work will normally be returned within four weeks after submission. Deadlines for the essays are respectively: **5.12.94**, **27.2.95** and **15.5.95**.

Recommended textbooks:

No single book covers the course as it is taught. However, the following books are of use for substantial sections of the course. They should be seen as complementary to the lectures.

For the **first term**:

> **Ricketts**, M, 1994, The Economics of Business Enterprise 2nd edition, Harvester/Weatsheaf.
>
> **Milgrom**, P. and J. **Roberts**, 1992, Economics, Organization and Management, Prentice-Hall.

For the **second term**:

> **Carlton**, D.W. and J.M. **Perloff**, 1994, Modern Industrial Organization 2nd edition, Harper/Collins.
>
> **Martin**, S., 1993, Advanced Industrial Economics, Blackwell

In addition to the attached reading list you will be able to find other material by using the CD ROM in the PC's in the Library. In particular the two databases ECONLIT and ABI INFORM may prove useful in your quest for more knowledge about a given area.

The remainder of the current handout concerns term 1. An outline and reading list for term 2 will be issued towards the end of term 1.

October 1994
Morten Hviid and Mike Waterson

Term 1: Theories of the firm.

1. Introduction to the theories of the firm. (2 hours)
   i) Types of contracts.
   ii) Property rights.
   iii) What is a firm and how is its boundaries defined?
   iv) The Coase question: Why do firms exist? Transaction costs. Attitudes to risk.
      Monitoring.
   v) The limits to integration (why not just one firm?). Technology. Incomplete
      contracts. Monitoring.

2. Separation of ownership and control. (2 hour)
   i) The Berle and Means hypothesis. Day to day decisions not taken by owners but by
      managers.
   ii) Organisational forms. U-form firms. M-form firms. Matrix organisations. Their
      relative merits. Empirical evidence.
   iii) The consequences of separation. Loss of control. Differences in goals.
      Differences in information.
   iv) What are the objectives of the firm? Profit maximisation. Maximising v.
      satisficing. Other corporate goals. Altruism. Concern for stake-holders.

3. The agency problem/incentive theory. (3 hours)
   i) Decision making under uncertainty.
   ii) Game theory.
   iii) The simple principal-agent model. Assumptions. Solution methods.
   iv) Applications of the principal-agent framework.

4. The various solutions to the problem of separation. (2 hours)
   i) Product/labour market discipline.
   ii) Market for corporate control. Mergers.
   iii) Managerial incentive schemes. Compensation plans. Sharing rules.
   iv) Empirical evidence.
   v) Discussions of the problems with the various solutions.

5. Internal Hierarchies (introducing workers). (3 hours)
   i) The depth of a hierarchy.
   ii) Supervisors. Supervisors as monitors. The incentives of supervisors. Tirole's
      model.
   iii) Internal labour markets. Career concerns. Promotions. Up-or-out contracts.
   iv) Introduction to overlapping generations of managers.

6. Theory of vertical relationships. (4 hours)
   i) Vertical integration.
   ii) Vertical separation.
   iii) Vertical restraints.
   iv) A halfway house - Franchising.

7. So why do firms exist? (3 hours)
   i) Williamson. The four assumptions.
   ii) Corporate culture. Kreps' model.
   iii) Example: Hudson Bay Company.

127

Reading List.

First: You should aim to read either the suggested reading in Ricketts(1994) <u>The Economics of Business Enterprise 2nd edition</u>, or in Milgrom and Roberts(1992) <u>Economics, Organization and Management</u>. Preferably you should read both as their perspective is very different.

Second: You should read some of the papers on the reading list below. This list contains additional suggested readings. I have tried to allocate the papers to the different sections. This only indicates that a paper is especially relevant for that topic, **not** that is **only** relevant for that topic. The lectures should give a guide to which parts are particularly relevant. Other reading may be suggested in the lectures. It is not enough to rely on the textbooks!

Surveys.

The following four surveys are useful guides to the literature. Don't just read one of them, each have their own perspective on the theory of the firm. They will help you to form your own.

Hart, O., 1989, "An Economist's Perspective on the Theory of the Firm", <u>Columbia Law Review</u> 89, 1748-1774.
Holmstrom, B. and J. Tirole, 1989, "The Theory of the Firm", in R. Schmalensee and R. Willig (Eds.), <u>Handbook of Industrial Organization</u>, North-Holland. (Sections of this survey are very demanding, but also very rewarding, so don't be deterred.)
Milgrom, P. and J. Roberts, 1988, "Economic Theories of the Firm: Past, Present, and Future", <u>Canadian Journal of Economics</u> 21, 444-458.
Stewart, G., 1994, "Economics of the Firm", in Cable(Ed.) <u>Current issues in Industrial Economics</u>, MacMillan.

Other relevant articles and books.

1. Introduction to the theories of the firm.
Milgrom and Roberts: Chapters 1 and 2.
Ricketts: Chapters 2, 4 and 7.
Alchian, A. and H. Demsetz, 1972, "Production, Information Costs, and Economic Organization", <u>American Economic Review</u> 62, 777-795.
Coase, 1937, "The Theory of the Firm", <u>Economica</u>.
Cowling, K. and R. Sugden, 1994, "Behind the Market Facade: an assessment and development of the theory of the firm", discussion paper, University of Warwick.
Kreps, D.M., 1990, <u>A Course in Microeconomic Theory</u>, Harvester Wheatsheaf. Chapters 19 and 20.
Putterman, L., 1993, "Ownership and the Nature of the Firm", <u>Journal of Comparative Economics</u> 17, 243-63.
Williamson, O.E., 1985, <u>The Economic Institutions of Capitalism</u>, Free Press. Chapter 6.

2. Separation of Ownership and Control.

Ricketts: Chapter 8.

Baker, G., M. Jensen and K. Murphy, 1988, "Competition and Incentives: Practice vs Theory", Journal of Finance 43, 593-616.

Berle, A.A. and G.C. Means,1932, The Modern Corporation and Private Property, MacMillan.

Cable, J, 1988, "Organisational Form and Economic Performance", in R.S. Thompson and M. Wright(Eds.)International Organisation, Efficiency and Profits, Philip Allen.

Carlos, A.M. and S. Nicholas, 1993, "Managing the Manager: An Application of the Principal Agent Model to the Hudson's Bay Company", Oxford Economic Papers 45, 243-256.

Leech, D. and J. Leahy, 1991, "Ownership Structure, Control Type Classification and the Performance of Large British Companies", Economic Journal 101, 1418-1437.

Kreps, D.M., 1990, A Course in Microeconomic Theory, Harvester Wheatsheaf. Ch. 19.

Williamson, O.E., 1985, The Economic Institutions of Capitalism, Free Press. Chapter 11.

3. Agency theory.

Milgrom and Roberts: Chapter 5.

Ricketts: Chapters 5 and 8.

Carlos, Ann M., Principal-Agent Problems in Early Trading Companies: A Tale of Two Firms. American Economic Review papers and proceedings 82, 140-45.

Eisenhardt, K.M., 1989, "Agency Theory: An Assessment and Review", Academy of Management Review vol. 14, 57-74.

Milgrom, P. and J. Roberts, 1987, "Informational Asymmetries, Strategic Behaviour, and Industrial Organization", American Economic Review papers and proceedings 77, 184-193.

Ross, S.A., 1973, "The Economic Theory of Agency: The Principal's Problem", American Economic Review papers and proceedings 63, 134-139.

Sappington, D.E.M., 1991, "Incentives in Principal-Agent Relationships", Journal of Economic Perspectives 5, 45-66.

4. The various solutions to the problem of separation.

Ricketts: Chapters 8 and 9.

Milgrom and Roberts: Chapters 12 and 13.

Carlos, A.M. and S. Nicholas, 1990, "Agency Problems in Early Chartered Companies: The Case of the Hudson's Bay Company", Journal of Economic History 50, 853-75.

5. Internal Hierarchies.

Ricketts: Chapter 9.

Bohn, H., 1987, "Monitoring Multiple Agents: The Role of Hierarchies", Journal of Economic Behaviour and Organization 8, 279-305.

Tirole, J., 1993, "Collusion and the theory of Organizations", in J.J. Laffont(Ed.) Advances in Economic Theory, Cambridge University Press.

Tirole, J., 1988, "The Multicontract Organization", Canadian Journal of Economics 21, 459-466.

Williamson, O.E., 1985, The Economic Institutions of Capitalism, Free Press. Chapter 9.

6 Vertical relationships.

Ricketts: Chapter 7.

Aoki, M., B. Gustafsson and O.E. Williamson, 1990, The Firm as a Nexus of Contracts, Sage Publication.

Brickley, J. and F. Dark, 1987, "The Choice of Organizational Form: The Case of Franchising", Journal of Financial Economics 25, 27-48.

Krueger, A., 1992, "Ownership, Agency and Wages: An Examination of Franchising in the Fast Food Industry", Quarterly Journal of Economics 101.

Lafontaine, F., 1992, "Agency Theory and Franchising: Some Empirical Results", Rand Journal of Economics 23,263-283.

Lafontaine, F., 1993, "Contractual Arrangements as Signalling Devices: Evidence from Franchising", Journal of Law Economics and Organization 9, 256-289.

Mahoney, J.Y., 1992, "The Choice of Organizational form: Vertical Financial Ownership versus other Methods of Vertical Integration", Strategic Management Journal 13, 559-584.

Norton, S.W., 1988, An empirical look at franchising as an organizational form, Journal of Business 61, 197-218.

Waterson, M., 1993, "Vertical Integration and Vertical Restraints", Oxford Review of Economics Policy 9(2), 27-40.

7. What is it then?

Ben-Ner, A., J.M. Montias and E. Neuberger, 1993, "Basic Issues in Organizations: A Comparative Perspective", Journal of Comparative Economics 17, 207-42.

Carlos, A. M. and S. Nicholas, 1988, "Giants of an Earlier Capitalism': The Chartered Trading Companies as Modern Multinationals", Business History Review 62, 398-419.

Carlos, A.M. and S. Nicholas, 1993, "Managing the Manager: An Application of the Principal Agent Model to the Hudson's Bay Company", Oxford Economic Papers 45, 243-56.

Kreps, D.M., 1990, "Corporate Culture and Economic Theory" in, J.E. Alt and K.A. Shepsle(Eds.) Perspectives on Positive Political Economy, Cambridge University Press.

Michael, S.C., 1994, "Competition in Organizational Form: Mail order retail stores, 1910-1940", Journal of Economic Behavior and Organization 23, 269-286.

Williamson, O.E., 1985, The Economic Institutions of Capitalism, Free Press.

Outline and Reading List (Spring 1995)

Lectures and classes will proceed as in term 1. Rough lecture allocations are given in brackets. Assessment 2 and 3 will be issued at the start of this term.

Theory of the Industry

I   Introduction (1 lecture)

Structure-conduct-performance and other organising paradigms
Competitive forces and their impact on the firm
The nature of the industry.

II   Oligopoly (4 lectures)

The Cournot framework; interaction. Reaction functions, Price and quantity as strategic variables. Nash equilibrium; Capacity constraints and rationing. Switching costs. Collusion and its problems; tacit collusion and punishment strategies. Concentration and profitability-concentration models-empirical analysis.

III Product Differentiation (3 lectures)

Approaches to modelling product differentiation. Horizontal v Vertical product differentiation. Modelling horizontal product differentiation - spatial or address models (Hotelling). Non address or utility function models. Vertical product differentiation and its implications.

IV   Potential Competition, Entry & Strategic Behaviour (3 lectures)

Contestable markets, their properties and the limiting nature of the assumptions. Limit pricing and barriers to entry. Entry deterrence by credible threats, sunk cost and strategic behaviour. Reputation for toughness and strategic behaviour.

V   Price Discrimination (1 lecture)

Types of price discrimination; two-part tariffs; tie-ins, quantity discounts etc.

VI   Information and Advertising (2 lectures)

Search, provision of information, signalling of quality; search and experience goods; Dorfman - Steiner condition; linkages to barriers and market structure.

VII Information, Technical Change and Patents (3 lectures)

The "knowledge production function", incentives to invent; uncertainty, innovation, diffusion and imitation; modelling patenting activity and effects.

VIII Determinants of Industry Structure (3 lectures)

Measures of concentration. Technology in production; sunk costs in product/advertising/R & D; stochastic factors; and implications for cross-country studies.

Reading List

Carlton and Perloff chs 5-17 (in the second edition) roughly covers this section of the course, though there are some elements it does not cover. Illustrations and empirics will be drawn much more from UK than US experiences.

Where several texts are listed, there is usually a large element of substitutability, but different people like different treatments and there is no uniformly best book.

I   Introduction

        Carlton and Perloff Ch1
        Tirole "Introduction"
        Martin Ch1
        Davies et.al. Ch1 Economics of Industrial Organisation
        Waterson Ch1 Economic Theory of the Industry
        J. Kay "Identifying the strategic market" Business
            Strategy Review, 1990

II   Oligopoly

        Carlton and Perloff Chs 5-7 and 9
        Tirole chs5 & 6
        Davies et.al. ch4
        Waterson Ec. Theory chs2, 3 and 10
        Martin chs 2, 5, 16
        R. Rees "Tacit Collusion" Oxford Review of Economic
            Policy no.2, 1993
        K. Cowling and M. Waterson "Price-cost margins and market
            structure" Economica, 1976
        J. Sutton "Explaining everything, explaining nothing?"
            European Economic Review, 1990
        M.E. Slade and A. Jacquemin "Strategic behaviour and
            collusion" in G. Norman & M. La Manna (eds.) The New
            Industrial Economics

III Product Differentiation

        Carlton & Perloff Ch8
        Tirole Ch7
        Martin Ch10
        Waterson Ec. Theory Ch6
        M. Waterson "Models of product differentiation" in J.
            Cable "Current Issues in Industrial Economics"

A. Shaked & J. Sutton "Multiproduct firms and market
structure" Rand Journal of Economics, 1990

J. Sutton "Vertical product differentiation : some basic
themes" American Economic Review (papers &
proceedings), 1986

IV   Potential Competition

Tirole Chs 4 & 10
Martin Chs3, 4 & 10
Carlton & Perloff Chs 4 & 10
Waterson Ec. Theory Ch4
R. Gilbert "Mobility barriers and the value of
incumbency" Ch8 of Schmalensee and Willig (eds.)
Handbook of Industrial Competition
R. Smiley "Empirical evidence on strategic entry
deterrence" International Journal of Industrial
Organisation, 1988
C. Baden-Fuller "Exit from declining industries" Economic
Journal, 1989
P.A. Geroski "Entry and Market Share Mobility" in Cable
(ed) Current Issues in Industrial Economics

V   Price Discrimination

Carlton & Perloff Chs 11 & 12
Tirole Ch 2
Varian Ch 10 in Handbook of Industrial Organisation

VI   Information and Advertising

Carlton & Perloff Ch 14-15
Tirole Ch 2
Waterson Ec Theory Ch 7

VII   Information, Technical Change and Patents

Carlton & Perloff Chs 16-17
Tirole Ch10 & part of 9
Martin Ch13
Waterson Ec. Theory Ch8
P. Stoneman The economic analysis of technological change
parts I & II
M. Waterson "The Economics of product patents" American
Economic Review, 199
P. Milgrom & J. Roberts "Information asymmetries,
strategic behaviour and industrial organisation"
American Economic Review Papers & proceedings, 1987
J. Beath et al. Strategic R&D and Innovation in J. Cable
(ed) Current Issues

VIII Determinants of Industry Structure

Carlton & Perloff Ch3
Martin Ch7
Waterson Ec. Theory Ch9

J. Sutton "Endogenous sunk costs and the structure of advertising-intensive industries" <u>European Economic Review</u> 1989

B. Curry and K. George "Industrial concentration: a survey" <u>Journal of Industrial Economics</u> 1983

S. Davies and B. Lyons: "Seller concentration: the technological explanation and demand uncertainty" <u>Economic Jounal</u> 1982

S. Davies "Concentration" in Davies et al. <u>Economics of Industrial Organisation</u>

M. Waterson
December 1994

134

Spring 1995

Texts: <u>Economics</u>, by Joseph Stiglitz, Norton 1993.
<u>Study Guide for Stiglitz</u> by Lawrence Martin, Norton 1993.
(optional)

Grading 25% homework, 25% midterm exam, 50% final exam.

<u>Course Outline</u>
1. Introduction
    Chapter 2: Thinking Like an Economist
    Chapter 3: Exchange and Production
2. Demand and Supply Analysis
    Chapter 4: Demand, Supply and Prices
    Chapter 5: Using Demand and Supply
    Chapter 8: The consumption decision
    Chapter 9: The savings decision
    Chapter 11: The labor supply decision
3. Theory of the Firm
    Chapter 12: The firm's costs
    Chapter 13: The Firm's production decision
    Chapter 15: Monopolies and Imperfect Competition
    Chapter 22: Managing the firm
4. Free Market Failures
    Chapter 18: Technological Change
    Chapter 23: Externalities
    Chapter 41: Development
5. Macro
    Chapter 36

Mid-Term March 1994)

<u>Instructions</u>: This is a 90 minute exam. Answer all questions.
Partial credit will be awarded so do not leave any question
<u>Advice</u>: Allocate only 9 minutes to each problem, If you can't
solve a problem, give your intuition and move on to the next
question. You might have time at the end of the exam to take a
second look at the problem. Good Luck!

1.A. Consider the markets for two substitute goods; tapes and
compact disks. Suppose technological progress makes it cheaper to
produced compact disks. Diagramatically explain:
i.   what happens in the market for compact disks
ii. what happens in the market for tapes
B. How are the following demand curves likely to respond to the
indicated change; (explain the reason for the change if there is
one)
i.   Demand for Mozart albums if Mahler albums are given away for
free
ii. Demand for umbrellas when rainfall decreases

2. In Mexico, each unit of a resource can produce either one
professional computer or three computer-game systems. Mexico is
endowed with 10,000 units of this resource. In Japan each unit of
this resource can produce either two professional computers or
eight computer-game systems. Suppose Japan also has 10,000 units

of this resource.

A. Draw Mexico's and Japan's production possibilities frontier.

B. What is the opportunity cost of producing a professional computer in each country? Is the production of computers subject to increasing or constant costs?

C. Which country has comparative advantage in professional computers production? (explain)

D. Assuming that in a world with no trade between Mexico and Japan, each country devoted exactly half of its resource to production of each good, show how world output of both goods can increase if trade is allowed.

3. Assume that the price elasticity of demand for pizza is 1.3 and the supply curve is upward sloping. If a $1 per pizza tax is now placed on the sale of pizza, then how will the equilibrium price change? (Answer with a diagram)

4. A firm can invest an amount of $1,000 in one of two alternative projects. Project A pays off $500 after the first year, $500 after the second year and $200 after the third year. Project B pays off $1,400 after the third year. If the equilibrium interest rate in the economy is 6%, then use the present discounted value criterion to decide which investment project the firm should undertake. Would your answer be likely to change if the interest rate were 1%? Explain intuition. (you do not have to calculate this).

5. The widget industry currently generates 6 tons of air pollution per month. The widget industry does create jobs for its employees and produces a valuable product; widgets. The following table depicts the total costs and benefits to society of reducing pollution (i.e. reducing widget production) to lower levels.

pollution level	total benefit of reducing pollution	total cost of reducing pollution to this level
5	$15	$2
4	$25	$5
3	$32	$11
2	$37	$16
1	$40	$36
0	$42	$60

A. What is the marginal cost of reducing pollution from 5 to 4? What is the marginal benefit?
What does this say about the current level of pollution?

B. From society's perspective, what is the optimal level of pollution? (explain)

C. Why isn't the optimal level of pollution equal to 0?

6. There are two goods in the world, pizza and mountain lions. Everyone in a society has an initial endowment of 200 pieces of pizza and no mountain lions. Suppose that the government offers to find 10 mountain lions if each citizen pays 50 pieces of pizza in tax. Graph indifference curves for 3 citizens, 1. those citizens who would vote in favor of this "mountain lion initiative". 2. Those citizens who are indifferent between the initiative passing and not passing. 3. Those citizens who would be made worse off by having this "mountain lion initiative" become law.

7. Jennifer enjoys bowling and golf. Her enjoyment is given by the following utility schedules.

Games of Bowling	Total Utility from Bowling	Games of Golf	Total Utility from Golf
0	0	0	0
1	8	1	12
2	12	2	20
3	15	3	24
4	17	4	26

A. Compute her marginal utility for each activity
B. Assume the price per game of golf is the same as the price per game of bowling and equals $2. Given, a budget of $6, how many games of each will Jennifer play? Use a diagram to present her best choice.
C. Suppose the price of bowling falls to $1 per game and the price of golf stays at $2, find her new preferred consumption bundle. Use a graph to explain your answer.

8. Consider an economy populated with individuals who live for two periods. In the first period each individual works and earns an after tax income of $1000. In the second period, people retire and do not earn wage income but receive a social security payment of $100 from the government. The interest rate is 10%. Use clearly labelled graphs to discuss the impact of the following government policies on savings.

A. The government decides to abolish social security but does not cut income taxes
B. The government decides to levy a 50% tax on interest income (it institutes a capital gains tax).

Mid-Term (Fall 1994)

Instructions: This is a 100 point exam. You have 100 minutes to complete the exam. Plan to allocate one minute per point. Answer all questions. For the multiple choice questions only answer with a letter for example "Z". If you cannot answer a question, provide your intuition and move on. Partial credit will be awarded. Good luck.

Questions 1-5 are Multiple Choice (five points each)
1. At a tuition price of $22,000, the elasticity of demand for attending Columbia is .4. If George Rupp is trying to maximize columbia's revenue,
A. He will lower tuition
B. He will raise tuition
C. He will not change tuition

2. Social security is more likely to be a popular government program among all voters when:
A. the number of old people is small relative to the number of young people.
B. the interest rate is very high
C. people love consumption when young

3. Below is a budget constraint for eggs and bacon. If the budget constraint changes from Y to Z. What happened?

A. the price of eggs fell and income increased
B. the price of eggs stayed the same, income fell, and the price of bacon fell.
C. the price of eggs and bacon did not change, and income fell
D. the price of bacon increased and income fell

4. Mexico and the United States are trading partners. Originally, the U.S can produce 20 computers or 10 sneakers. Mexico can produce 10 computers or 10 sneakers. If Mexico experiences a 100% productivity growth in its computer industry;
A. Mexico will now have a comparative advantage in computers
B. Mexico will now have a comparative advantage in sneakers
C. There will be no gains to trade
explain your answer

5. If a tropical storm raises a pizza maker's marginal product of labor, then;
A. wages will rise
B. the firm's revenue will rise and the firm will hire less workers
C. the firm's cost per pizza produced will fall and the firm will hire more workers
D. the firm will shut down

Questions 6-10 are each worth 15 points.
6. Consider the New York City real estate market. For each statement, declare whether it shifts supply, demand, both, or neither.
A. Princess Di moves to New York
B. Global Warming occurs and New York's climate becomes much nicer
C. the government sells all abandoned lots and sells the land to Don Trump (the developer) who converts them into houses
D. New Jersey is destroyed by a comet.
E. An engineering breakthrough such that 200 story buildings can cheaply be constructed.

7. Suppose that a pizza maker has a production function that uses labor, L, and capital, K, to make pizza. The production function is;

pizza = 2*(L + K)

Suppose the wage = 2, and the price of capital = 4, price of pizza = .50
A. Graph the firm's isoquant at 200 pizza.
B. Graph the cheapest isocost line that the firm car reach subject to producing 200 pizza
C. Will a profit maximizing firm with this technology use any capital in production?
D. Show that the profit maximizing firm would choose to produce zero pizza. (hint: compare revenue and costs at first piece of pizza)
E. If the wage falls from 2 to .5, will the firm produce zero?

8. Use indifference curves and budget constraints to illustrate why someone who loves pizza and likes beer has inelastic demand curves for pizza.

9. Assume that married couples share their work income. Explain why married men are more likely to reduce their hours worked when

their wife receives a large wage increases versus when the man
receives a large wage increase. (hint: graph the husband's
leisure and pizza budget constraint. Is the husband's pizza
consumption zero, when leisure = 24?)

10. You get utiles from eating pizza and from living far from a
toxic waste site. Your utility function is;

U(pizza,distance) = pizza + 2*distance.

Assume that you are endowed with 100 pieces of pizza and you live
at ground zero, distance = zero.

A. Graph your indifference curve and your initial endowment in
pizza, distance space.
B. What is the most (measured in pizza) that you are willing to
pay to move 1 unit of distance away from the toxic waste site?
C. Suppose that farmers own the land away from the waste site and
can either sell land to you or use it to produce one piece of
pizza, do you think that farmers will sell their land? Where will
people choose to live?

Final Exam   (Fall 1994)

Instructions: You have 180 minutes to complete the exam. Answer
all questions. For the multiple choice questions only answer with
a letter for example "Z", and briefly explain your answer. If you
cannot answer a question, provide your intuition and move on.
Partial credit will be awarded. Good luck.

Multiple Choice
1. A pizza maker who is a monopolist and uses both labor and
capital to produce has not maximized her profit if she produces
such that;
A.   price does not equal marginal cost
B.   the marginal product of labor does not equal the marginal
product of capital
C.   marginal revenue is positive
D.   the slope of the isoquant does not equal the slope of the
isocost line

2. Suppose that the upper West Side neighborhoods are expected to
improve in the near future. How will this affect the NYC real
estate market?
A. rentals will rise and condo prices will not change because
supply increases
B. rentals will not change and condo prices will rise because
supply increases
C. rentals will not change and condo prices will rise because
demand increases
D. nothing happens

3. A new Federal Report declares that there is a shortage of
patents and new scientific ideas in the United States. Policies
that would be effective in solving this problem include;
A. Scholarships to people who major in the sciences
B. An increased emphasis on poetry in the Core Curriculum
C. Increased federal funding of PHD science research
D. Increased liability law suits directed at malfunctioning new
products

E. A and C

4. The Soviet Union's currency (The Rubble) was not freely convertible into other currencies. The Soviet Union official exchange rate was much higher than the free market rate (i.e. if you wanted to exchange a $ for rubbles you would receive less rubbles than the free market price);
An economist would predict;

A. Since demand exceeds supply, there will be a surplus of rubbles
B. Since supply exceeds demand, there will be a surplus of rubbles
C. Since demand exceeds supply, there will be a shortage of rubbles
D. Since supply exceeds demand, there will be a shortage of rubbles

5. Suppose that a high school graduate discovers that he has won the lottery. He will work less at his job if;
A. the substitution effect of winning the lottery outweighs the income effect
B. the income effect of winning the lottery outweighs the substitution effect
C. if he has a low opportunity cost
D. the present value of lottery payment exceeds the present value of his wages

Explain
6. Certain charities such as the "Anti-Blindness Association" have tax exempt status. People who donate money can deduct such money from their taxes. Explain why such associations hate income tax cuts.

7. If a republican Congress does not enforce environmental law, then explain using revenue and cost curves why a highly polluting electric utility is likely to be pro-republican.

8. You can only perform medical procedures if you are accredited by the american medical association. This organization licenses doctors. Does this organization convey monopoly power to the set of people it licenses?

9. Cab drivers implicitly sign short term contracts with their riders. They drive you to a specifice location and you pay them. If New York City were to be struck with a plague such that 50% of all riders no longer paid their fare, use supply and demand to explain how this would affect the supply of cabs on the road and the price that people (who do pay) pay for riding a cab.

10. A person gains utility from clean air and pizza. If he locates in Chicago, he will receive 20 pizza and 5 units of air quality. If he locates in New York City, he will receive 40 pizza. If his utility function is U(pizza,air) = 5*pizza + 2*air. Give conditions for when he will choose to live in New York City, when he choose to live in Chicago and when he would indifferent between where he lives.

11. Assume that a university can be expressed as a ranking of fun and academics. Assume that students gain utility from both fun and academics and that Harvard has an index of 14 for fun and 7

for academics while columbia receives a 2 for fun and an 18 for academics. (Assume that the larger is the number the greater the level)

Use indifference curves to identify an individual who will attend Columbia and another individual who will attend Harvard.

12. Suppose that a pizza maker has a production function that uses labor, L, and capital, K, to make pizza. The production function is;

$$pizza = 4*(L + K)$$

Assume that the pizza maker is a monopolist in the pizza market and that it can buy production inputs, L and K, at prices, wage = 4, and the price of capital = 8; and assume that monopolist faces the aggregate demand curve;

$$P_{pizza} = 20-2*pizza$$

A. Make a table of the firm's revenue, and marginal revenue from selling pizza
B. Make a table of the firm's cost, and marginal cost from producing pizza
C. How much pizza will this firm produce? and at what price will it sell?
D. Will the firm use both labor and capital in producing pizza?
E. If the pizza monopolist was broken up by the Federal Trade Commission, and a competitive industry took its place, make a graph of how many more jobs would be created in this industry.

13. Two nations; england has an endowment of 20 computers and 10 sneakers. US has 1 hour of time and two production technologies. Can produce 40 computers with one and 10 sneakers per/hour with the other.

A. graph the ppf for each nation and the world ppf
B. If consumers in both nations only gain utility from computers, graph the highest indifference curve each can reach.
C. Given the preferences in B., will they trade?

14. My Neighbor's radio keeps me awake at night. Our lease says that if I complain then he can't play his radio. Under what conditions will I shut him down?

15. A firm can invest an amount of $100 in one of two alternative projects. Project A pays off $50 after the first year, $75 after the second year and $125 after the third year. Project B pays off $400 after the third year. If the equilibrium interest rate in the economy is 6%, then use the present discounted value criterion to decide which investment project the firm should undertake. Would your answer be likely to change if the interest rate were 1%? Explain intuition. (you do not have to calculate this).

Final Exam 2   (December 1994)

Instructions: You have 180 minutes to complete the exam.   Answer all questions. For the multiple choice questions only answer with a letter for example "Z", and briefly explain your answer. If you

cannot answer a question, provide your intuition and move on.
Partial credit will be awarded. Write down concise brief answers.
Good luck.

Multiple Choice (worth 5 points each, give brief explanation)
1. In a two good economy, if matt's income is held constant and
the price of both goods doubles then;
A. The substitution effect says he will reduce consumption of
both goods
B. The budget constraint does not change
C. Relative prices will change
D. Relative prices will not change and the budget constraint will
shift inward

2. Suppose that the upper West Side neighborhoods are expected to
decline in the near future. How will this affect the upper West
Side real estate market?
A. rental prices will rise and condo prices will not change
because supply increases
B. rental prices will not change and condo prices will rise
because supply increases
C. rental prices will not change and condo prices will rise
because demand increases
D. rental prices will not change and condo prices will fall
because demand decreases

3. The end of the Cold War will affect the military. College and
high school graduates must choose between joining the civilian
sector or joining the military. The decline of the military will
lead to:
A. Lowered wages and a lower number of jobs for privates
B. Fewer 18 year olds applying to West Point Army Academy
C. Increased cross-state migration away from "military-industrial
complexes"
D. A and B and C
E. none of the above

4. In the labor market, assume that there is a minimum wage law
such that wages are set at above the equilibrium wage. Assume
that every person is either out of the labor force, unemployed,
or has a job. Now president Clinton mandates that employers must
also provide generous health insurance benefits. This will:
A. Lower unemployment because supply of workers shifts out
B. Raise unemployment because demand for workers decreases and
the supply of workers increases
C. Raise unemployment because demand for increases and the supply
of worker does not change
D. Has no impact on employment but raises wages

5. Suppose a firm has hired 11 workers and must choose to hire a
12th or not. If the wage equals 8 and the price of the output the
firm sells is 2 then;
A. The firm will hire the worker if his marginal product is
greater than or equal to 4
B. The firm will hire the worker if his average product is
greater than or equal to 4
C. The firm will not hire the worker because price is less than
the wage
D. The firm will only hire the worker if his margin product is
greater than the 10th worker hired

142

Explain

6. (5) If the United States opened its borders to allow any immigrant into the country, use supply and demand analysis of the labor and product markets to discuss who would be the winners and losers from this new law.

7. (5) Suppose that a Delta Shuttle airplane crashed on November 5, 1997. Use supply and demand analysis to discuss how this event affects the price and quantity of Delta Shuttle tickets sold in December of 1997. Under what conditions would this crash actually lower the price and quantity of its competitor "U.S Air" shuttle tickets sold in December of 1997 and when would this event raise "U.S Air"'s revenue?

8. (5) You can only perform medical procedures if you are accredited by the american medical association. This organization licenses suppliers of health care (doctors). Graph the supply and demand for medical procedures and use this graph to discuss how this organization affects the price and quantity of health care. Also discuss how this organization affects the quality of health care.

9. (5) The Blink company sells both computers and computer software in an industry where it has some monopoly power (it does not take prices as given). If it is a profit maximizer, then give conditions when it would give its computer software away for free. Does your answer depend on the demand elasticity for computers?

10. (5) A person gains utility from clean air and pizza. If he locates in Chicago, he will receive 20 pizza and 5 units of air quality. If he locates in New York City, he will receive 25 pizza. If his utility function is U(pizza,air) = 10*pizza + 5*air. Give conditions for when he will choose to live in New York City, when he choose to live in Chicago and when he would indifferent between where he lives.

11. (5) Assume that all people have identical ability and must choose an occupation. Every occupation can be expressed as a salary and as a "status". Assume that workers gain utility from both salary and status. Assume that there are two occupations; Construction and Teaching. Construction has a salary of $32,000 and a status rating of 2 while teaching has a salary of $12,000 and a status rating of 25.
Graph indifference curves for an individual who will choose to be a teacher and another individual who will choose to go into construction.

12. (20) Suppose that a pizza maker has a production function that uses labor, L, and capital, K, to make pizza. The production function is;

pizza = 4*(L + K)

Assume that the pizza maker is a monopolist in the pizza market and that it can buy production inputs, L and K, at prices, wage = 6, and the price of capital = 8,

Assume that monopolist faces the aggregate demand curve;

9

$$P_{pizza} = 24 - 2*pizza$$

A. Make a table of the firm's revenue, and marginal revenue from selling pizza
B. Make a table of the firm's cost, and marginal cost from producing pizza
C. How much pizza will this firm produce? and at what price will it sell?
D. Now assume that a new large influx of immigrants enters the labor market, how will this affect the firm's choice to use labor and/or capital in production?

13. (15) Two nations; england can produce 10 sneakers in one hour or 20 computers in one hour while the U.S. can produce 40 computers in one hour or 10 sneakers in an hour.

A. graph the ppf for each nation and the world ppf, who has a comparative advantage at what?
B. If consumers in both nations only gain utility from computers, graph the highest indifference curve each can reach.
C. Given the preferences in B., will they trade?

14. (5) I love smoking and I have the right to do so. I gain $10 worth of pleasure when I smoke a cigar but when I smoke I impose damage of $6 on frank and $5 of damage on Jill. Is the Coase theorem relevant for predicting what will happen and what do you predict will be the resulting trades made?

15. (5) Suppose that you gain utility from consumption today and consumption tomorrow. You are paid $1000 dollars today and $0 tomorrow. You can save at a market rate of interest of 5%.

Graph your budget constraint
Now the government mandates a social security program that taxes you $100 today and gives you $105 dollars tomorrow. Graph your new budget constraint and graph the indifference curves of a person whose utility is lowered by this new social security program.

Final Exam   (May 9, 1994)

Instructions: This is a three hour 100 point exam. Answer all questions. Total points per question are indicated in the parentheses. When you are finished with the exam, you must hand in the exam questions with your answers. Any specific discussion of the contents of this exam with other students before May 11th will be viewed as cheating.
1. (5)   Why does economic theory predict that if the land market is competitive, deaf people will live near noisy airports?

2. (12) Robinson Crusoe lives in a world of two goods: milk and bread. He has an income of $100. Answer the following questions and diagramatically illustrate your answer. Crusoe likes consuming milk as much as he likes bread (they are perfect substitutes) so he is ready to trade-off in a one-to-one ratio.

a.   Explain what his indifference map is in the two goods space.
b.   If the price of milk is $2 per gallon and bread is $5 a loaf, what is Crusoe's equilibrium consumption bundle?

144

c.   If the price of bread falls to $3 per loaf, everything else unchanged, what is Crusoe's new equilibrium consumption?
d.   From your answer in (c) what can you say about the price elasticity of demand for bread?

3. (5) A factory located on a river bank can costlessly dump its chemical waste into the river-water. Fishermen using the river notice that, on an average their catch is decreasing due to the factory's dumping.

a.   What are the social and private cost of the chemical waste?
b.   Do you think that the Coase theorem would be useful in resolving the above problem? How?

4. (6) Mark owns and operates a farm. His total revenue this year is $180,000. His expenses include $27,000 to hire farm labour, $12,000 for fertilizer and seed, $10,000 to rent an adjacent farm, and $20,000 for gas and other costs. Although his accountant tells him that he is extremely successful, he considers giving up farming to take a job managing a farm supply business where he has been offered a $65,000 salary. If he did so, he would sell his farm and invest the proceeds in government bonds to receive $62,000 a year in interest income.
a.   What is his accounting profit and his economic profit?
b.   Assuming that he finds farming and managing the farm supply business equally attractive, which would you recommend he do? Why?

5. (12) NewStore has the following total revenue and total cost schedules.

Q	Total Revenue	Total Cost
0	0	100
1	200	350
2	400	500
3	600	630
4	800	850
5	1000	1100

a.   What is the marginal revenue of the second unit of output? What is the marginal cost of this unit?
b.   Which market structure best characterizes this product market? On what basis did you reach this conclusion?
c.   How many units of output should be produced to maximize profits? Give the general profit maximization condition for this kind of firm and show how you derived your answer on the basis of the above schedules. What is the corresponding profit for this choice?
d.   If the firm uses capital and labour as inputs in its production process and if labour costs $3 per unit and capital costs $10 per unit, show the firm's costs minimizing decision in hiring inputs on a diagram. State the general condition for cost minimization.

6.   (14) The martian pizza company sells its product (pizza) at the price of $2 a slice.   The price for the pen produced by Bic corporation is $1. Suppose currently that the Pizza company hires 4 units of labor, while Bic corporation hires 2 units of labor.

Units of Labor	Total Pizza	marginal product of labor for pizza	Total Pen	Marginal product of labor for pen
1	10		20	
2	15		30	
3	19		38	
4	22		44	
5	24		48	

a. fill in the blank for marginal products.

b. What is the maximum wage that the martian Pizza company is willing to pay for its labor?

c. Suppose each firm pays the maximum wage calculated in b. If you are currently working at martian Pizza, will you move to Bic?
If you are currently working at Bic, will you move to Italian Pizza? why?

d. If you answered "yes" to either or both questions in (c), how many workers will move to the other firm?

e. What will be the eventual competitive equilibrium wage in this two firm economy?

7. (7) New Jersey and Pittsburgh make jets and steel. Ten thousand hours in New Jersey produces four jets or three tons of steel. A hundred thousand hours of labor in Pittsburgh can produce one jet or two tons of steel. You observe that New Jersey is producing 20 jets and five tons of steel. Pittsburgh is producing one jet and two tons of steel. Show how the global total output of one good can be increased without having anyone work any longer or harder or decreasing the global output of the other good.

8. (8) Consider an economy producing only one good, pizza. Suppose that the aggregate demand for pizza is a decreasing function of the price of pizza. Furthermore, the aggregate supply curve is upward-sloping, but not perfectly inelastic. The government decides to increase government spending and finances the additional spending by issuing government bonds (=Treasury bills). Discuss the impact of this government policy on GNP, employment, price level, and interest rate. How would your answer change if the aggregate supply curve were perfectly inelastic?

9. (8) Imagine two individuals, you and M. Kahn, both expecting to earn the same income "in the average", i.e. their permanent income is identical. However, M. Kahn had recently a disproportionate number of bad years, whereas you have been quite lucky. Consequently, right now M. Kahn is only a Columbia assistant professor earning a yearly salary of $8,000, whereas you are a young, successful lawyer making $ 100,000 per year (without bonus!). According to Friedman's permanent income hypothesis, how does your current consumption compare to M. Kahn's current consumption. Would your answer change if you were told that M. Kahn is credit rationed? Now assume that after ten years M. Kahn is still earning $8,000 (now he is a lecturer at NYU) and disappointedly realizes his inferiority (in the meantime you have tripled your salary). Taking into account this additional information, how does your consumption level compare to M. Kahn's consumption.

10. (10) A firm uses labour (L) and capital (K) to produce a

single output. The input prices of labour and capital are the same.

a.   Show on a diagram the firm's cost-minimizing input mix. Label them as L* and K*.
b.   Assume the price of capital is doubled. Repeat question (1) and show your answer on the same diagram. Compare the labour capital ratio with the one you found in (1). If they are different, explain why.
c.   The price of labour and capital remain equal. Suppose a technology progress make the firm's production process more efficient (i.e., same labour capital mix gives a higher output level with the new technology). Draw the isoquant Q* for the new technology on the same diagram. Do you expect the firm's cost minimizing labour capital ratio different from that of (1)? Explain.

11. (10) John lives for two time periods. He earns $40,000 in the first period. The economy-wise interest rate is 10%. He may borrow or save but default is not allowed. Draw and label diagrams clearly to answer this question, no calculations.

a.   If John expects to earn zero income in the second period, how much would he consume in period 1?
b.   Assume John continues to earn $40,000 in the second period. Repeat (1).
c.   Assume the possibility of earning zero and $40,000 in the second period is fifty and fifty. Repeat question a.
d.   Suppose the interest rate of borrowing money is now 20% and of saving is still 10%. How might this change your answers to question (1) and (2)?

HW #1 due (9/28)

1. Two Good economy featuring pizza and coke. The price of pizza is $1 per unit, and the price of coke is $2 per unit.

A. If you have $100, graph your budget constraint
B. If prices double and Income does not change, graph new budget constraint
C. Suppose that a benevolent government gives "pizza food stamps" to people who have only $100 income. Thus in addition to having $100 such a person also receives 20 extra units of pizza. Graph the new budget constraint. Under what conditions do you predict that there would be a black market for people attempting to sell the "pizza food stamps"?

2. In some states, hunting licenses are allocated by lottery; if you want a license, you send in your name to enter the lottery. If the purpose of the system is to ensure that those who want to hunt the most get a chance to do so, what are the flaws of this system? How would the situation improve if people who won licenses were allowed to sell them to others?

3. In the 1980s, the Reagan Administration wanted to help the Contras in Nicaragua. The Contras wanted military support (guns) and medical support (medicine). Congress demanded that the Reagan Administration only provide medical support. Graph the Contras budget constraint (assume that they had $500 and that the price of guns and medicine is both $1). Now assume that the Reagan

administration sends in $200 of medicine.

A. Show how this infusion of support affects the Contra budget constraint
B. Use your graph to show why might this increase in humanitarian support increase the Contra military muscle.

4. In Mexico, each unit of a resource can produce either one professional computer or three computer-game systems. Mexico is endowed with 10,000 units of this resource. In Japan each unit of this resource can produce either two professional computers or eight computer-game systems. Suppose Japan also has 10,000 units of this resource.
A. Draw Mexico's and Japan's production possibilities frontiers.
B. Which country has comparative advantage in professional computers production? (explain)
C. Assuming that in a world with no trade between Mexico and Japan, each country devoted exactly half of its resource to production of each good, show how world output of both goods can increase if trade is allowed.

HW #2
Graph all answers)

Supply and Demand
1. Old cars (car built before 1980) pollute more than new cars. New car regulation requires that expensive emissions control devices be placed on cars built after 1994. Graph the supply and demand for new and used cars and explain why this stringent new vehicle emissions control regulation may actually lower air quality in the short run. (hint: discuss scrappage of old cars in the absence of the regulation)

2. Suppose President Clinton passes a crime bill that places a 24 day wait for buying a gun. Draw the supply and demand for guns in the legal and illegal markets. Explain how this policy affects the two diagrams. Would an economist predict that armed crimes will fall? Suppose Clinton places a tax on buying bullets in the legal market, why may the number of bullets bought not decrease?

3. More states are passing laws allowing gambling. The goal is to raise revenue by taking a percentage of the gambling. Graph the supply and demand for gambling and discuss conditions such that total tax revenue from gambling would actually fall as more entry into this industry occurs.

4. Why does economic theory predict that deaf people will live next to airports? (hint: the supply and demand for locations)

5. The Wall Street Journal reported that a Scotch company lowered its product's price in Japan one holiday season. It was shocked to learn that demand fell. Consumers' demand had increased as price fell (as theory predicts!) but gift givers bought less of the Scotch as the price fell. Give an information theory of prices to explain this true story.

6. The government wants manufacturing plants to pollute less. It passes a law stating that polluters must buy pollution permits for each ton of emissions. If a fixed number of permits are to be supplied, graph supply and demand to show how the permits' equilibrium price is determined. When will firms cheat and not

148

buy the permits?

7. I am saving part of my Columbia pay check so that I can still eat at Mamma Joy's when I am an old man. Why am I delighted that developing countries are very eager to increase infrastructure? (hint: graph the capital market's supply and demand) Under what conditions would I not care about LDC growth?

8. (Chapter 7 Tietenberg) Why is the american car owner better off if OPEC is unable to collude? Why is OPEC better off if natural gas is price controlled?

9. Why does Madonna earn more than firemen?

10. Firms invest in advertising. These advertisements convey information about the product. Use a graph to show the goal of advertising.

HW #3

1. (Comparative Advantage again) There are two nations, Korea and the US, and they both have the technology to produce two goods called computers (C) and sneakers (S). For each labor unit the production possibilities are:

	computers	Sneakers
Korea	5	5
US	20	5

Assume that the US has two units of labor and Korea has one unit of labor.
(in english, this means that we are assuming that US has more workers than korea)

A.   Graph the NO-TRADE ppf for each nation
B.   Graph the world ppf if labor cannot move across nations
C.   Graph the world ppf if labor can move across nations
D.   Why would the Korean worker be willing to pay up to 15 computers for the right to work in the US?
E.   Use supply and demand curves in the US labor market to show conditions such that US workers would sharply oppose Korean worker immigration.

2. I am saving part of my Columbia pay check so that I can still eat at Mamma Joy's when I am an old man. Why am I delighted that developing countries are very eager to increase infrastructure? (hint: graph the capital market's supply and demand) Under what conditions would I not care about LDC growth?

3. Vehicle Import Quotas - Only Toyota and Ford make cars. Assume that each car maker views the industry as competitive. The cars are identical. Toyota can ship cars for free to the United States from Japan. In the initial equilbrium in the car market. The equilibrium price of cars was $12 and 2000 total cars were sold. Toyota sold 1,000 and Ford sold 1,000.

A. The Clinton Administration puts a 500 car quota on Toyota (the company can only sell 500 cars to the U.S). How does this affect the supply and demand for cars in the United States? How does the new equilibrium quantity and price of cars differ from the inital equilibrium? Why does Lee Iaccocca lobby Congress for Japanese import restrictions?

149

15

4. What is the present value of a stream of $1,000 checks each year if the interest rate is 0%? What is the present value of a stream of $1,000 checks each year if the interest rate is 10%?

5. A bond is a financial instrument that promises to pay a fixed quantity of money (maybe $10,000) in the future. Why do bond prices fall when interest rates rise?

HW #4 (Chapters 5 and 6)

1. Bill Clinton announces that college students will each receive a $5000 tuition subsidy to make college increasingly affordable for more americans.

Draw supply and demand curves for college education and present cases when the subsidy will lower the price consumers pay and increase college enrollment. Draw another scenario when the policy will simply lead to higher tuition prices such that the University endowments are the big winner from the President's new program. (hint: see page 124 of stiglitz)

2. You have won the lotto! The lotto pays $50,000 each year for the next 20 years. If the market rate of interest is 10%, explain why you are not a millionare. (page 141) Write down the present value of your winnings.

3. Moodys and Standard and Poor are two companies that rank other companies' credit worthyness. If Nabisco has recently defaulted on paying back a large loan to its creditors, Moodys and Standard and Poor are likely to lower its ranking. Why do companies such as Nabisco worry about their credit ranking? (p 163)

4. Suppose that there is no legal system to sue to recover "bad loans". Would companies have an incentive to pay back their debts?

5. Do debtor nations have the same incentives as these companies to pay back their debts? Why does Poland pay higher interest rates to borrow money than Japan?

6. In World War II, the U.S. government needed to raise money to pay for its war effort. U.S. citizens collected income from their jobs and bought consumption goods with part of their income and saved the remainder (income - consumption = savings). These folks had many options for saving their money. They could put in the bank, or under their bed, or buy War Bonds. Why did the U.S government start an advertising campaign that it was patriotic to buy War Bonds?

7. Suppose that one share of Microsoft entitles its owner to a stream of dividends. Assume that all investors expect it to pay out a dividend of $2 next year and $4 the year after that. If the interest rate in the economy is 5%, write down what you expect the price of Microsoft shares to sell for on Wall Street. Now suppose that you observe in the Wall Street Journal that Dell Computer shares sell for the same price as a share of Microsoft. If Dell is expected to pay a dividend of $1 next year, what must its dividend be in the second year?

8. If you want to sell your used car, why might demand for your vehicle actually fall if you lower the price?

150

9. Why is the average rental car in such terrible condition?

10. Why do farmers never buy flood insurance?
(read 153-158)

HW #5

1. (Read Stiglitz page 238-240) You live for two periods. When you are young, you work and earn $4000 income. When you are old you earn nothing. The interest rate in the economy is 10%. Your utility function is;

$$U(C_{young}, C_{old}) = 5 * C_{young}^{.5} + C_{old}^{.5}$$

A. Graph your intertemporal budget constraint and your utility maximizing consumption when young and when old. If the interest rate were to rise to 15%, will savings rise or fall?

B. Now assume that when you are old, a new generation of young people are born. There is a social security program that pays each old person $2000. Explain why if the government runs a balanced budget and the young pay for the old's social security, then each young person must pay;

$$(N_{old} * 2000) / (N_{young})$$

Where N represents the number of people in that birth cohort.
C. Following part B, explain why it is very costly for Generation X kids to live after the Baby Boomers. Graph the case, where a given generation would vote for Congress people who campaign to abolish social security.
D. Give conditions when a generation is greatly enriched by social security.

2. (read stiglitz 240-242) Your great aunt has given you a generous gift of $22,000 today and $28,000 next year. Assume the local bank pays 4% interest if you save your money today. Suppose you know a loan shark who is willing to lend you money today to buy consumption today at a 50% interest rate in return for the $28,000 you will collect next year. If the price of consumption is one both today and tomorrow, graph the consumption possibilities that your aunt's gift makes possible.

3. Discuss the incentive problems introduced by paying the police paid per arrest, versus paying them an hourly wage.

4. Assume there are two occupations, medicine and law. Pay fluctuates wildly in both occupations with the strange occurence that when medicine is paying well the law does not pay well and vice versa.   If people do not have access to capital markets to borrow and lend, why does economic theory predict that doctors will marry lawyers? (read page 272 and explain why this is a portfolio.

HW #6
Firm Labor Demand
A pizza company makes pizza using only one input labor, labelled

L (measured in hours of labor). This company has the production function;

$$pizza = 20 * L^{.5}$$

1. Fill in a table that has the following columns, pizza output, workers, total pizza output, marginal pizza output, average pizza output.

2. If the price of pizza is $4 a piece, add a new column to your table which indicates total firm revenue from selling pizza, and marginal revenue.

3. If the wage equals $5 per unit of labor input, add a new column indicting the the total wage bill per unit of labor employed.

4. Use this table, to solve for how many workers the firm will hire. Explain your answer.

5. If this firm experiences a productivity shock, such that the new production function is;

$$pizza = 30 * L^{.5}$$

and if the wage stays at 5 dollars per unit, by how much will this firm increase

its workforce?

6. Go back to question #5, if this productivity shock occurs, under what conditions would the firm want to make its current workers work longer days rather than hiring more workers who work the same number of hours as before?

7. Suppose that Robots (labelled as R) now are invented and can be used to produce pizza. In particular suppose that robots and labor can be used to produce pizza as;

$$pizza = 20 * R * L^{.5}$$

Assume that the firm has received two robots for free and cannot buy anymore. Make a new table and show why workers would not fear losing their jobs to these machines.

8. Use the consumption/Leisure indifference curve framework to present the conditions such that a wage
tax cut would increase the government's revenue.

9. If the demand for high skilled labor has increased in the 1980s and the demand for low skilled labor has decreased in the 1980s, explain why the income distribution has become more skewed (higher variance) in the 1980s.

10. (extra-credit) Return to question #7 and give a case where the introduction of robots does reduce the firm's demand for

152

labor.

HW #7

A pizza company makes pizza using only one input labor, labelled L (measured in hours of labor). This company has the production function;

$$pizza = 20*L^{.5}$$

It is the only pizza maker in the industry; the market demand for pizza is;

$$pizza=100-4*price$$

1. Fill in a table that has the following columns, price of pizza, revenue, marginal revenue per pizza sold,
2. Fill in a table that has the following columns; labor, pizza production, marginal pizza production.

3. If the wage =6, how much does it cost the firm (measured in $) to produce the first piece of pizza? to produce two pieces of pizza? to produce 10?

4. Use this table, to solve for how many workers the firm will hire and how much pizza the profit maximizing monopolist will produce.

5. If this firm experiences a productivity shock, such that the new production function is;

$$pizza = 30*L^{.5}$$

and if the wage stays at 6 dollars per unit, re-do question #4.

6. An economy features a manager whose utility is only a function of money and a worker whose utility is a function of money and leisure. The worker lives for 24 hours. There exists a production function that transforms worker's time into money such that; $ = 5*work.

A. What will be the pareto-optimal allocation of resources if the manager owns the machine and the worker?

B. What will be the pareto-optimal allocation of resources if the worker owns the machine and owns himself? (hint: graph indifference curves in consumption/leisure space and compare the two regimes)

7. There are two types of people in society, pizza lovers and pizza likers. All "lovers" are identical. Their demand for pizza is; pizza = 20 - 2*pizza. Pizza likers have demand functions of; pizza = 10 - 4*pizza. There are 100 pizza lovers and 100 pizza

likers.

If a pizza maker can produce pizza for zero cost and he is a monopolist, what would be his profit maximizing output choice if he could not discriminate? What would be his profit maximizing choices if he could? How much profit would he gain if he could treat the two groups differently?

8. Assume that Mick Jagger knows that attending a Rolling Stones concert is a complement of buying their CDs, why do the Rolling Stones set ticket prices below their market clearing prices?

9. A drug company has a monopoly for producing a hair growth tonic which some men want to buy. If the company has a monopoly on this product but also is developing an AIDS cure using federal government research funds, why might it choose not to "price gouge" and charge the monopoly price for the bald drug. What is the general lesson for multi-product firms?

HW #8:

The Coase Theorem (Solving externalities without government intervention)
The Model;
An Electric utility, named E, receives $8 for every unit of power it creates. It can create 0, 1, 2, 3, 4, 5, 6 units of power. In the table, I give you the marginal cost for producing each additional unit of power. Each unit of power created by E creates one unit of air pollution that falls on the person who lives in New York, named N. N hates air pollution because it raises the costs of her producing flowers and she makes her living selling flowers. Suppose if N chooses to farm she receives $9 for her flowers. If she chooses not to farm, her profit is 0. (Note: she does not choose how many flowers to plant, her only decision is to farm or not farm)

Power generation by E	Revenue for E	Marginal revenue for E	Marginal cost for E	Profit for E	Revenue for N	marginal Cost for N	Profit for N	Total society profit
0			0		9	1		
1			1		9	2		
2			2		9	3		
3			3		9	4		
4			4		9	5		
5			8		9	6		
6			10		9	7		

1. fill in the table's entries

2. What is society's total profit if N does not farm?

3. How much power will E create if there is no government

20

regulation and no bargaining with N?

4. What level of power creation maximizes total society profit?

5. If N has the right to clean air (meaning that she can always costlessly force E to stop polluting), will N allow E to pollute? How much money will E transfer to N?

6. If E has the right to pollute (meaning that he can dump on N without compensating N), will the outcome match your answer to question 4? Will N farm?

Oxford University
Institute of Economics and Statistics

Instructor: P.D. Klemperer
Game Theory: (9 x 1 1/2-hour lectures)

1. Introduction. What is Game Theory: how does we model a game? K 11.1-11.3; F 1.2.1-1.2.2
2. Zero Sum Games. (Owen § 2); Bacharach § 3
3.&4. Simple examples of Nash Equilibrium; Alternative rationales for Nash Equilibrium (Kreps Game Theory and Economic Modelling 12.6); Mixed strategy equilibria and their computations. G 1.3A; Cournot and Bertrand. G 1.2A,B; Bayesian-Nash Equilibrium. G3.1-3.2A, Existence and N.E. G1.3B, F 3.2 Friedman Oligopoly and the Games II.7.2-II.7.3
5. Correlated Equilibrium. F&T 2.2; Handbook of I.O. pp. 272-74; M 6.2; Dominance Arguments. G 1.1B; Rationalizability etc. F&T 2.1
6. Introduction to refinement including Focal Points. K 12.6; Schellings § 3 & Appendix Backwards Induction (subgame Perfection) K 12.7.2; (G2.4B); Forwards Induction. K 12.7.4 pp. 432-33; M4.9
7. Sequential Equilibrium. K12.7.3; G4.2A; Trembling Hand Perfection, Properness etc. K12.7.5; K12.7.6
8. Refinements of Sequential Equilibrium (esp. Intuitive Criterion). K12.7; G4.4; Summary Comments about refinement.
9. Co-operative solution concepts including Nash bargaining, Shapley Value, Core. Friedman Oligopoly and the Theory of Games 7.1.2.2, 7.1.4, 11.1-11.3, 12.1; F 6.2.1-6.2.2, 7.3.1-7.3.2, 7.6.1-7.6.2; M8.2, 9.1-9.4.

Multiple readings for a topic are alternatives; (Readings in parenthesis are less recommended.); K=Kreps "A Course in Microeconomic Theory." (1990), G=Gibbons (1992), F=Friedman (1991), F&T=Fudenberg and Tirole (1991), M=Myerson (1991).

Introduction:

Bacharach, M. 1976, Economics and the Theory of Games, London: MacMillan.
Dixit, A., and Nalebuff, B., 1991, Thinking Strategically, New York: Norton.
*Fudenberg, D., and Tirole, J, 1989, Chapter 5 of Handbook of Industrial Organization, Richard Schmalensee and Robert D. Willig (eds.), New York: North Holland.
*Kreps, D., 19890, Game Theory and Economic Modelling, Oxford University Press (forthcoming).
*Myerson, R.B., 1984, An Introduction to Game Theory, Discussion Paper No. 623, Northwestern University.
*Tirole, J., 1989, Chapter 11 of the Theory of Industrial Organization, MIT Press.

Books: Theory

*Binmore, K., 1992, Fun and Games, D.C. Heath and Co.
*Friedman, J.W., 1991 (2,d. Ed.) Game Theory with Applications to Economics, Oxford University Press.
*Fudenberg, D., and Tirole, J., 1991, Game Theory, MIT Press.
*Gibbons, R., 1992, A Primer in Game Theory, Harvester Wheatsheaf.
Harsanyi, J.C., 1977, Rational Behavior and Bargaining Equilibrium in Games and Social

Situations, Cambridge University Press.

Harsanyi, J.C., and R. Selten, 1988, A General Theory of Equilibrium Selection in Games, MIT Press.

Jones, A.J., 1980, Game Theory: Mathematical Models of Conflict, Ells Horwood.

*Kreps, D., 1990, part III of A Course in Microeconomic Theory, Harvester Wheatsheaf.

Luce, R.D., and H. Raiffa, 1957, Games and Decisions, New York: Wiley.

Moulin, H., 1982, Game Theory for the Social Sciences, New York university Press.

*Myerson, R.B., 1991, Game Theory: Analysis of Conflict, Harvard University Press.

Owen, G., 1968, Game Theory, Academic Press.

Rapoport, A., 1970, n-Person Game Theory, University of Michigan Press.

Rasmusen, E., 1989, Games and Information: An Introduction to Game Theory, Basil Blackwell.

Shubik, M., 1982, Game Theory in the Social Sciences, MIT Press.

van Damme, E., 1991, (2nd ed.) Stability and Perfection of Nash Equilibrium, Springer-Verlag.

Books: Application

*Friedman, J.W., 1977, Oligopoly and the Theory of Games, Amsterdam, Elsevier, North Holland.

Ordeshook, P., 1986, Game Theory and Political Theory, Cambridge University Press.

Osborne, M., and Rubinstein, A., 1990, Bargaining and Markets, Academic Press.

*Schelling, T.C., 1960, The Strategy of Conflict, Cambridge, Mass, Harvard University Press.

Schubik, M. with R. Levitan, 1980, Market Structure and Behavior, Cambridge, Mass, Harvard University Press.

Telser, L.g., 1978, Economic Theory and the Core, Chicago: University of Chicago Press.

Zagare, F.C., 1984, Game Theory: Concepts and Applications (to international relations), Sage Publication.

Oxford University
Institute of Economics and Statistics

Instructor: P.D. Klemperer
The Economics of Auctions: (6 x 11/2-hour lectures)

Bulow, Jeremy I. and Klemperer, Paul D. "Auctions vs Negotiations." St. Catherine's College, Oxford, Working Paper (1993).

_____ "Rational Frenzies and Crashes." *J. Pol. Econ.* 102 (Feb. 1994): 1-23.

Bulow Jeremy, I. and Roberts D. John. "The Simple Economics of Optimal Auctions." *J. Pol. Econ.* 97 (Oct. 1989): 1060-90.

Cramton, Peter, Gibbons, Robert, and Klemperer, Paul. "Dissolving a Partnership Efficiently." *Econometrica* 55 (May 1987): 615-32.

Cremer, Jacques and McLean Richard. "Optimal Selling Strategies under Uncertainty for a Discriminatory Monopolist When Demands are Independent." *Econometrica* 53 (March 1985): 345-361.

Gilbert, Richard and Klemperer, Paul. "An Equilibrium Theory of Rationing." St. Catherine's College, Oxford, Working Paper (1993).

McAfee, R. Preston, and McMillan, John. "Auctions and Bidding." *Journal of Economic Literature* 25 (June 1987b): 699-738.

Milgrom, Paul R. " The Economics of Competitive Bidding: A Selective Survey." In *Social Goals and Social Organizations: Essays in the Memory of Elisha Pazner*, edited by Leonid Hurwicz, David Schmeidler, and Hugo Sonnenschein. Cambridge: Cambridge University Press, 1985.

_____. "Auction Theory." In *Advances in Economic Theory: Fifth World Congress*, edited by Truman F. Bewley. Cambridge: Cambridge University Press, 1987.

_____. "Auctions and Bidding: A Primer." *Journal of Economic Perspectives* 3 (Summer 1989) (and other articles in the same issue of J.E.P).

Milgrom, Paul R., and Weber, Robert, J. " A Theory of Auctions and Competitive Bidding." *Econometrica* 50 (September 1982): 1089-1122.

Myerson, Roger B. "Optimal Auction Design." *Math Operations Res.* 6 (February 1981): 58-73.

Riley, John G., and Samuelson, william F. "Optimal Auctions." *AER* 71 (June 1981): 381-92.

University of Pennsylvania G

Economics 703
Microeconomics II

Fall 1994

George J. Mailath
McNeil 436
phone 8-7908
Office hours: Mondays 3–4 p.m. and Fridays 2–3 p.m.

This is a graduate level introduction to game theory, decision making under uncertainty, and information economics.

There will be weekly problem sets, a midterm, and a final exam. The midterm will be given on October 19 in class. Your grade will be determined as 10% problem sets, 40% midterm, and 50% final exam. The problem sets are an important part of the course; you should spend a great deal of time and effort on them. You are encouraged to work in groups on the problem sets. However, before meeting in the group you should have attempted each question—groups work well when they allow you to learn from each other, they do *not* work well when they are used to facilitate a division of labor (you learn nothing from copying another student's answer).

The teaching assistants for the course are Matthias Kahl and Andrea Moro. Their office is McNeil 442; their office hours will be announced.

The texts for the course are:

[G] Robert Gibbons, *Game Theory for Applied Economists*, Princeton University Press, Princeton, 1992.

[K] David M. Kreps, *A Course in Microeconomic Theory*, Princeton University Press, Princeton, 1990.

In addition, the following (optional) text contains succinct descriptions of much of the material:

[V] Hal Varian, *Microeconomic Analysis*, W.W. Norton, New York, third edition, 1992. (Note that this edition is significantly different from earlier editions.)

Other useful books are:

Avinash Dixit and Barry Nalebuff, *Thinking Strategically*, W.W. Norton, New York, 1991. (An entertaining and easy introduction to game theoretic reasoning.)

Drew Fudenberg and Jean Tirole, *Game Theory*, MIT Press, Cambridge, 1991. (An encyclopedic graduate level text on modern noncooperative game theory.)

David M. Kreps, *Game Theory and Economic Modelling*, Oxford University Press, Oxford, 1990. (A collection of non-mathematical essays on game theory, emphasizing the strengths and weaknesses as Kreps sees them—many of the points are also in his text.)

Roger Myerson, *Game Theory: Analysis of Conflict*, Harvard University Press, Cambridge, 1991. (Graduate level text. Includes some treatment of cooperative game theory.)

Jean-Jacques Laffont (ed.), *Advances in Economic Theory: Sixth World Congress*, Vol 1, Cambridge University Press, Cambridge, 1992. (Contains surveys on various aspects of game theory and its applications.)

1

Martin Osborne and Ariel Rubinstein, *A Course in Game Theory*, MIT Press, Cambridge, 1994 (Graduate level text. Includes some treatment of cooperative game theory.)

All of these books should be on reserve in Lippincott.

Course Outline

You should read the indicated sections of the texts. They cover material that every serious economist should have seen. For those with an interest in a particular topic, the literature discussions at the end of the relevant chapters in Gibbons and Kreps, as well as the surveys in Laffont (the titles are self-explanatory), are important sources for more advanced papers. I have also included one or two (usually more recent) readings in some topics (their references will also point you to other papers).

1. **Normal form games.** (2 classes)
   (a) Iterated deletion of dominated strategies. [G 1.1.A, 1.1.B; K. 12.1–2; V. 15.1–3, 15.8–9, 23.1–2, 23.4, 23.8–9]
   (b) Nash equilibrium. [G 1.1.C; K. 12.4; V. 15.4, 16.1–5, 23.3, 23.5–6]
2. **Extensive form games.** (5 classes)
   (a) Definition of extensive form games. [G 2.4; K. Ch. 11]
   (b) Backward induction, subgame perfection, and credible threats. [G 2.1–2; K. 12.3, 12.7.1, 12.7.2; V. 15.10, 16.6–7]
       i. For more on the relationship between normal and extensive form: G.J. Mailath, L. Samuelson, and J.M. Swinkels (1993), "Extensive Form Reasoning in Normal Form Games," *Econometrica*, 61, 273–302.
       ii. For a criticism of backward induction: P.J. Reny (1993), "Common Belief and the Theory of Games with Perfect Information," *Journal of Economic Theory*, 59, 257–274.
   (c) Repeated games and the folk theorem. [G 2.3; K. 14.1–2, 14.4–5; V. 15.6, 15.11]
       i. For renegotiation in repeated games: J.-P. Benoit and V. Krishna (1993), "Renegotiation in Finitely Repeated Games," *Econometrica*, 61, 303–323.
3. **Decision making under risk and uncertainty.** (3 classes)
   (a) Risk and von Neumann-Morgenstern expected utility. [V. 11.1–4, 11.8; K. 3.1]
   (b) Measures of risk aversion. [V. 11.5–7; K. 3.2–3]
   (c) Uncertainty and subjective probability. [V. 11.9; K. 3.4]
       i. For "Savage"-like decision making that is consistent with admissibility: L.E. Blume, A. Brandenburger, and E. Dekel (1991), "Lexicographic Probabilities and Choice Under Uncertainty," *Econometrica*, 59, 61–79.
4. **Mixed strategies, domination, and equilibria.** (2 classes)
   (a) Mixed strategies and existence of Nash equilibria. [G 1.3; K. 12.5; V. 15.5]
   (b) Rationalizability, learning and evolution. [K. 12.6]
       i. For an approach to rationalizability more consistent with Savage: T. Börgers (1993), "Pure Strategy Dominance," *Econometrica*, 61,

2

423-430.

    ii. For recent symposia on learning and evolution: *Journal of Economic Theory*, August 1992, volume 57 (#2) and *Games and Economic Behavior*, July and October 1993, volume 5 (#3 and 4).

5. **Games of incomplete information.** (3 classes)
   - (a) Bayesian Nash equilibrium. [G 3.1, 3.2; V. 15.12–13]
   - (b) Sequential equilibria, perfect Bayesian equilibria [G 4.1–2; K. 12.7.3, 13.1–2]
     - i. A recent reputation paper: K. Schmidt (1993), "Reputation and Equilibrium Characterization in Repeated Games with Conflicting Interests," *Econometrica*, 61, 325-351.
   - (c) Refinements [G 4.4; K. 12.7.4]
     - i. For criticism of equilibrium domination argument: G.J. Mailath, M. Okuno-Fujiwara, and A. Postlewaite (1993), "Belief Based Refinements in Signaling Games," *Journal of Economic Theory*, 60, 241-276.

6. **Moral hazard and incentives.** (4 classes)
   - (a) Principal-agent model. [K. Ch. 16; V. 25.1–5]
   - (b) Incomplete contracts
     - i. Survey: O. Hart and B. Holmstrom (1987), "The Theory of Contracts," in *Advances in Economic Theory: Fifth World Congress*, ed. T. Bewley, Cambridge University Press, Cambridge.
     - ii. Example of recent work on incomplete contracts: P. Aghion and P. Bolton (1992), "An Incomplete Contracts Approach to Financial Contracting," *Review of Economic Studies*, 59, 473-494.

7. **Adverse selection and market signaling.** (4 classes)
   - (a) Akerlof's model of lemons. [K. 17.1; V. 25.9]
   - (b) Signaling. [G 4.2; K. 17.2–4, 18.1; V. 25.6–8, 25.10–11]
     - i. An interesting (but hard) paper: D. Gale (1992), "A Walrasian Theory of Markets with Adverse Selection," *Review of Economic Studies*, 59, 229-255.

8. **Social choice, the revelation principle, and mechanism design.** (3 classes)
   - (a) Arrow's theorem [K. 5.5]
   - (b) The Revelation Principle. [G 3.3; K. 18.2]
     - i. Classic application to bilateral bargaining: R.B. Myerson and M. Satterthwaite (1983), "Efficient Mechanisms for Bilateral Trading," *Journal of Economic Theory*, 28, 265-281.
     - ii. To public goods: G.J. Mailath and A. Postlewaite (1990), "Asymmetric Information Bargaining Problems with Many Agents," *Review of Economic Studies*, 57, 351-367.
   - (c) Gibbard-Satterthwaite theorem. [K. 18.4]

3

Fall 1994

George J. Mailath

There are three questions. Do all questions. The exam is worth 60 points in total. Justify all answers and show all work. Label all diagrams clearly. Write legibly. If you need to make additional assumptions, state them clearly.

1. Prove that a dominant strategy $s_i' \in S_i$ is a strictly dominant strategy if and only if $\arg\max_{s_i} u_i(s_i, s_{-i})$ is a singleton for all $s_{-i} \in S_{-i}$.

2. Consider the following game between Bruce and Sheila, denoted G: Bruce first decides between taking an outside option, "O", or playing a battle of the sexes with Sheila. If Bruce takes the outside option then the game is over, Bruce receives a payoff of 2, and Sheila a payoff of 0. The battle of the sexes payoff matrix is:

		Sheila	
		L	R
Bruce	U	1,3	0,0
	D	0,0	3,1

(a) What is the normal form of G? [5 points]

(b) Describe a subgame perfect equilibrium strategy profile in which Bruce takes the outside option O. [10 points]

(c) What is the reduced normal form of G? [5 points]

(d) What is the result of the iterated deletion of weakly dominated strategies? [5 points]

(e) Compare your answer in parts 2.b and 2.d. [5 points]

3. Suppose the following game is infinitely repeated:

		Sheila	
		L	R
Bruce	U	2,0	x,0
	D	0,5	1,1

Let δ denote the common discount factor for both players and consider the strategy profile that induces the outcome path DL, UR, DL, UR,$\cdots$, and that, after a deviation, specifies one period of UL and then returning to the outcome path DL, UR, DL, UR,$\cdots$.

(a) Suppose $x = 5$, i.e., the payoff to Bruce from UR is 5. For what values of δ is this strategy profile subgame perfect? [10 points]

(b) Suppose now $x = 4$. How does this change your answer to part 3.a? [5 points]

1

Economics 703
Midterm Solutions

George J. Mailath

1. If $s_i' \in S_i$ is a dominant strategy, then $s_i' \in \arg\max_{s_i} u_i(s_i, s_{-i})$ $\forall s_{-i} \in S_{-i}$.

   If $\arg\max_{s_i} u_i(s_i, s_{-i})$ is a singleton, then, for any $\hat{s}_i \neq s_i'$, $\hat{s}_i \notin \arg\max_{s_i} u_i(s_i, s_{-i})$. That is, $u_i(\hat{s}_i, s_{-i}) < \max_{s_i} u_i(s_i, s_{-i}) \equiv u_i(s_i', s_{-i})$. But then $u_i(\hat{s}_i, s_{-i}) < u_i(s_i', s_{-i})$ $\forall \hat{s}_i \neq s_i'$, and since this holds for all $s_{-i} \in S_{-i}$, s_i' is a strictly dominant strategy.

   Conversely, suppose $\arg\max_{s_i} u_i(s_i, s_{-i})$ is not a singleton for some $s_{-i} \in S_{-i}$. That is, $\hat{s}_i \in \arg\max_{s_i} u_i(s_i, s_{-i})$ with $\hat{s}_i \neq s_i'$. Then, $u_i(s_i', s_{-i}) = u_i(\hat{s}_i, s_{-i})$ and so s_i' is not a strictly dominant strategy.

   (a) The normal form of G is:

		Sheila L	Sheila R
	O,U	2,0	2,0
Bruce	O,D	2,0	2,0
	not O,U	1,3	0,0
	not O,D	0,0	3,1

   (b) A subgame perfect equilibrium strategy profile in which Bruce takes the outside option O is ((O,U),L). Note that the profile specifies the Nash equilibrium (U,L) on the battle of the sexes subgame.

   (c) The reduced normal form of G is:

		Sheila L	Sheila R
	O	2,0	2,0
Bruce	not O,U	1,3	0,0
	not O,D	0,0	3,1

   (d) The iterative deletion of weakly dominated strategies yields the profile ((not O,D),R). [In the first round, O dominates (not O, U). Then R dominates L, and finally, (not O,D) dominates O.]

   (e) The subgame perfect equilibrium does not survive the iterative deletion of dominated strategies. Subgame perfection "uncouples" the decision of Bruce at his first information set from his decision in the battle of the sexes. This allows Sheila to (behave as if she) believe that, even though Bruce made a mistake by playing "not O", in the battle of the sexes, he will play his part of the original equilibrium, UL.

   Iterative deletions, however, does not allow the decision to be uncoupled in this way. In particular, Sheila concludes (according to this logic) that the only reason Bruce did not play O is that he intends to play D in the battle of the sexes.

   Which argument do you find compelling?

(a) Note first that Sheila is always playing a myopic best reply to the specified behavior of Bruce, and that any deviation by Sheila can at best only postpone by one period the alternating sequence of $5, 0, 5, 0, \cdots$ payoffs, so that Sheila is always playing a best reply on every subgame for every value of δ (including $\delta = 0$!). There are three classes of subgames to check.

Consider first the class of subgame in which the first period action profile is DL. The payoff to Bruce from following the profile is $0 + 5 \cdot \delta + 0 \cdot \delta^2 + 5 \cdot \delta^3 + \cdots = 5 \cdot \delta / (1 - \delta^2)$. The only one shot deviation is to play U in the first period and then follow the profile. The outcome path this induces is UL, UL, DL, UR, DL, UR,$\cdots$. The payoff from this is $2 + 2 \cdot \delta + 5 \cdot \delta^3 / (1 - \delta^2)$. This deviation is not profitable if

$$5 \cdot \delta / (1 - \delta^2) \geq 2 + 2 \cdot \delta + 5 \cdot \delta^3 / (1 - \delta^2)$$

$$\Leftrightarrow 0 + 5 \cdot \delta + 5 \cdot \delta^3 / (1 - \delta^2) \geq 2 + 2 \cdot \delta + 5 \cdot \delta^3 / (1 - \delta^2)$$

$$\Leftrightarrow 5\delta \geq 2 + 2\delta \Leftrightarrow 3\delta \geq 2 \Leftrightarrow \delta \geq \frac{2}{3}.$$

The next class of subgame to consider is the one in which the first period action profile is UR. The payoff to Bruce from following the profile is $5 / (1 - \delta^2)$ (note that the payoff on the previous subgame is this payoff, discounted by one period). The one shot deviation leads to the outcome: DR, UL, DL, UR, DL, UR,$\cdots$. Its payoff is $1 + 2\delta + 5\delta^3 / (1 - \delta^2)$. This is clearly not a profitable deviation for $\delta \geq 2/3$, since the payoff on this profile is larger than on the previous subgame and the payoff from the deviation lower.

Finally, we must consider the class of subgame in which the first period action profile is UL. Clearly, the one shot deviation is not profitable since, Bruce loses in the first period, and he delays by one period when he receives the alternating sequence of payoffs.

(b) When $x = 4$, the indicated profile is not subgame perfect for any value of $\delta < 1$: Consider the class of subgame in which the first period action profile is DL. The payoff to Bruce from following the profile is $0 + 4 \cdot \delta + 0 \cdot \delta^2 + 4 \cdot \delta^3 + \cdots = 4 \cdot \delta / (1 - \delta^2)$. The payoff from the one shot deviation is $2 + 2 \cdot \delta + 4 \cdot \delta^3 / (1 - \delta^2)$. This deviation is profitable, since

$$4 \cdot \delta / (1 - \delta^2) < 2 + 2 \cdot \delta + 4 \cdot \delta^3 / (1 - \delta^2)$$

$$\Leftrightarrow 0 + 4 \cdot \delta + 4 \cdot \delta^3 / (1 - \delta^2) < 2 + 2 \cdot \delta + 4 \cdot \delta^3 / (1 - \delta^2)$$

$$\Leftrightarrow 4\delta < 2 + 2\delta \Leftrightarrow \delta < 1.$$

Note that the min max value for Bruce in this game is 2, and the indicated profile yields a payoff of $x \cdot \delta / (1 - \delta^2)$. A necessary condition (from the folk theorem) is that this payoff exceed the (appropriately normalized) min max value, i.e.,

$$\frac{x\delta}{(1 - \delta^2)} > \frac{2}{(1 - \delta)},$$

but this is equivalent to

$$x > \frac{2(1 + \delta)}{\delta} = 2 + \frac{2}{\delta} > 4.$$

Economics 703
Final Exam

George J. Mailath

Do all questions. There are three questions; questions 1 and 2 are worth 30 points each, and question 3 is worth 60 points. Justify all answers and show all working. Label all diagrams clearly. Write legibly. If you need to make additional assumptions, state them clearly.

1. Consider the game:

		L	C	R
I	T	1,4	9,0	1,0
	M	0,0	7,7	0,0
	B	0,0	0,0	4,1

II (L C R across top)

(a) What are the pure strategy Nash equilibria of this game?   [5 points]

(b) What are the mixed strategy Nash equilibria?   [10 points]

(c) Suppose the game is played twice, with payoffs added. Describe a subgame perfect equilibrium in which (M,C) is played in the first period. [Of course, you also need to verify that the described profile is in fact a subgame perfect equilibrium.]   [15 points]

2. A worker for a firm can either work hard (i.e., choose effort $a = a_H$) or shirk (effort $a = 0$). (Note that a denotes effort, and e denotes the base of natural logarithms, $e \approx 2.7183$.) If the worker works hard, the output of the firm is $\bar{y} = (e+1)^2$ with probability $\frac{1}{2}$ and $\underline{y} = 4e$ with probability $\frac{1}{2}$. (Note that $\underline{y} < \bar{y}$.) If the worker shirks, output is $\underline{y}$ with probability one. The von Neumann-Morgenstern utility function for the worker is $u(w) = \ln w$. Suppose the worker receives a utility of zero from not working for the firm. Suppose further that working hard incurs a disutility of 1, while shirking incurs a disutility of zero. As usual, the disutility of effort is additively separable from the expected utility of income. Finally, the firm is risk neutral. **NOTE: Leave answers in terms of e!**

(a) Suppose effort is contractible. What wage contract does the firm offer the worker? [10 points]

(b) Suppose output is contractible, but effort is not. What wage contract does the firm offer the worker?   [20 points]

Question 3 is on next page.

1

3. Consider a seller (Sheila) selling a nondurable good to a buyer (Bruce). There are two periods, and Bruce can purchase one unit in both, either, or neither periods. Both Bruce and Sheila discount by rate $\delta \in (0,1)$. Denote Bruce's reservation price by v, so that Bruce's payoff is given by

$$d_1(v - p_1) + d_2\delta(v - p_2),$$

where p_t is the price charged by Sheila in period t, and $d_t = 1$ if Bruce purchases in period t and $d_t = 0$ otherwise. Similarly, Sheila's payoff is

$$d_1 p_1 + d_2 \delta p_2.$$

It is common knowledge that Sheila has zero costs of production. There is incomplete information about Bruce's reservation price.

The game is as follows: In the first period, Sheila announces a price p_1. Nature then determines Bruce's reservation price (type) according to the probability distribution that assigns probability $\frac{1}{2}$ to $v = v_H$ and probability $\frac{1}{2}$ to $v = v_L$. Bruce learns his type and then decides whether to buy or not to buy. In the second period, Sheila again announces a price (knowing whether Bruce had bought or not in the first period) and Bruce then decides whether to buy or not.

Assume $0 < 2v_L < v_H$. Restrict attention to pure strategies.

(a) Describe Sheila's and Bruce's (extensive form) strategies of the two period game. [10 points]

(b) Consider a subgame starting at $p_1 \in [v_L, \delta v_L + (1-\delta)v_H]$. Describe a separating perfect Bayesian equilibrium of this subgame(naturally, the separation should occur in the first period). [Of course, you also need to verify that the described profile is in fact a perfect Bayesian equilibrium.] Hint: How will Sheila price in the second period if she assigns probability 1 to the value $v = v_H$? To $v = v_L$? [10 points]

(c) Consider now subgames starting at $p_1 \in (v_L, \delta v_L + (1-\delta)v_H]$. Note that now $p_1 \neq v_L$. Is there a pooling equilibrium in these subgames (i.e., an equilibrium in which both types of Bruce behave the same way in period 1)? Hint: How will Sheila price in the second period if her beliefs equal her prior on v (remember that $v_H > 2v_L$)? [10 points]

(d) Suppose that $\delta v_L + (1-\delta)v_H < p_1 < v_H$. Show that there is no pure strategy equilibrium in this subgame. [10 points]

(e) Suppose $p_1 \leq v_L$. Describe the pooling perfect Bayesian equilibrium in this subgame. Why is this the unique equilibrium when $p_1 < v_L$? [10 points]

(f) Suppose that Bruce always accepts when he is indifferent. Suppose there is a price ceiling $\bar{p} = \delta v_L + (1-\delta)v_H$ on first period prices. What price $p_1 \leq \bar{p}$ will Sheila charge in the first period? [10 points]

(g) [EXTRA CREDIT] What is the mixed strategy equilibrium in the subgame reached by $p_1 \in (\delta v_L + (1-\delta)v_H, v_H)$? What price will Sheila charge in the first period in the absence of a price ceiling (assume that if there are multiple equilibria at any price p_1, the one advantageous to Sheila is played)? [10 points]

2

1. (a) The pure strategy equilibria are (T,L) and (B,R).

   (b) Note first that T strictly dominates M for player 1, so M will not be played in any Nash equilibrium. Moreover, both L and R weakly dominate C for player 2 once M has been eliminated. Thus, the only additional equilibrium has player 1 randomizing between T and B and player 2 randomizing between L and C. Let p denote the probability that 1 places on T, and q the probability that 2 places on L. If 2 is randomizing, then 2 is indifferent between L and R, and so

$$4p = (1-p) \Rightarrow p = \frac{1}{5}.$$

Similarly, if 1 is indifferent between T and B,

$$q + (1-q) = 4(1-q) \Rightarrow q = \frac{3}{4}.$$

   (c) Consider the strategy profile in which (M,C) is played in the first period, (B,R) is played in the second period if player 1 had played M in the first, and (T,L) is played in the second period if player 1 had not played M in the first. If player 2 deviates from C in the first period, his first period payoff falls and there is no benefit in the second period, so player 2 has no incentive to deviate. If player 1 follows the profile, he earns $7 + 4 = 11$. If he deviates, the most he can earn is $9 + 1 = 10 < 11$, and so player 1 also has no incentive to deviate. Finally, a Nash equilibrium is played in the second period after every possible play in the first period. Thus the profile is subgame perfect.

2. (a) The firm can either offer w_L, a wage contingent on low effort (shirking), or w_H, a wage contingent on hard work. Then, participation constraint requires

$$\ln w_L \geq 0 \text{ and } (\ln w_H) - 1 \geq 0,$$

that is,

$$w_L \geq 1 \text{ and } w_H \geq e.$$

The firm's profits from offering w_L is $4e - 1$, while the firm's profit from offering w_H is $\frac{1}{2}((e+1)^2 + 4e) - e = \frac{1}{2}(e^2 + 4e + 1)$. Now, $4e - 1 - \frac{1}{2}(e^2 + 4e + 1) = \frac{1}{2}(-e^2 + 4e - 3) = \frac{1}{2}(1 - (e-2)^2) > 0$, so the firm offers the low effort contingent wage of $w_L = 1$.

   (b) Let $\underline{w}$ denote the wage after low output, and $\overline{w}$ the wage after high output. The incentive efficient implementation of low effort is obtained by setting $\underline{w} = \overline{w} = 1$, and yields a profit of $4e - 1$. Consider the incentive efficient implementation of high effort. Incentive compatibility requires

$$\frac{1}{2}\ln\overline{w} + \frac{1}{2}\ln\underline{w} - 1 \geq \ln\underline{w},$$

$$\Rightarrow \ln\overline{w} \geq 2 + \ln\underline{w} \Rightarrow \overline{w} \geq e^2\underline{w}.$$

Minimizing wages given this constraint implies $\overline{w} = e^2\underline{w}$. Participation constraint is

$$\frac{1}{2}\ln\overline{w} + \frac{1}{2}\ln\underline{w} - 1 \geq 0,$$

1

substituting for $\overline{w}$ yields

$$\frac{1}{2}(2 + \ln \underline{w}) + \frac{1}{2} \ln \underline{w} - 1 \geq 0 \Rightarrow \ln \underline{w} \geq 0 \Rightarrow \underline{w} \geq 1.$$

Again, minimizing wages gives $\underline{w} = 1$, and so $\overline{w} = e^2$. Profit from high effort wage contract is $\frac{1}{2}(\overline{y} - e^2) + \frac{1}{2}(\underline{y} - 1) = \frac{1}{2}((e+1)^2 - e^2 + 4e - 1) = 3e < 4e - 1$, and so low effort contract is offered. (Given the answer to the last part, this should not be a surprise.)

3. (a) A strategy for Sheila is (p_1, ζ_2), where $p_1 \in \Re_+$ is first period price and $\zeta_2 : \Re_+ \times \{0, 1\} \to \Re_+$ is second period price as a function of first period price and whether Bruce had purchased in the first period (0 means no, 1 means yes). A strategy for Bruce is (ξ_1, ξ_2), where $\xi_1 : \{v_L, v_H\} \times \Re_+ \to \{0, 1\}$ is first period purchase decision as a function of his valuation and first period price, and $\xi_2 : \{v_L, v_H\} \times \Re_+ \times \{0, 1\} \times \Re_+ \to \{0, 1\}$ is second period purchase decision as a function of his valuation, first period price, his first period decision, and second period price.

(b) First observe that if Sheila assigns probability 1 to the value $v = v_H$ in the second period, then she will charge a price of $p_2 = v_H$ (and Bruce will accept). Similarly, if Sheila assigns probability 1 to the value $v = v_L$, then she will charge a price of $p_2 = v_L$. Separating behavior requires that Bruce accepts if and only if he is of one type. The only candidate is to have low value type not buy in the first period and the high value type buy. Then after observing a purchase in the first period, Sheila concludes she is facing a high value Bruce and so charges $p_2 = v_H$ in the second period. After observing no purchase in the first period she concludes Bruce has low value and charges $p_2 = v_L$. Since $p_1 \geq v_L$, the low value type has no incentive to buy in period 1. The only issue is the high value type. By buying in period 1, Bruce receives a total payoff of $v_H - p_1 + \delta(v_H - v_H) = v_H - p_1$. By not buying, he convinces Sheila that he is of low type and so receives a payoff of $\delta(v_H - p_2) = \delta(v_H - v_L)$. Now,

$$v_H - p_1 \geq \delta(v_H - v_L) \Leftrightarrow (1 - \delta)v_H + \delta v_L \geq p_1,$$

and so the high type has no incentive to deviate.

(c) In a pooling equilibrium, in the second period Sheila's beliefs equal her prior on v. If she wants to sell to both types, she prices at $p_2 = v_L$, giving profit of v_L. If she wants to extract more money from the high value type, she prices at $p_2 = v_H$, only sells to the high value type, and so earns a profit of $\frac{1}{2}v_H$. Since $v_H > 2v_L$, it is more profitable to sell to only the high type. Since $p_1 > v_L$, the low type is strictly better off not purchasing (second period price is never lower than v_L). Thus, a candidate pooling equilibrium must involve neither type purchasing. But second period price after not purchasing is $p_2 = v_H$, and so high type earns zero from following the candidate pooling equilibrium. Deviating by purchasing in the first period yields strictly positive profits, since $v_H - p_1 > 0$ (from part (3.b)).

(d) When $p_1 > (1 - \delta)v_H + \delta v_L$, the separating strategy profile of part (3.b) is not an equilibrium (the high type prefers to not buy in period 1). The only other possible pure strategy equilibrium is to have neither type buy in the first period, but, since $p_1 < v_H$, the analysis of part (3.c) shows that is not an equilibrium.

(e) If $p_1 \leq v_L$, then a pooling perfect Bayesian equilibrium in this subgame is: both types buy in the first period, Sheila prices at $p_2 = v_H$ in the second, high type Bruce buy and low type not buy. This is the unique equilibrium when $p_1 < v_L$ because the separating strategy profile of part (3.b) is no longer an equilibrium (the low type strictly prefers to buy in the first period).

2

(f) When $p_1 = v_L$, the separating equilibrium has the low type not buy when he is indifferent. The assumption that Bruce accepts whenever he is indifferent, serves to select the pooling equilibrium in this case. Thus, the comparison is between charging a first period price of $p_1^p = v_L$ (and the pooling equilibrium results) and charging $p_1^s = \bar{p} = \delta v_L + (1 - \delta)v_H$ and the separating equilibrium results. The profit from the pooling price p_1^p is $v_L + \delta(\frac{1}{2}v_H)$, while the profit from the separating price p_1^s is $\frac{1}{2}\left(\delta v_L + (1 - \delta)v_H + \delta v_H\right) + \frac{1}{2}\delta v_L = \frac{1}{2}\left(v_H + 2\delta v_L\right) = \frac{1}{2}v_H + \delta v_L$. Thus, Sheila charges $p_1 = p_1^s$ in the first period, since

$$\frac{1}{2}v_H + \delta v_L > v_L + \delta(\frac{1}{2}v_H) \Leftrightarrow \frac{(1 - \delta)}{2}v_H > (1 - \delta)v_L \Leftrightarrow v_H > 2v_L.$$

(g) Suppose $p_1 \in (\delta v_L + (1 - \delta)v_H, v_H]$. Any mixed strategy equilibrium must have Sheila randomizing between $p_2 = v_L$ and $p_2 = v_H$ after no purchase in the first period. Let $\rho = \Pr(v_H | \text{no purchase})$ be Sheila's posterior probability that Bruce is high type after no purchase in the first period. In order for Sheila to be indifferent between $p_2 = v_L$ and $p_2 = v_H$, it must be the case that $v_L = \rho v_H$, that is $\rho = v_L/v_H$. Since $v_L/v_H < \frac{1}{2}$, Bruce must be randomizing between buying and not buying. Let q denote the probability that Bruce buys when $v = v_H$ in the first period. Then,

$$\rho = \frac{(1 - q)\frac{1}{2}}{(1 - q)\frac{1}{2} + \frac{1}{2}} = \frac{1 - q}{2 - q},$$

so

$$q = \frac{1 - 2\rho}{1 - \rho} = \frac{v_H - 2v_L}{v_H - v_L}.$$

Finally, letting r be the probability that Sheila charges $p_2 = v_H$ after no purchase, Bruce is willing to randomize if

$$v_H - p_1 = \delta\left(v_H - rv_H - (1 - r)v_L\right)$$

$$\Rightarrow v_H - p_1 = \delta(1 - r)\left(v_H - v_L\right) \Rightarrow r = 1 - \frac{(v_H - p_1)}{\delta(v_H - v_L)}.$$

The profit to Sheila from the mixed strategy equilibrium is $\frac{1}{2}\left(q(p_1 + \delta v_H) + (1 - q)\delta v_L\right) + \frac{1}{2}\delta v_L = \frac{1}{2}\left(q(p_1 + \delta v_H) + (1 - q)\delta v_H\right)$. Note that q only depends upon the reservation values of Bruce, and not on p_1, so profits are increasing in p_1 for $p_1 \in (\delta v_L + (1 - \delta)v_H, v_H]$, and maximized at $p_1 = v_H$ with value $\frac{1}{2}(q + \delta)v_H$.

Note that there is no other equilibrium (the only other possibility is separation at $p_1 = v_H$, but this has been ruled out in earlier parts). For $p_1 > v_H$, the only equilibrium is pooling with no types purchasing in the first period, yielding profits of $\delta v_H/2$, which is less than the profit from $p_1 = p_1^s = \delta v_L + (1 - \delta)v_H$. The profit maximizing price is either p_1^s or v_H. Profit from p_1^s is greater than that from v_H iff

$$\frac{1}{2}v_H + \delta v_L > \frac{1}{2}(q + \delta)v_H$$

$$\Leftrightarrow v_H + 2\delta v_L > (\frac{v_H - 2v_L}{v_H - v_L} + \delta)v_H \Leftrightarrow (v_H + 2\delta v_L)(v_H - v_L) > (v_H - 2v_L + \delta(v_H - v_L))v_H$$

$$\Leftrightarrow v_H^2 + 2\delta v_L v_H - v_L v_H - 2\delta v_L^2 > v_H^2 - 2v_L v_H + \delta v_H^2 - \delta v_L v_H \Leftrightarrow v_L v_H > \delta v_H^2 - 3\delta v_L v_H + 2\delta v_L^2$$

$$\Leftrightarrow v_L v_H > \delta\left(v_H^2 - 3v_L v_H + 2v_L^2\right) \Leftrightarrow v_L v_H > \delta(v_H - v_L)(v_H - 2v_L).$$

Thus, Sheila charges $p_1 = p_1^s = \delta v_L + (1 - \delta)v_H$ if $v_L v_H > \delta(v_H - v_L)(v_H - 2v_L)$, she charges $p_1 = v_H$ if $v_L v_H < \delta(v_H - v_L)(v_H - 2v_L)$, and she is indifferent if $v_L v_H = \delta(v_H - v_L)(v_H - 2v_L)$.

3

Fall 1994

George J. Mailath

1. Gibbons Problem 1.2.

2. There are two firms who each offer one good for sale. Firm i charges p_i, the demand for firm 1's product is

$$q_1 = (p_2/p_1)^\alpha,$$

and the demand for firm 2's product is

$$q_2 = (p_1/p_2)^\beta.$$

Assume that firm i has constant marginal cost of c_i. What is the normal form game when the firms choose prices simultaneously? Compute the dominant strategy equilibrium. Do you need to make any assumptions about α and β?

3. [**Extra credit**] Gibbons Problem 1.3.

4. Gibbons Problem 1.4.

5. Gibbons Problem 1.6. For the case $0 < c_i < a/2$, what happens to firm 2's equilibrium output when firm 1's costs, c_1, increase? Can you give an intuitive explanation?

6. Consider again the Cournot duopoly model with $P(Q) = a - Q$, but firm i's *total* costs are now given by $C(q_i, \alpha_i)$, where α_i is a cost parameter. Assume that C is twice continuously differentiable, $\partial C(0, \alpha_i)/\partial q_i = 0$, $\partial^2 C/\partial q_i^2 > 0$, and $\partial^2 C/\partial q_i \partial \alpha_i > 0$.

    (a) Prove that, locally, an increase in α_i implies a decrease in the equilibrium production of firm i, but an increase in the production of firm j. [Hint: Apply the implicit function theorem.]

    (b) [**Extra credit**] What are the weakest conditions on C that you can provide that imply uniqueness of Nash equilibria? [Hint: Think about contraction mappings.]

7. Gibbons Problem 1.7.

8. [**Extra credit**] Gibbons Problem 1.8.

Economics 703
Problem Set 2

Fall 1994   George J. Mailath

1. Consider the following Cournot duopoly game: The two firms are identical. The cost function
   facing each firm is $C(q)$, with $C(0) = 0, C'(0) = 0, C'(q) > 0 \ \forall q > 0$. Firm i chooses
   $q_i, i = 1, 2$. Inverse demand is given by $p = P(Q)$, where $Q = q_1 + q_2$ is total supply. Assume
   $P(Q) > 0$ for $Q \in [0, \overline{Q}), \overline{Q} > 0$, and $P(Q) = 0$ for $Q \geq \overline{Q}$. Assume firm i's profits are strictly
   concave in q_i for all $q_j, j \neq i$.

   (a) Prove that for each value of q_j, firm i ($i \neq j$) has a unique profit maximizing choice.
       Denote this choice $R_i(q_j)$. Prove that $R_i(q) = R_j(q)$, i.e., the two firms have the same
       reaction function. Thus, we can drop the subscript of the firm on R.

   (b) Prove that $R(0) > 0$ and that $R(\overline{Q}) = 0 < \overline{Q}$.

   (c) We know (from the maximum theorem) that R is a continuous function. Use the In-
       termediate Value Theorem to argue that this Cournot game has at least one symmetric
       Nash equilibrium, i.e., a quantity q^*, such that (q^*, q^*) is a Nash equilibrium. [Hint:
       Apply the Intermediate Value Theorem to the function $f(q) = R(q) - q$. What does
       $f(q) = 0$ imply?]

2. Suppose $(T, \prec)$ is a finite arborescence, i.e., T is finite set and $\prec$ is a binary relation on T
   satisfying: asymmetry ($t \prec t' \Rightarrow t' \not\prec t$), transitivity ($\forall t, t', t'' \in T, t \prec t', t' \prec t'' \Rightarrow t \prec t''$)
   and if $t \prec t''$ and $t' \prec t''$ then either $t \prec t'$ or $t' \prec t$. Define $W \equiv \{t \in T : \not\exists t' \in T, t' \prec t\}$; W
   is the set of *initial* nodes. A *path* to t is a sequence of nodes, $t_0 t_1 t_2 \cdots t_k$ such that $t_0 \in W$,
   t_κ is an immediate successor of $t_{\kappa-1}$, and $t_k = t$. Prove that $\forall t \in T \backslash W$, there is a unique node
   $w \in W$ and a unique path from w to t.

3. This question concerns the vetoing game discussed in class. Two agents must select a public
   project from three possibilities: x, y, and z. Agent I first vetoes one project. Agent II, seeing
   which project was vetoed by agent I, then vetoes one of the remaining two projects. The
   remaining project is the one that is undertaken. Agent I's utility from the projects is given
   by $u_1(x) = 2$, $u_1(y) = 1$, and $u_1(z) = 0$. Agent II's utility from the projects is given by
   $u_2(x) = 1$, $u_2(y) = 2$, and $u_2(z) = 0$.

   (a) Draw the tree describing this game. What is the normal form for this game?

   (b) What is the backward induction solution for this game? Is it a Nash equilibrium out-
       come? Would you rather be agent I or agent II?

   (c) Are there any other Nash equilibria?

4. Gibbons problem 2.1.

5. Consider the canonical Stackelberg model. There are two firms, I and II, producing the
   same good. Their inverse demand function is $P = 6 - Q$, where Q is market supply. Each
   firm has a constant marginal cost of \$4 per unit and a capacity constraint of 3 units (the
   latter restriction will not affect optimal behavior, but assuming it eliminates the possibility
   of negative prices). Firm I chooses its quantity first. Firm II, knowing firm I's quantity
   choice, then chooses its quantity. Thus, firm I's strategy space is $S_1 = [0, 3]$ and firm II's
   strategy space is $S_2 = \{\tau_2 \mid \tau_2 : S_1 \to [0, 3]\}$. A strategy profile is $(q_1, \tau_2) \in S_1 \times S_2$, i.e., an
   action (quantity choice) for I and a specification for *every* quantity choice of I of an action

1

(quantity choice) for II. The strategy profile (q_1, τ_2) implies the outcome $(q_1, \tau_2(q_1))$. Note that $\tau_2(q_1)$ is a quantity while τ_2 is a function. Given (q_1, τ_2), payoff for I is $u_1(q_1, \tau_2) = (6 - q_1 - \tau_2(q_1))q_1 - 4q_1 = (2 - q_1 - \tau_2(q_1))q_1$, and for II is $u_2(q_1, \tau_2) = (2 - q_1 - \tau_2(q_1))\tau_2(q_1)$. Observe that II's payoff is not affected by the values that τ_2 takes for quantities other than q_1.

(a) Show that the following strategy profile does not constitute a Nash equilibrium: $(\frac{1}{2}, \tau_2)$, where $\tau_2(q_1) = (2 - q_1)/2$. Which firm(s) is (are) not playing a best response?

(b) Prove that the following strategy profile constitutes a Nash equilibrium: $(\frac{1}{2}, \hat{\tau}_2)$, where $\hat{\tau}_2(q_1) = \frac{3}{4}$ if $q_1 = \frac{1}{2}$ and $\hat{\tau}_2(q_1) = 3$ if $q_1 \neq \frac{1}{2}$, i.e., II threatens to flood the market unless I produces exactly$\frac{1}{2}$. Is there any other Nash equilibrium which gives the outcome path $(\frac{1}{2}, \frac{3}{4})$? What are the firms' payoffs in this equilibrium?

(c) Prove that the following strategy profile constitutes a Nash equilibrium: $(0, \bar{\tau}_2)$, where $\bar{\tau}_2(q_1) = 1$ if $q_1 = 0$ and $\bar{\tau}_2(q_1) = 3$ if $q_1 \neq 0$, i.e., II threatens to flood the market unless I produces exactly 0. What are the firms' payoffs in this equilibrium?

(d) Given $q_1 \in [0, 2]$, specify a Nash equilibrium strategy profile in which I chooses q_1. Why is it not possible to do this for $q_1 \in (2, 3]$?

(e) What is the unique backward induction equilibrium of this game?

Economics 703
Problem Set 3

Fall 1994   George J. Mailath

1. (Rubinstein's alternating offers bargaining game.) Prove that the infinite horizon alternating offer bargaining game has a unique backward induction solution (we will *assume* that all backward induction solutions involve immediate agreement—this can be relaxed), using the following steps:

   (a) Let s_H denote the supremum of 1's share in any backward induction solution to the game when 1 makes the inital offer. Argue that

   $$s_H \leq 1 - \delta(1 - \delta s_H).$$

   [Hint: Assume that there is an backward induction solution with 1's share s satisfying $s > 1 - \delta(1 - \delta s_H)$. Argue to a contradiction by showing that 2 rejecting 1's offer and counteroffering $\delta s_H + \epsilon$, where $0 < \epsilon < \delta(1 - \delta s_H) - (1 - s)$ is a profitable deviation. Is it still a profitable deviation if $\epsilon = 0$?]

   (b) Let s_L denote the infimum of 1's share in any backward induction solution to the game when 1 makes the inital offer. Argue that

   $$s_L \geq 1 - \delta(1 - \delta s_L)$$

   as follows: Assume that there is an backward induction solution with 1 offering $(s, 1-s)$ and 2 accepting in which 1's share s satisfies $s < 1 - \delta(1 - \delta s_L)$. Suppose 1 deviates by offering $\delta(1 - \delta s_L) + \epsilon$ to 2, $\epsilon > 0$. There are three possibilites: 2 accepts; 2 refuses and makes a counteroffer that 1 accepts; and 2 refuses and makes a counteroffer that 1 refuses. Argue that 2 will accept by showing that the payoffs in the other two cases are strictly less than $\delta(1 - \delta s_L) + \epsilon$. (Would 1 ever accept an offer strictly less than δs_L?) For what values of ϵ is the initial offer of $\delta(1 - \delta s_L) + \epsilon$ to 2 a profitable deviation by 1? (The existence of a profitable deviation shows that $(s, 1-s)$ is not the result of a backward induction solution.)

   (c) From the above two inequalities, argue that $s_L = s_H = (1 + \delta)^{-1}$.

   (d) What is the only strategy profile satisfying backward induction?

2. (An extension of the Stackelberg problem.) Suppose there are four firms, I, II, III and IV, producing the same good. The inverse demand function is $P = 12 - Q$, where Q is market supply. Each firm has a constant marginal cost of \$4 per unit and a capacity constraint of 3 units. Firms I and II simultaneously choose their quantities first. Firms III and IV, knowing I's and II's quantity choices, then simultaneously choose their quantities. Thus firm i's strategy space $S_i = [0, 3]$ for $i = $ I, II, and $S_i = \{\tau_i \mid \tau_i : S_1 \times S_2 \to [0, 3]\}$ for $i = $ III, IV. A strategy profile is $(q_1, q_2, \tau_3, \tau_4) \in S_1 \times S_2 \times S_3 \times S_4$, i.e., an action (quantity choice) for I and II and a specification for every quantity choice of I and II of an action (quantity choice) for III and IV. The strategy profile $(q_1, q_2, \tau_3, \tau_4)$ implies the outcome $(q_1, q_2, \tau_3(q_1, q_2), \tau_4(q_1, q_2))$. Given $(q_1, q_2, \tau_3, \tau_4)$, payoff for i is

$$U_i(q_1, q_2, \tau_3, \tau_4) = \begin{cases} (8 - q_1 - q_2 - \tau_3(q_1, q_2) - \tau_4(q_1, q_2))q_i, & \text{if } i = \text{I, II,} \\ (8 - q_1 - q_2 - \tau_3(q_1, q_2) - \tau_4(q_1, q_2))\tau_i(q_1, q_2), & \text{if } i = \text{III, IV.} \end{cases}$$

173

(a) Every pair of quantity choices for I and II defines a subgame of the original game. What is the normal form of the subgame starting at (q_1, q_2), i.e., given the pair (q_1, q_2) of quantity choices for I and II? Compute the unique Nash equilibrium of this subgame. Let $\theta_i : S_1 \times S_2 \to [0, 3]$ be the function whose value at (q_1, q_2) is given by i's action (quantity choice) in the Nash equilibrium of the subgame starting at (q_1, q_2). That is, $(\theta_3(q_1, q_2), \theta_4(q_1, q_2))$ is the Nash equilibrium of the subgame starting at (q_1, q_2).

(b) Show that the following strategy profile is a Nash equilibrium: $(1, 1, \hat{\tau}_3, \hat{\tau}_4)$ where $\hat{\tau}_i(q_1, q_2) = 2$ if $(q_1, q_2) = (1, 1)$, and $\hat{\tau}_i(q_1, q_2) = 3$ if $(q_1, q_2) \neq (1, 1)$ for $i =$ III, IV. What is the relationship between $\hat{\tau}_i(1, 1)$ and $\theta_i(1, 1)$ for $i =$ III and IV? What is the outcome path and what are firms' payoffs?

(c) Show that the following strategy profile is subgame perfect: $(\frac{8}{3}, \frac{8}{3}, \tilde{\tau}_3, \tilde{\tau}_4)$ where $\tilde{\tau}_i(q_1, q_2) = (8 - q_1 - q_2)/3$ for $i =$ III and IV. What is the relationship between $\tilde{\tau}_i$ and θ_i for $i =$ III and IV? What is the outcome path and what are firms' payoffs?

(d) Show that the following strategy profile has the same outcome path as $(\frac{8}{3}, \frac{8}{3}, \tilde{\tau}_3, \tilde{\tau}_4)$ and that it is Nash: $(\frac{8}{3}, \frac{8}{3}, \overline{\tau}_3, \overline{\tau}_4)$ where $\overline{\tau}_i(q_1, q_2) = \frac{8}{9}$ if $(q_1, q_2) = (\frac{8}{3}, \frac{8}{3})$, and $\overline{\tau}_i(q_1, q_2) = 3$ if $(q_1, q_2) \neq (\frac{8}{3}, \frac{8}{3})$, for $i =$ III, IV. Is this profile subgame perfect? Why or why not?

3. Let $G(2)$ denote the game where Bruce and Sheila play the following Prisoner's Dilemma game twice:

		Sheila	
		L	R
Bruce	T	1,1	4,0
	B	0,4	3,3

After the first round of play, they observe the choices made and then they make their second round choices. Payoffs for the two rounds are added together. Be precise and clear in your description of and notation for strategies.

(a) Draw the extensive form for $G(2)$ (i.e., the Prisoner's Dilemma played twice). What is its reduced normal form (note that the normal form is 32×32, while the reduced normal form is 8×8)?

(b) Is there any Nash equilibrium of $G(2)$ in which Bruce plays B or Sheila plays R in the first round? (Note that this is a question about Nash, not subgame perfection). What is the intuition for your answer?

4. Consider now the following modification of the Prisoner's Dilemma, where $x \in \Re$:

		Sheila		
		L	R	P
	T	1,1	4,0	-2,0
Bruce	B	0,4	3,3	-2,0
	Q	0,4	3,3	-1,x

Let $G^*(2)$ denote the repeated "modified" Prisoner's Dilemma. As before, be precise and clear in your description of and notation for strategies.

(a) Describe a Nash equilibrium of $G^*(2)$ in which Bruce plays B in the first round. Give bounds on x for which this equilibrium is subgame perfect.

(b) For $x \geq 4$, describe a subgame perfect equilibrium in which Sheila plays R in the first period.

(c) Suppose $x \geq 4$. Is there a subgame perfect equilibrium of $G^*(2)$ in which Bruce plays B and Sheila plays R in the first round? If so, describe it. If not, reconcile this with your answers to the previous two parts.

174

Fall 1994   George J. Mailath

1. Suppose $G \equiv \{(A_i, u_i)\}$ is an n-person normal form game (i.e., A_i is i's strategy space and u_i is i's payoff function), and $G(2)$ is G played twice. Let $A \equiv \prod_i A_i$. The strategy profile $s \equiv (s^1, s^2)$ of $G(2)$ is history independent if, for all i, $s^2(a)$ is independent of $a \in A$ (i.e., $s^2 : A \to A$ is a constant function). Let $N(1)$ be the set of Nash equilibria of G. Suppose s is history independent. Prove that s is a subgame perfect equilibrium of $G(2)$ if and only if $s^1, s^2(a) \in N(1)$. Provide examples to show that the assumption of history independence is needed in both directions.

   How does this generalize to the T-fold repetition of G?

2. Gibbons problem 2.13.

3. Gibbons problem 2.15.

4. Gibbons problem 2.17.

5. [**Extra credit**] Consider the following modification of the Stackelberg game. The leader, firm 1, chooses $q_1 \in \Re_+$. Rather than observing q_1, the follower, firm 2, observes the noisy signal $\tilde{q}_1 = q_1 e^\epsilon$, where $\epsilon \sim N(0, \sigma^2)$. After observing $\tilde{q}_1$, firm 2 chooses its quantity q_2. Both firms have identical constant marginal cost, of production given by $c = 1$. Price is determined by $P = 10 - q_1 - q_2$. Note that P is independent of $\tilde{q}_1$. For simplicity, allow prices to be negative, so that firm i's profit is $\pi_i(q_1, q_2) = (9 - q_1 - q_2)q_i$, $i = 1, 2$.

   (a) Describe the extensive form game.

   (b) What is the unique subgame perfect equilibrium when $\sigma^2 > 0$? What happens as $\sigma^2 \to 0$?

   (c) What is the unique subgame perfect equilibrium when $\sigma^2 = 0$, so that $\tilde{q}_1 = q_1$? Discuss.

1

Fall 1994

George J. Mailath

1. Let G_x denote the game (note that x is I's payoff from TR):

		II			
		L	C	R	P
I	T	4,2	0,0	x,0	0,1
	M	0,0	2,4	0,0	−1,0
	B	0,0	0,0	4,4	−1,0

Let $G_x(n)$ denote G_x played n times, with payoffs given by adding payoffs in the n periods.

(a) Suppose $x = 7$. Describe a subgame perfect equilibrium strategy profile of $G_7(3)$ in which II *never* chooses P that implies the outcome BR, TL, TL.

(b) Suppose $x = 9$. Why is there no subgame perfect equilibrium strategy profile of $G_9(3)$ in which II never chooses P that implies the outcome BR, TL, TL?

(c) Again suppose $x = 9$. Describe a subgame perfect equilibrium strategy profile of $G_9(2)$ that implies the outcome TP, MC (note that $n = 2$ here).

(d) Still supposing $x = 9$, describe a subgame perfect equilibrium strategy profile of $G_9(3)$ that implies the outcome BR, TL, TL.

2. Prove that in an extensive form game, any *Nash* equilibrium strategy profile induces a Nash equilibrium on any subgame *on the equilibrium path*. You don't need to be formal in your argument, as long as the idea is clear. If you have trouble with the general case, consider the special case of repeated games; the case of a stage game played twice is particularly simple.

3. Kreps problem 14.8.3. (This question and the next assume you have read Kreps section 14.5.)

4. Kreps problem 14.8.4.

5. Gibbons problem 2.14.

Economics 703
Problem Set 6

Fall 1994

George J. Mailath

1. This question concerns the example on the demand for insurance discussed in Kreps, page 91. Call state 1 the state in which, in the absence of insurance, the consumer loses L (e.g., the state in which his house burns), and state 2 the other state. The probability of state 1 is p. Let (x_1, x_2) represent the outcome in which the consumer has wealth x_1 in the state 1, and wealth x_2 in state 2. Thus, (x_1, x_2) is a state contingent commodity bundle. For example, the consumer's state contingent endowment vector (and, without insurance, state contingent consumption vector), is $(W - L, W)$. We can think of the consumer as having preferences over bundles in $\Re_+^2$, given by $v(x_1, x_2) = pu(x_1) + (1-p)u(x_2)$. Suppose the consumer is risk averse, so that u is strictly concave.

   (a) Show that v is strictly concave.

   (b) What is the consumer's marginal rate of substitution between x_1 and x_2? Does this have any particular interpretation when $x_1 = x_2$, i.e., on the certainty line? [Note that bundles of the form (x, x) have the particular property that the consumer's wealth is independent of the state.]

   (c) Interpret the purchase of insurance (where π is the premium per dollar of coverage) using standard consumer theory. In particular, what is the budget constraint facing the consumer in $\Re_+^2$? How is the budget constraint affected if the consumer is allowed to sell as well as buy insurance? Interpret the tangency condition between the budget constraint and indifference curves at the consumer's optimal bundle. When (in terms of π and p) will this tangency occur on the certainty line, i.e., when $x_1 = x_2$? [Hint: The discussion is easier using a diagram.]

2. Kreps problem 3.8.5.

1

Fall 1994

George J. Mailath

1. Consider a consumer with risky wealth also facing randomness from a second source: Let $\tilde{w} = w_1$ with probability p and $\tilde{w} = w_2$ with probability $1 - p$. Let $\tilde{\epsilon} = 0$ if $\tilde{w} = w_2$. If $\tilde{w} = w_1$, $\tilde{\epsilon} = \epsilon$ with probability $\frac{1}{2}$ and $\tilde{\epsilon} = -\epsilon$ with probability $\frac{1}{2}$. Define a risk premium π_u for $\tilde{\epsilon}$ by

$$E[u(\tilde{w} - \pi_u)] = E[u(\tilde{w} + \tilde{\epsilon})].$$

(a) Show that if ϵ is sufficiently small,

$$\pi_u \approx \frac{-\frac{1}{2}pu''(w_1)\epsilon^2}{pu'(w_1) + (1 - p)u'(w_2)}.$$

[HINT: Take a first order Taylor series of the left hand side and a second order of the right hand side of the equation defining π_u.]

(b) Let $u(w) = -e^{-aw}$ and $v(w) = -e^{-bw}$. Compute the Arrow-Pratt measure for u and v.

(c) Suppose that $a > b$. Show that if $p < 1$, there exists a value $w_1 - w_2$ large enough to make $\pi_v > \pi_u$. What does this tell you about the Arrow-Pratt measure?

2. Bruce has a von Neumann-Morgenstern utility function given by $u(w) = \ln w$. He is offered the opportunity to bet on the flip of a coin that has a probability p of coming up heads. If he bets $\$x$, he will have $w + x$ if head comes up and $w - x$ if tails comes up. Solve for the optimal x as a function of p. What is his optimal choice of x when $p = \frac{1}{2}$?

3. Kreps problem 3.8.6.

4. Kreps problem 3.8.8.

5. [Extra credit.] Kreps problem 3.8.11.

6. Complete the proof of Nash's existence theorem as follows:

(a) Recall that $X_i = \Delta(S_i)$, $X = \prod_i X_i$, $\phi_i(\sigma_{-i}) = \arg\max u_i(\sigma_i, \sigma_{-i})$, and $\phi = (\phi_1, \ldots, \phi_n)$. Then $\phi : X \mapsto X$ and σ^* is a Nash equilibrium if and only if $\sigma^* \in \phi(\sigma^*)$. Prove that $\phi(\sigma)$ is convex for all $\sigma \in X$.

(b) Prove that ϕ is upperhemicontinuous.

7. Suppose $\{(S_1, u_1), (S_2, u_2)\}$ is a finite two player normal form game.

(a) Suppose $u_1(s_1', s_2^*) > u_1(s_1, s_2^*)$, for two strategies, $s_1, s_1' \in S_1$, and for some $s_2^* \in S_2$. Demonstrate that there exists $\epsilon > 0$ such that $u_1(s_1', \sigma_2) > u_1(s_1, \sigma_2)$ if $\sigma_2(s_2^*) > 1 - \epsilon$.

(b) Suppose now s_1 is not a best reply to any mixed strategy with support in $S_2^* \subset S_2$ (i.e., $\sigma_2 \in \Delta(S_2^*)$). Show that there exists $\epsilon > 0$ such that s_1 is not a best reply to any mixed strategy $\sigma_2 \in \Delta(S_2)$ satisfying $\sigma_2(S_2^*) > 1 - \epsilon$.

1

Economics 703
Problem Set 8

Fall 1994   George J. Mailath

1. Consider the stage game:

$$
\begin{array}{c c c}
 & A & B \\
A & 1,1 & 2,2 \\
B & 2,2 & 1,1
\end{array}
$$

Suppose players are randomly and repeatedly matched to play this game. In contrast to the discussion in class, row and column players are drawn from two distinct populations. Denote by α the fraction of the row population playing A, and by β the fraction of the column population playing A. Assume $\dot\alpha > 0$ if $u_1(A,\beta) > u_1(B,\beta)$, $\dot\alpha = 0$ if $u_1(A,\beta) = u_1(B,\beta)$, and $\dot\alpha < 0$ if $u_1(A,\beta) < u_1(B,\beta)$. Also, $\dot\beta > 0$ if $u_2(A,\alpha) > u_2(B,\alpha)$, $\dot\beta = 0$ if $u_2(A,\alpha) = u_2(B,\alpha)$, and $\dot\beta < 0$ if $u_2(A,\alpha) < u_2(B,\alpha)$. Assume that $(\dot\alpha, \dot\beta)$ has a unique solution for each interior initial condition $(\alpha, \beta) \in (0,1)^2$.

   (a) What are the rest points of the dynamical system, $(\dot\alpha, \dot\beta)$ (i.e., for what values of α and β does $(\dot\alpha, \dot\beta) = (0,0)$)?

   (b) Characterize each rest point as a sink (i.e., there is a neighborhood of the rest point such that every path starting in the neighborhood converges to it), a source (i.e., there is a neighborhood of the rest point such that every path starting in the neighborhood eventually leaves the neighborhood and never returns), or a saddle point (i.e., there is a neighborhood of the rest point such that some paths starting in the neighborhood converge to it and some paths starting in the neighborhood eventually leave the neighborhood and never return).

   (c) Compare your answer to the one population case (i.e., when there is no role identification, so that players are drawn from the same population) discussed in class.

2. Suppose there are two equally likely states of the world $\{s_1, s_2\}$. There are two players, S and R. Player S knows s_k and sends message $m \in \{m_1, m_2\}$ to player R, who chooses response $r \in \{r_1, r_2\}$. von Neumann-Morgenstern payoffs are given by:

$$
\pi_i(s_k, m, r_j) = \begin{cases} 2, & \text{if } k = j, \\ 0, & \text{if } k \neq j. \end{cases}
$$

Thus, messages are costless and players' interests coincide.

   (a) What is the normal form of this game?

   (b) Calculate all of its *pure* strategy Nash equilibria.

   (c) Are all of these equilibria equally plausible? Which equilibria are asymptotically stable under myopic adjustment dynamics?

3. Suppose $G \equiv \{A_1, \ldots, A_n; T_1, \ldots, T_n; u_1, \ldots, u_n; p\}$ is a normal form game of incomplete information with T_i finite and $p(t) > 0 \ \forall t \in T \equiv \prod_j T_j$. Let $S_i \equiv \{s_i : T_i \to A_i\}$ denote the set of strategies for player i. Define

$$
v_i(s_1, \ldots, s_n) = \sum_{t \in T} u_i(s(t); t) p(t),
$$

1

where $s(t) = (s_1(t_1), \ldots, s_n(t_n))$. Then $G^\bullet \equiv \{(S_1, v_1), \ldots, (S_n, v_n)\}$ is a normal form game. Prove that $s^\bullet = (s_1^\bullet, \ldots, s_n^\bullet) \in \prod_j S_j$ is a Bayesian Nash equilibrium of G if and only if it is a Nash equilibrium of $G^\bullet$.

For the more mathematically inclined: What is the appropriate version of this equivalence if T_i is a continuum, such as $[0,1]$?

4. Gibbons problem 3.3.

5. Gibbons problem 3.4.

6. Gibbons problem 3.6.

7. Gibbons problem 3.7.

8. Suppose there are n bidders with valuations independently and uniformly distributed on $[0, 1]$. Show that the expected revenue raised in the dominant strategy equilibrium of the sealed bid second price auction equals the expected revenue raised in the Bayes-Nash equilibrium of the first price auction. (Do the case $n = 2$ if you are having difficulty with general n).

(**Extra credit**) Suppose now that are 2 bidders with valuations independently and identically distributed according to the strictly positive density f on $[0, 1]$. Show again the equivalence of the two auctions in terms of their expected revenues.

2

Fall 1994   George J. Mailath

1. Gibbons problem 3.8.

2. Kreps problem 12.10.6.

3. Gibbons problem 4.2.

4. Gibbons problem 4.3.

5. Gibbons problem 4.4.

6. Gibbons problem 4.16.

7. Consider the following signaling game:

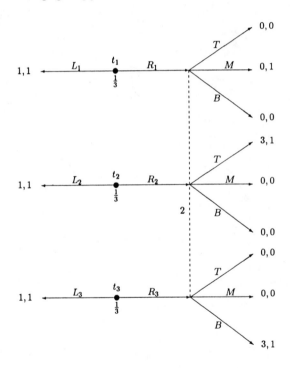

(a) Describe all of the pure strategy perfect Bayesian equilibrium.

(b) Which of these equilibria pass the test of equilibrium domination?

1

(c) **(Only for those with spare time)** Cho and Kreps (*Quarterly Journal of Economics*, May 1987) define the intuitive criterion (a weaker test than the test of equilibrium domination) as follows: Define $BR(T', m)$ as the set of best replies by R to beliefs with support contained in $T' \subset T$. Fix an equilibrium, with equilibrium payoffs $u_S^*(t)$. For each out-of-equilibrium message m, define $S(m) \equiv \{t \in T : u_S^*(t) > \max_{a \in BR(T,m)} u_S(m, a, t)\}$. If there exists an out-of-equilibrium message m and type $t' \in T$ such that

$$u_S^*(t') < \min_{a \in BR(T \setminus S(m), m)} u_S(m, a, t'),$$

then the equilibrium fails the intuitive criterion.

Which equilibrium passes the intuitive criterion and fails the test of eq domination?

(d) **(Only for those with spare time)** How does your answer change if the payoff to $R_2 B$ and $R_3 T$ are changed to $-2, 0$ (don't restrict restrict yourself to pure strategies for the receiver)?

2

Economics 703
Problem Set 10

Fall 1994

George J. Mailath

1. Kreps problem 16.6.1.

2. Suppose a risk neutral principal wishes to hire an agent. The agent chooses effort level of either low or high, $e \in \{e_L, e_H\}$. The principal's payoff is $x - w$, where x is output and w is wage. The agent's payoff is $\ln(1 + w) - v(e)$, where $v(\cdot)$ measures disutility of effort and $v(e_L) = 0$ and $v(e_H) = \bar{v} > 0$. The agent's reservation utility is u_0. Suppose the technology is such that if $e = e_H$, $x = \bar{x}$ for sure, while if $e = e_L$,

$$x = \begin{cases} \bar{x}, & \text{with probability } p, \\ \underline{x}, & \text{with probability } 1 - p, \end{cases}$$

where $\bar{x} > \underline{x}$ and $0 < p < 1$. Assume $\bar{x} > e^{u_0 + \bar{v}} - 1$.

(a) Suppose effort choice is contractible (that is, wage can be written contingent on effort choice). When will the principal's optimal contract force the agent to choose e_H? When will it force e_L?

   For the remainder of this question, as usual in principal-agent models, assume effort is contractible, so that wages can only be contingent on output.

(b) Suppose that $w \geq 0$. Describe the principal's optimal wage profile offer. Show that, in general, the participation constraint and incentive constraint cannot simultaneously bind. Suppose that if effort were contractible, the principal would have the worker choose e_H. Is it ever optimal for the principal to have the worker put in low effort, when effort is not contractible?

(c) Suppose the principal can require a payment from the agent in order for the agent to be hired (for example, the firm may require the agent to post a bond when hired). The agent is still free not to work for the principal and receive u_0 in utility. Show that the principal can now guarantee an effort level of e_H whenever it would have been optimal to do so when effort is contractible.

(d) How does your answer to the previous question change if the technology is such that if $e = e_H$, then

$$x = \begin{cases} \bar{x}, & \text{with probability } q, \\ \underline{x}, & \text{with probability } 1 - q, \end{cases}$$

   where $1 > q > p$.

3. (Two agent version of Varian example, pages 453-454). Suppose a principal wishes to hire two agents, B (Bruce, of course) and S (Sheila). Agent i chooses an action, denoted $a^i \in \Re$. Agent i produces output (observed by the principal) of $x^i = a^i + \epsilon^i$. The error terms (ϵ^B, ϵ^S) are jointly normally distributed, with mean zero and variance-covariance matrix Σ, where:

$$\Sigma = \sigma^2 \begin{bmatrix} 1 & \rho \\ \rho & 1 \end{bmatrix}.$$

Agent i has a CARA utility function of wealth: $u_i(w) = -e^{-r_i w}$, where r_i is the coefficient of risk aversion, and cost of effort is $c(a)$ (so both agents have identical disutilities of effort).

1

Agent i's reservation utility is $\bar{u}^i$. Payoff to principal is: $x^B - w^B + x^S - w^S$, where w^i is wage paid to agent i. Assume that the principal chooses a linear incentive scheme for Bruce and Sheila,

$$w^B(x) = \delta^B + \gamma_1^B x^B + \gamma_2^B x^S,$$

and

$$w^S(x) = \delta^S + \gamma_1^S x^S + \gamma_2^S x^B.$$

(a) Describe the optimal incentive scheme for Bruce if $\rho = 0$. Interpret your answer. [Hint: Are the constraints for the principal's problem linked across agents? Can the principal's problem be analyzed agent by agent? What about the agents?]

(b) Describe the optimal incentive scheme for Bruce if $\rho \neq 0, 1$. Interpret your answer.

2

Economics 703
Problem Set 11

Fall 1994

George J. Mailath

1. Kreps problem 17.5.2. (Consider the case of non-productive education. The analysis can be a little loose as long as the ideas are clear. Diagrams may be helpful.)

2. Kreps problem 17.5.5.

3. Kreps problem 17.5.6. (If you are having trouble with randomizations by the worker, consider only pure strategy equilibria.)

4. Consider the Spence model as a signaling game as discussed in class with three types, i.e., $\alpha \in \{1, 2, 3\}$, with $\Pr(\alpha = i) = \frac{1}{3}$, $i = 1, 2, 3$. Consider the following strategy profile: $(\hat{e}_1, \hat{e}_2, \hat{e}_3, \hat{w}(\cdot))$, where $\hat{e}_1 = \hat{e}_2 = 0$, and

$$\hat{w}(e) = \begin{cases} \bar{w}, & \text{if } e = 0, \\ 3, & \text{if } e = \hat{e}_3, \\ 1, & \text{if } e \notin \{0, \hat{e}_3\}. \end{cases}$$

   (a) For what values of $\bar{w}$ and $\hat{e}_3$ does this describe a perfect Bayesian equilibrium?

   (b) Show that a profile of this form with $\hat{e}_3 > 3$ cannot describe a perfect Bayesian equilibrium that passes the test of equilibrium domination.

   (c) Specify a weakly increasing wage function, $\tilde{w}$, for the case $\hat{e}_3 = 3$ such that $(\hat{e}_1, \hat{e}_2, \hat{e}_3, \tilde{w}(\cdot))$ is a perfect Bayesian equilibrium.

   (d) Specify out-of-equilibrium wages, $w^*(e)$, $e \notin \{0, \hat{e}_3\}$, so that the profile with $\hat{e}_3 = 3$ passes the test of equilibrium domination. Why is this possible?

5. Kreps problem 17.5.8.

1

1. Consider the monopolist in an adverse selection environment discussed in class. In particular, there is a risk neutral monopolist making a take-it-or-leave-it offer of an insurance contract (y_1, y_2) to a consumer with a risky endowment, (Y_1, Y_2), with $Y_2 < Y_1$. The consumer is either high risk, π_H, or low risk, $\pi_L < \pi_H$, where π_i is the probability of state 2. The monopolist assigns probability ρ to the consumer being high risk. Show that the monopolist's problem is a principal-agent problem, providing the participation constraint is reinterpreted. Be precise about the possible action choice of the consumer and the outcomes that the principal observes.

2. Kreps problem 17.5.11.

3. Consider the first price auction when there are n bidders with valuations independently and uniformly distributed on $[0, 1]$. You showed in Problem Set 8 that this game had a Bayes-Nash equilibrium in which each bidder bid $(n-1)/n$ times his or her valuation. What is the direct revelation mechanism induced by this equilibrium? Show by direct calculation that truth-telling is an equilibrium of this direct revelation game. (Do the case $n = 2$ if you are having difficulty with general n).

4. Show that if a direct revelation mechanism has a non-truth-telling equilibrium, then there is another direct revelation game with truth-telling as an equilibrium and whose outcome induced by truth-telling coincides with the non-truth-telling equilibrium outcome of the original direct revelation game.

5. **[EXTRA CREDIT]** Consider the signalling game below, Game 1.

    (a) Consider the following behavior strategy profile: $((1 - \epsilon) \circ L + \epsilon \circ R,\ \eta \circ L + (1 - \eta) \circ R,\ (1 - \delta) \circ U + \delta \circ D)$. Given this strategy profile, what is 2's posterior beliefs about 1's type after R, i.e., what is $\Pr[\alpha = 1 \mid R]$? What pure strategy profile does the mixed strategy profile converge to as $\epsilon, \eta, \delta \to 0$? What do 2's posterior beliefs about 1's type after R converge to as $\epsilon, \eta, \delta \to 0$, i.e., what is $\lim_{\epsilon, \eta, \delta \to 0} \Pr[\alpha = 1 \mid R]$?

    (b) Consider the following mixed strategy profile: $((1 - \epsilon) \circ L + \epsilon \circ R,\ (1 - \eta) \circ L + \eta \circ R,\ (1 - \delta) \circ U + \delta \circ D)$. What pure strategy profile does the mixed strategy profile converge to as $\epsilon, \eta, \delta \to 0$? Suppose $\eta = 2\epsilon$. What do 2's posterior beliefs about 1's type after R converge to as $\epsilon, \delta \to 0$, i.e., what is $\lim_{\epsilon, \delta \to 0} \Pr[\alpha = 1 \mid R]$? What is the limit posterior if $\eta = \epsilon^2$? What is the limit posterior if $\eta = \sqrt{\epsilon}$? Show that any posterior on α after R can be "justified" as the limit (as $\epsilon, \eta, \delta \to 0$) of beliefs obtained using Bayes' rule.

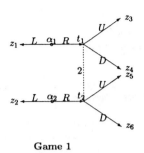

Game 1

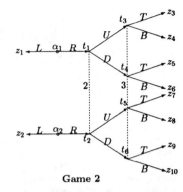

Game 2

6. **[EXTRA CREDIT]** Consider the above game, Game 2, inspired by the Spence job market model and the following mixed strategy profile: $((1-\epsilon)\circ L+\epsilon\circ R,\ (1-\eta)\circ L+\eta\circ R,\ (1-\delta)\circ U+\delta\circ D,\ (1-\beta)\circ T+\beta\circ B)$. What pure strategy profile does the mixed strategy profile converge to as $\epsilon, \eta, \delta, \beta \to 0$? Suppose $\eta = 2\epsilon$. What do 2's posterior beliefs about 1's type after R converge to as $\epsilon, \delta, \beta \to 0$, i.e., what is $\lim_{\epsilon,\delta,\beta\to 0} \Pr[t_1 \mid R]$? What about 3's posterior, i.e., what is $\lim_{\epsilon,\delta,\beta\to 0} \Pr[t_i \mid R]$, $i = 3, \ldots, 6$? Show that $\lim_{\epsilon\to 0} \Pr[t_1 \mid R] = \lim_{\epsilon\to 0} \Pr[\{t_3, t_4\} \mid R]\ \forall \delta, \beta$.

2

UNIVERSITY COLLEGE DUBLIN
DEPARTMENT OF ECONOMICS
M.A./M.Econ.Sc.: ECN 421 Microeconomics II, Spring 1995

J. Peter Neary
Thursday 4.00-6.00, C214
(Office Hours: Tues, Thur, 11.30-12.45)

The objective of this course is to illustrate some recent applications of microeconomic theory. The specific applications considered deal with open economies but no familiarity with international trade theory is assumed. The first part of the course deals with competitive general equilibrium models, using dual techniques. Results on shadow prices, optimal intervention and piecemeal policy reform are derived. Extensions to measuring the restrictiveness of trade policy are examined. The second part of the course deals with oligopolistic models and reviews recent work in the theory of industrial organisation and of strategic trade and industrial policy. The topics covered include policy choice in one-period games, the choice of solution concept and the implications of commitment in simple dynamic games.

A satisfactory performance in the M.A. Core Micro course and a modest background in mathematics and microeconomic theory will be assumed. Assessment will be on the basis of a take-home test at Easter (10%) and of the final exam (90%). References marked with two asterisks are recommended.

General References

Deardorff, A.V. (1985): "Major recent developments in international trade theory," in T. Peeters, P. Praet and R. Reding (eds.): *International Trade and Exchange Rates*, Amsterdam: North-Holland, 3-27.

Dixit, A. (1985): "Tax policy in open economics," in A.J. Auerbach and M. Feldstein (eds): *Handbook of Public Economics, Volume 1*, Amsterdam: North Holland.

Dixit, A.K. and V. Norman (1980): *Theory of International Trade: A Dual, General Equilibrium Approach*, London: Cambridge University Press.

Ethier, W.J. (1987): "The theory of international trade," in L.H. Officer (ed.): *International Economics*, Dordrecht: Kluwer Academic Publishers, 1-63.

Grossman, G. (ed.) (1992): *Imperfect Competition and International Trade*, Cambridge, Mass.: MIT Press.

Helpman, E. and P. Krugman (1985): *Market Structure and Foreign Trade*, Cambridge, Mass.: MIT Press.

Helpman, E. and P.R. Krugman (1989): *Trade Policy and Market Structure*, Cambridge, Mass.: MIT Press.

Jones, R.W. (1979): *International Trade: Essays in Theory*, Amsterdam: North-Holland.

Jones, R.W. and P.B. Kenen (eds.) (1984): *Handbook of International Economics: Volume 1 International Trade*, Amsterdam: North-Holland.

Neary, J.P. (ed.) (1995): *Readings in International Trade* (Volumes 1 and 2), Cheltenham: Edward Elgar.

Tirole, J. (1988): *The Theory of Industrial Organisation*, Cambridge, Mass.: MIT Press.

Woodland, A.D. (1982): *International Trade and Resource Allocation*, Amsterdam: North-Holland.

1. Introduction

* Introductory overview of the course
* Representation of consumer and producer behaviour using duality
* Properties of the trade expenditure function
* Comparative statics of a small open economy

** Dixit and Norman, Chap. 2 (esp. Sections 2.1, 2.4)

** Neary, J.P. (1988): "Determinants of the equilibrium real exchange rate," *American Economic Review*, 78 (March), 210-215; reprinted in Neary (1995).

Edwards, S. and S. van Wijnbergen (1987) "Tariffs, the real exchange rate and the terms of trade: On two popular propositions in international trade," *Oxford Economic Papers*, 39, 458-464.

Connolly, M. and J. Devereux (1992): "Commercial policy, the terms of trade and real exchange rates," *Oxford Economic Papers*, (July).

Devereux, J. and M. Connolly (1993): "Public sector pricing and the real exchange rate," *Economica*, 60, 295-309.

Falvey, R.E. and N. Gemmell (1991): "Explaining service-price differences in international comparisons," *American Economic Review*, 81 (December), 1295-1309.

2: Effects of Tariffs

* Positive and normative effects of tariffs
* Shadow prices in the presence of tariffs

Neary, J.P. and F.P. Ruane (1988): "International factor mobility, shadow prices and the cost of protection," *International Economic Review*, 21, 571-585.

** Neary, J.P. (1995): "Trade liberalisation and shadow prices in the presence of tariffs and quotas," *International Economic Review* (forthcoming).

3. Quantitative Trade Restrictions

* Shadow prices and piecemeal policy reform in the presence of tariffs, quotas and voluntary export restraints
* Rent-sharing and the welfare costs of quotas
* Measuring the restrictiveness of trade policy

Neary, J.P. (1988): "Tariffs, quotas and voluntary export restraints with and without international capital mobility," *Canadian Journal of Economics*, 21, 714-735; reprinted in Neary (1995).

** Anderson, J.E. and J.P. Neary (1992): "Trade reform with quotas, partial rent retention and tariffs," *Econometrica*, 60:1, January, 57-76.

Anderson, J.E. (1988): *The Relative Inefficiency of Quotas*, Cambridge, Mass.: MIT Press.

** Anderson, J.E. and J.P. Neary (1993): "A new approach to evaluating trade policy," mimeo., University College Dublin.

4: Trade Policy in the Presence of Market Power

* The optimal tariff argument
* Export subsidies in competitive markets
* Export subsidies in oligopolistic markets

** Neary, J.P. (1988): "Export subsidies and national welfare," *Empirica - Austrian Economic Papers*, 15, 243-261.

** Brander, J.A. and B.J. Spencer (1985): "Export subsidies and international market share rivalry," *Journal of International Economics*, 18, 83-100; reprinted in Neary (1995).

6: Aspects of Strategic Trade Policy

* Critique of the Brander-Spencer thesis
* Tariffs and quotas in oligopolistic markets

Dixit, A. (1984): "International trade policies for oligopolistic industries," *Economic Journal (Supplement)*, 94, 1-16.

Eaton, J. and G.M. Grossman (1986): "Optimal trade and industrial policy under oligopoly," *Quarterly Journal of Economics*, 100, 383-406; reprinted in Grossman (1992) and Neary

190

(1995).

Helpman and Krugman (1989), chap. 5.

Bulow, J.I., J.D. Geanakoplos and P.D. Klemperer (1985): "Multimarket oligopoly: Strategic substitutes and complements," *Journal of Political Economy*, 93, 488-511.

Spencer, B.J. and J. Brander (1983): "International R&D rivalry and industrial strategy," *Review of Economic Studies*, 50, 707-722.

de Meza, D. (1986): "Export subsidies and high productivity: Cause or effect?," *Canadian Journal of Economics*, 19, 347-350.

Dixit, A.K. and A.S. Kyle (1985): "The use of protection and subsidies for entry promotion and deterrence," *American Economic Review*, 75, 139-152.

Dixit, A. and G.M. Grossman (1986): "Targeted export promotion with several oligopolistic industries," *Journal of International Economics*, 21, 233-249; reprinted in Neary (1995).

Venables, A.J. (1985): "Trade and trade policy with imperfect competition: the case of identical products and free entry," *Journal of International Economics*, 19, 1-19; reprinted in Neary (1995).

Horstmann, I.J. and J.R. Markusen (1986): "Up the average cost curve: Inefficient entry and the new protectionism," *Journal of International Economics*, 20, 225-247; reprinted in Neary (1995).

** Markusen, J.R. and A.J. Venables (1988): "Trade policy with increasing returns and imperfect competition: Contradictory results from competing assumptions," *Journal of International Economics*, 24, 299-316; reprinted in Grossman (1992).

** Harris, R. (1985): "Why voluntary export restraints are 'voluntary'," *Canadian Journal of Economics*, 18, 799-805; reprinted in Neary (1995).

Brander, J.A. and B.J. Spencer (1984): "Tariff protection and imperfect competition," in H. Kierzkowski (ed.): *Monopolistic Competition and International Trade*, Oxford University Press, 194-206; reprinted in Grossman (1992).

Krugman, P. (ed.): *Strategic Trade Policy*, Cambridge, Mass.: MIT Press, 1986.

Neary, J.P. (1991): "Export subsidies and price competition," in E. Helpman and A. Razin (eds.): *International Trade and Trade Policy*, Cambridge, Mass.: MIT Press.

** Neary, J.P. (1994): "Cost asymmetries in international subsidy games: Should governments help winners or losers?", *Journal of International Economics*, 37, 197-218.

4

7. Dynamic Issues in Strategic Trade Policy

* Strategic investment
* Learning by doing and infant industry protection

Smith, A. (1987): "Strategic investment, multinational corporations and trade policy," *European Economic Review*, 31, 89-96; reprinted in Neary (1995).

Krugman, P. (1984): "Import protection as export promotion: International competition in the presence of oligopoly and economies of scale," in H. Kierzkowski (ed.): *Monopolistic Competition in International Trade*, Oxford University Press, 180-93; reprinted in Grossman (1992).

Venables, A.J. (1990): "International capacity choice and national market games," *Journal of International Economics*, 29, 23-42; reprinted in Neary (1995).

Fudenberg, D. and J. Tirole (1983): "Learning by doing and market performance," *Bell Journal of Economics*, 14, 522-30.

Fudenberg, D. and J. Tirole (1984): "The fat-cat effect, the puppy-dog ploy, and the lean and hungry look," *American Economic Review, Papers and Proceedings*, 74, 361-6.

Leahy, D. and J.P. Neary (1994): "Time consistency, learning by doing and infant industry protection: The linear case," *Economic and Social Review*, 26, 59-68.

Leahy, D. and J.P. Neary (1994): "Learning by doing, precommitment and infant industry protection," mimeo, University College Dublin.

1. Consider a competitive small open economy producing traded and non-traded goods and with no trade restrictions. Show that equilibrium is characterised by:

$$E(p,q,u,v) = 0$$

$$E_q(p,q,u,v) = 0,$$

where p is the domestic (and world) price vector of imported goods; q is the price vector of non-traded goods; u is utility (welfare); v is a vector of factor endowments; and $E(p,q,u,v)$ is the trade expenditure function, defined as the difference between the household expenditure function $e(p,q,u)$ and the GNP function $g(p,q,v)$.

(a) Derive the effects of endowment growth on welfare and on the prices of non-traded goods. Comment on the role of the matrix g_{qv} in influencing the results.

(b) Show that the effects of an increase in import prices on the prices of non-traded goods are given by:

$$(-E_{qq})^{-1}dq = (x_{ql}m' - E_{qp})dp,$$

where m is the import vector and $x_{ql} = E_{qu}(e_u)^{-1}$ is the vector of marginal propensities to consume non-traded goods.

(c) Assume for simplicity that there is only one non-traded good and one import good. Denote by π the "real exchange rate" (the relative price of non-traded to traded goods). Discuss the likelihood that an improvement in the terms of trade will lead to a real appreciation (a rise in π).

2. Derive the "Little-Mirrlees rule," which states that the social profitability of public projects in a tariff-distorted small open economy should be evaluated at world rather than at domestic prices. Evaluate the robustness of this rule if:

(a) In addition to tariff-restricted goods, some other goods are subject to quotas, with all the rents returned in a lump-sum manner to the private sector.

(b) The only form of trade restriction is quotas, with a fraction ω of the resulting rents lost to the domestic economy.

(c) Tariffs are the only form of trade restriction, but the economy is large enough to exert some influence on world prices.

3. Consider the problem of deriving an "average" measure of trade restrictiveness in a small open economy in which tariffs are the only form of trade restriction.

(a) What problems may arise with measures which use average weights, such as the trade-weighted average tariff?

(b) Explain how a measure of trade restrictiveness, Δ, may be derived by applying the compensation principle to the balance of trade function, defined as:

$$B(p,u) \equiv E(p,u) - t'E_p(p,u).$$

Discuss the intuitive basis and the possible uses of such a measure.

(c) By totally differentiating the balance of trade function evaluated at $(p^1/\Delta, u^0)$, show how changes in Δ may be expressed in terms of marginal rather than average weights.

4. Consider a Cournot duopoly model in which a home and a foreign firm produce output levels x and y respectively of a differentiated product, the market demand curves for which are $p(x,y)$ and $q(y,x)$, respectively.

(a) Illustrate the determination of equilibrium and discuss its stability when the two goods are "strategic substitutes" (i.e., the marginal profitability of each firm is decreasing in its rival's output).

(b) Derive the effect of a small home subsidy on the output of each firm and on the market price.

(c) Derive the optimal home subsidy by the home government, assuming that neither good is consumed at home.

(d) How are your answers to (a), (b) and (c) affected if either or both of the goods is a strategic complement for the other?

(e) How are your results affected as the cross-elasticity of demand between the two goods falls in absolute value (i.e., as the two goods become less and less closely related in demand)?

194

5. Consider a two-period Cournot duopoly model in which in period t $(t=1,2)$ a home and a foreign firm produce output levels x_t and y_t respectively of a homogeneous product. All output is exported to a third market where the demand curve is linear and time-invariant: $p_t=a-b(x_t+y_t)$. The foreign firm has a constant marginal cost in each period equal to c^*. The home firm's marginal cost in the first period is c and in the second period it benefits from learning by doing: $c_2=c-\lambda x_1$. Each firm wishes to maximise its *undiscounted* profits: $\Pi=\pi_1+\pi_2$. The home government provides an export subsidy s_t in each period and seeks to maximise *undiscounted* *net* profits: $W=(\pi_1-s_1x_1)+(\pi_2-s_2x_2)$.

(a) Show that the foreign firm's reaction function in each period is:

$$2by_t = a - c^* - bx_t.$$

(b) Assume that firms can *commit* in the first period to their second-period outputs (i.e., at the beginning of period 1, each firm chooses its outputs in both periods, taking as given its rival's outputs in periods 1 *and* 2). Assume also that the government can commit in the first period to its subsidy levels in both periods. By manipulating the first-order conditions for the government and the home firms, show that the optimal subsidy in each period is:

$$s_t = bx_t/2.$$

Comment on the implications of this result.

(c) Suppose instead that the firms *cannot* commit to future outputs and the government cannot commit to the future subsidy level. How does this affect the home firm's incentive to produce in the first period?

(d) Show that the second-period subsidy is now related to first-period output by the following government reaction function:

$$4s_2 = \phi + 2\lambda x_1,$$

where ϕ is a measure of the home firm's cost competitiveness in the first period: $\phi=a-2c+c^*$.

(e) Hence, show that the optimal first-period subsidy equals:

$$s_1 = bx_1/2 - \lambda x_2.$$

Comment on the implications of this result.

University of Chicago
Graduate School of Business

Business Economics 300-03   Prof. Pashigian
Autumn, 1994

Reading List

Price Theory and Applications is a new microeconomics textbook that was published in May and will serve as your textbook for the course. You should also purchase a packet of articles at the bookstore. My goal in writing the book was to integrate theory with application more effectively by providing more in-depth empirical applications than is found in competing microeconomics textbooks. Each chapter develops the theory and then demonstrates the relevance of the theory. The applications perform two functions. Many are taken from the business press or from academic journals and illustrate the relevance of the theory. Others demonstrate how you can use the theory to address specific questions and help prepare you for the end-of-chapter exercises. Another distinctive feature of the book is the coverage of some topics not usually included in an intermediate textbook because I believe MBA students should be exposed to such topics as the cost of time, the governance of firms, etc. I do not intend to mislead you. While there are many applications, there will considerable doses of theory. Theory without applications or applications without theory both represent failings. You are expected to master the theory and to develop a facility for applying the theory. I consider the latter very important.

I will base my lectures on the material in the chapters with periodic digressions from the text . Reading the chapters and then listening to the lectures may be repetitive but yields considerable learning reinforcement. You can test your understanding of the core material in each chapter by answering the review questions and especially the exercises at the end of each chapter. Answers to some but not all exercises are included at the end of the book. Answers for some of the other exercises will be distributed during the quarter and discussed in review sessions which are tentatively scheduled for Fridays at 2:00 - 3:20 PM (except for the first and sixth week and the day after Thanksgiving.)

A special word of advice is appropriate for a student who has not had, or can only faintly remember registering for an introductory economics class sometime in the distant past. Many students with limited backgrounds in economics have successfully completed this course and there is no reason you cannot. However, it will take more time and effort on your part, especially at the beginning of the quarter. If you think that your background is weak, you may want to begin by completing the readings in <u>Microeconomics</u> (the 8th edition should be available in Regenstein) by E. Mansfield and then go on to read the material in <u>Price Theory and Applications</u>. What you do <u>not</u> want to do is fall behind and then hope to catch up with a last minute all-nighter just before the mid-quarter examination.

It is a good idea to work on the review questions and especially the exercises at the end of the chapter soon after you read the chapter. The best test of your understanding of price theory is your ability to apply the theory to new situations. The exercises at the end of each chapter vary from easy to difficult and many test your ability to apply the theory to new situations. Most of the exercises are based on questions taken from my old exams so they give you an inkling of what you can expect on the exams. You can test your understanding of the theory by correctly answering the exercises at the end of each chapter. You might want to join or form a small group of two or three persons (larger groups prove unworkable) to review questions and exercises. Do not wait until the fifth or sixth week before working the exercises <u>especially</u> if your background in economics is weak.

The mid-quarter examination is scheduled for Wednesday, November 9 of the <u>sixth week</u>. The final examination is given during the eleventh week and <u>only</u> covers the second half of the course. The mid-quarter and final examinations are each weighted 40% and homework accounts for 20% in the determination of your final grade. These examinations review material presented in class and in the required readings. Don't be a late starter. What you learn in the first week contributes as much to your final grade as what you learn in the last week.

A.   Introduction to Market Demand and Supply Curves

    1.   Pashigian, B. P., <u>Price Theory and Applications</u>, Chapter 1.

    2.   "Rental Roulette: Frustrated Torontonians Offer Cash Rewards to Tenants Willing to Pull Up Stakes," <u>Toronto Globe and Mail</u>, (July 25, 1985). (packet)

1st and 2nd Weeks

B.   Consumer Behavior and the Theory of Market Demand

    1.   Pashigian, B. P., <u>Price Theory and Applications</u>, Chapter 2.

    *2.   Mansfield, <u>Micro-Economics</u>, (8th Edition), pp. 53-71, 85-94, 116-126.

    3.   Hirsch, J. "Frequent Fliers Resist Forking Over Their Miles," <u>Wall Street Journal</u>, March 28, 1994. (packet)

    4.   Pashigian, B. P., Price Theory and Applications, Chapter 3, pp. 120-31.

    5.   Pashigian, B. P., <u>Price Theory and Applications</u>, Chapter 4.

    6.   Hwang, S., "From Choices to Checkout, the Genders Behave Very Differently in Supermarkets," <u>Wall Street Journal</u>, March 22, 1994. (packet)

    7.   Gorman, J., "Fast-Food Push Puts Time on Diner's Side," <u>Wall Street Journal</u>, (August 23, 1987). (packet)

    8.   Gray, P. B., "Remember Speed Reading? Nowadays, There are Speed Viewing and Listening," <u>Wall Street Journal</u>, (November 29, 1985). (packet)

3th and 4th Weeks

C.   The Short and Long Run Cost Curves of the Firm and the Theory of Firm Supply

    1.   Pashigian B. P., <u>Price Theory and Applications</u>, Chapters 6-7.

    *2.   Mansfield, <u>Micro-Economics</u>, 213-240.

    3.   Machalaha, D. "Shipping Firms Suffer as Boat Values Decline and Freight Rates Fall," <u>Wall Street Journal</u>, November 5, 1985. (packet).

    4.   Tanner, J., "Smaller U.S. Oil Producers Dropping Out," <u>Wall Street Journal</u>, (February 19, 1986). (packet)

    5.   Pashigian, B. P., "How Large and Small Plants Fare Under Environmental Regulation," <u>Regulation</u>, (September/October, 1983), pp. 19-23. (packet)

4

5th, 6th and 7th Weeks

D.   Price Determination Under Price Competition

    1.   Pashigian, B. P., <u>Price Theory and Applications</u>, Chapter 8, pp. 273-313.

    *2.   Mansfield, <u>Micro-Economics</u>, Chapter 9.

    3.   "Regulate Us, Please," <u>Economist</u>, January 8, 1994, p. 69. (packet)

    4.   Chapman, S., "Let Alaskan Oil Flow to Japan," <u>Chicago Tribune</u>, (April 21, 1985). (packet)

    5.   "Florida Officials Report Numerous Complaints of Price Gouging," <u>Chicago Tribune</u>, (August 30, 1992). (packet)

    6.   Lorh, S. "Lessons From a Hurricane: It Pays Not to Gouge," <u>New York Times</u>, (September 22, 1992). (packet)

6th Week

MID-QUARTER EXAMINATION on Wednesday, November 9.

7th and 8th Weeks

E.   Monopoly Pricing and Price Discrimination

    1.   Pashigian, B. P., <u>Price Theory and Applications</u>, Chapter 9, pp. 320-355.

    2.   Guyon, J., "Czechs Play a Tough Game of Monopoly," <u>Wall Street Journal</u>, October 12, 1993. (packet)

    3.   Pashigian, B. P., <u>Price Theory and Applications</u>, Chapter 12, pp. 437-59.

    *4.   Mansfield, <u>Micro-Economics</u>, pp. 296-308, 313-316

    5.   Solis, D., "To Avoid Cost of U.S. Prescription Drugs, More Americans Shop South of the Border," <u>Wall Street Journal</u>, (June 29, 1993) (packet)

    6.   Darlin, D., "Japanese Learn Thrills of Bargain Shopping From Mentors Abroad," <u>Wall Street Journal</u>, March 11, 1988. (packet)

9th Week

F.   Oligopoly

    1.   Pashigian, B. P., <u>Price Theory and Applications</u>, Chapter 10.

    *2.   Mansfield, <u>Micro-Economics</u>, pp. 345-357, 368-378.

3.   Lochhead, C., "Fruit Fight," <u>Insight</u>, July 29, 1991, pp. 13-19 (packet).

<u>10th Week</u>

G.   Governance of the Firm

1.   Pashigian, B. P. <u>Price Theory and Applications</u>, Chapters 11.

2.   Shleifer, A and Vishny, R., "The Takeover Wave of the 1980's," <u>Science</u>, Vol. 249, pp. 745 - 49 (packet).

<u>11th Week</u>

<u>FINAL EXAMINATION</u> (second half of course)

* Denotes optional reading.

Professor John Pencavel   Autumn 1994
Stanford University
Economics 202
PRICE AND ALLOCATION THEORY I

This is an introductory course in microeconomic analysis. Its purpose is to prepare students for work in applied economics and for further work in economic theory.   There are two texts:

Hal R. Varian, <u>Microeconomic Analysis</u>, third edition, Norton, 1992.

Angus Deaton and John Muellbauer, <u>Economics and Consumer Behavior</u>, Cambridge Univ. Press, 1980.

At the beginning of the course, students are presumed to be at ease with the techniques of calculus and during the term they are expected to pick up the essentials of linear and nonlinear programming. By the end of the course, students should have read pages 1-197, 215-58, and 313-57 of Varian and the first eight chapters (plus pages 380-405) of Deaton and Muellbauer.

Course Outline

I. Static Model of Consumer Behavior
    (a) Structure of preferences
    (b) Constrained utility maximization and expenditure minimization
    (c) Separability, aggregation, and multiconstraint problems

II. Static Model of Producer Behavior
    (a) Production technology and cost minimization
    (b) Profit maximization in competition and monopoly
    (c) Supply of factor inputs

III. Partial and General Equilibrium of Markets
    (a) Partial equilibrium: Comparative statics of single and many markets
    (b) General equilibrium: exchange economies
    (c) General equilibrium: exchange and production

IV. Information and Uncertainty
    (a) Expected utility and risk aversion
    (b) State preference approach to decision-making
    (c) Risk sharing, asymmetric information, and transaction costs

Reading List

I. Consumer Demand Analysis

W.M. Gorman, "Tricks with Utility Functions", in M.J. Artis and A.R. Nobay, eds., Essays in Economic Analysis, Proceedings of the Association of University Teachers of Economics (Sheffield 1975), Cambridge Univ. Press, 1976, pp. 211-44.

Alan P. Kirman, "Whom or What Does the Representative Individual Represent?", Journal of Economic Perspectives, Spring 1992, pp. 117-36.

Kenneth W. Clements, "Alternative Approaches to Consumption Theory", Chapter 1 of Henri Theil and Kenneth W. Clements, Applied Demand Analysis: Results from a System-Wide Approach, Ballinger, Cambridge, 1987, pp. 1-35.

II. Producer Behavior and Distribution

R.G.D. Allen, Mathematical Analysis for Economists, Macmillan, 1938, Sections, 12.7, 12.8, 12.9, 13.7, 14.8, 19.4, 19.5, and 19.6, pp., 315-22, 340-43, 369-74, and 502-9.

Robert Dorfman, Paul A. Samuelson, and Robert M. Solow, Linear Programming and Economic Analysis, 1958, Chapters, 6 & 7, pp. 130-85.

Armen A. Alchian, "Uncertainty, Evolution and Economic Theory", JPE, June 1950, pp. 211-21.

Louis Putterman, "On Some Recent Explanations of Why Capital Hires Labor", Economic Inquiry, April 1984, pp. 171-87.

III. Markets: Partial and General Equilibrium

R.A. Radford, "The Economic Organization of a P.O.W. Camp", Economica, November 1945, pp. 189-201.

Ronald W. Jones, "The Structure of Simple General Equilibrium Models", JPE, December 1965, pp. 557-72.

IV. Information and Uncertainty

Friedrich A. von Hayek, "The Use of Knowledge in Society", AER, September 1945, pp. 519-30.

Kenneth J. Arrow, "The Theory of Risk Bearing", Chapter 3 of Essays in the Theory of Risk Bearing, 1971, pp. 90-120.

3

Michael Rothschild and Joseph E. Stiglitz, "Increasing Risk: I A Definition", *Journal of Economic Theory*, 1970, pp. 225-43.

Michael Rothschild and Joseph E. Stiglitz, "Equilibrium in Competitive Insurance Markets: An Essay on the Economics of Imperfect Information", *QJE*, November 1976, pp. 629-49.

George A. Akerlof, "The Market for Lemons: Quality Uncertainty and the Market Mechanism", *QJE*, August 1970, pp. 488-500.

John Roberts, "Moral Hazard and the Principal-Agent Problem", Stanford University Graduate School of Business, undated.

203

John Pencavel   Stanford University   Autumn Quarter 1994-95

Economics 202: Price and Allocation Theory I

Final Examination

This is a closed book examination. You have three hours to answer three questions. Answer all questions. Please answer each of the three questions in a separate Blue Book.

Write coherently and lucidly. Provide the economic reasoning for your answers.

QUESTION ONE

Part A (15 points)

What are transaction costs? Identify components of these costs.

Part B (85 points)

To produce their outputs, two firms, 1 and 2, purchase a resource from a third firm, 3. The production functions of the two firms are $X_1 = 4(Z_1)^{1/2}$ and $X_2 = 2(Z_2)^{1/2}$ where X_i is the level of output and Z_i the level of the resource input of firm i. The total amount of the resource available is Z^*.

(a) Calculate the optimal allocation of this resource that yields the largest total output for the two firms together assuming that all of the resource is used up. What is the shadow price of the resource?

(b) Now suppose the fixed per unit output prices of firms 1 and 2 are p_1 and p_2. Firm 3 sells the resource for the fixed per unit price of r. Assuming $Z_1 + Z_2 < Z^*$, obtain the maximized profit functions for firms 1 and 2 and use these functions to derive the output supply functions for X_1 and X_2.

(c) Suppose c denotes firm 3's fixed unit cost of extracting the resource and suppose firm 3 unilaterally selects r to maximize its net revenues from the sale of this resource to firms 1 and 2. When $Z_1 + Z_2 < Z^*$, obtain an expression for the selling price of the resource as a function of other prices.

QUESTION TWO

(Each of the four parts of this question carries 25 points.)

1. In the analysis of consumer behavior, it might seem natural to define complementarity between commodities 1 and 2 as occurring when the marginal utility of consuming commodity 1 rises as more of commodity 2 is consumed, i.e., $\partial^2 U/\partial q_1 \partial q_2 > 0$. (Here U denotes

utility and q_i the consumption of commodity i.) In fact, complementarity is not defined this way. Why? How is complementarity usually defined?

2. Zoe's utility function is $U(F, G) = F.G$ where F indicates her consumption of food and G stands for her consumption of all other goods. If she buys her groceries at the "Price Club", she pays an annual membership fee of $m and receives a 19% discount on regular grocery store prices on her food purchases. Derive an expression for the maximum membership fee she is willing to pay as a fraction of her income to join the "Price Club"?

3. A strictly quasi-concave utility function over three commodities is written $U(q_1, q_2, q_3) = \Phi[f(q_1, q_2), q_3]$. Show that the demands for commodities 1 and 2 can be written as functions of only the prices of commodities 1 and 2 and the total amount spent on these two commodities. What property does this utility function exhibit?

4. Consider a two-household, two-commodity, exchange economy. Household A's utility function is

$$U^A(q_1^A, q_2^A) = -(0.5)(q_1^A)^{-2} - (0.5)(q_2^A)^{-2}$$

and household B's is

$$U^B(q_1^B, q_2^B) = q_1^B q_2^B .$$

A is endowed with Q_1 of commodity 1 and no endowments of commodity 2. B is endowed with Q_2 of commodity 2 and no endowments of commodity 1. Derive the excess demand functions for the two commodities.

QUESTION THREE

Part A (30 points)

You are presented with the following gamble. You draw a card from a deck. If the card is a spade, a coin is tossed and you win $1 if it comes down heads and lose $1 if it comes down tails. If the card drawn is a heart, diamond, or club, a die is rolled and you win $1 if it lands showing a 1 or 2 and lose $1 if it lands showing a 3, 4, 5, or 6.

(a) Is this gamble favorable, fair, or unfavorable?

(b) Your utility function is $U(W^* - 1) = 10$, $U(W^*) = 11$, and $U(W^* + 1) = 15$ where W^* denotes your current wealth. You behave in accordance with the expected utility hypothesis. Will you accept the gamble?

(c) Does the utility function in part (b) display aversion to risk? Why or why not?

Part B (30 points)

M denotes Jane's initial wealth, some of which is held in risky assets. If G represents the amount of Jane's risky assets, then her wealth changes to $M + \theta_i G$ in state of the world i where $i = 1, 2$, $\theta_1 > 0$, and $\theta_2 < 0$. Jane selects her holdings of risky assets to maximize her expected utility.

(a) Assuming G to be strictly positive, state the first-order and second-order conditions determining an optimum value of G and interpret them.

(b) How does an increase in Jane's initial wealth affect her purchase of the risky assets? Assume her coefficient of absolute risk aversion falls with her wealth.

Part C (40 points)

Max consumes two commodities in amounts q and r respectively. His utility function is $U(q,r) = q + \beta \log(r)$, $\beta > 0$. Each unit of q sells at a fixed price of unity and p denotes the given price of each unit of r. Max's income is y and he maximizes his utility.

Statement One: With respect to variations in r alone, given the form of his direct utility function, Max is risk-averse.

Statement Two: Max's indirect utility function suggests Max displays risk preference with respect to the price of r.

Do you agree with Statements One and Two? Are they paradoxical or inconsistent? Explain.

Instructor: Prof. Steve Pischke, E52-371a

TA: Lorenza Martinez, office TBA

Time and Location: Tuesday, Thursday 1:00-2:30, 1-190

Office Hours: Wednesday 1:30 - 3:30

Prerequisites: Introductory Microeconomics 14.01

Course Description: Microeconomics is the study of the behavior of individual economic agents like consumers, workers, and firms, and their interaction in markets or other social settings. Intermediate typically refers to the fact that the course should cover these topics at somewhat more depth than an introductory course, without the theoretical rigor of an advanced or graduate course. However, 14.01 at MIT essentially covers material that is traditionally thought of as "intermediate." What I plan to do in this course is to expose you to some issues and models that typically don't receive much attention in 14.01 but are really part of the core of modern microeconomics: choice under uncertainty, the economics of information and market failures associated with it, basic principles of game theory and its application to market structures, and the organization of firms. Many of these basic models are used again and again in economics, so this will provide you with a foundation for more topical courses in economics, like industrial organization, labor economics, public finance, or international trade. We will do some theory and math in this course, but unlike in 14.04, the focus will be on basic economic principles as well as on applications in a variety of situations (the label "applied" in the course title is mainly to distinguish it from the more rigorous 14.04). The applications will not be designed to give you a general or comprehensive overview of a particular area in economics (there are many topical courses offered in the department to do that) but rather to help you learn to think as economists and apply the basic principles in a particular situation. Thus, this is a course more interested in "means" rather than "ends" and it will be geared towards students with a general interest in economics who want to go on in their study to more specialized material (presumably mostly students who want to pursue a major or minor in economics). It will probably be less satisfying to those students looking for "another" economics class; you might be better served by taking a specific field course.

Textbook: The fact that this course doesn't exactly fit the design of a standard intermediate micro course means that there isn't really a single good textbook to go along with it. Nevertheless, you should purchase

- Walter Nicholson: *Microeconomic Theory. Basic Principles and Extensions.* Fort Worth: The Dryden Press, 5th edition 1992 which is available at the MIT Coop. It touches on all the relevant issues but we will fly through some chapters and do others in much more depth. Given that the course material does not exactly coincide with the text, you will probably not be able to do very well in the course with reading the text alone.

Since Nicholson isn't the perfect book, let me mention two others that might be useful. A superb book dealing with issues in information economics, contract design and the organization of firms is

- Paul Milgrom and John Roberts *Economics, Organization, and Management.* Englewood Cliffs: Prentice Hall, 1992

It contains little mathematics but a lot of examples and applications from management. I have thought of using it as a text for the course. While it treats very well what it covers, it is a little narrower in focus than the course. If you are interested in the management applications of economics, you may want to get a hold of this one. I will certainly consult it for my lectures.

In addition to these, this syllabus makes references to

- Robert S. Pindyck and Daniel L. Rubinfeld, *Microeconomics,* New York: Macmillan Publishing Company, 2nd edition 1992

which many of you own. It is slightly more basic than the level of this course but really a very nice text.

Grading: There will be (approximately) biweekly homework assignments (probably six of them), two quizzes and a final exam. The various parts will count toward the grade as follows.

Assignments	30%
Each Quiz	20%
Final	30%.

Exams: The tentative dates for the quizzes are October 6 and November 15, they will focus on the preceding segments of the course. The date of the final exam will be announced in the exam schedule. The final will cover all course material.

Tentative Course Outline
Economic Models: Toys or Tools?

- Nicholson, chapter 1, Pindyck and Rubinfeld, sections 1.1-1.3

- David A. Levy "Assumptions and Economists' Other Vices," *The Jerome Levy Economics Institute Report* April 1994, pp. 8-9

Consumer Choice: Some Old Material in a New Wrapper

Preferences and Utility: A Review of the Basics

- Nicholson, chapter 3, Pindyck and Rubinfeld, section

2

Consumer Choice: An Application of Constrained Optimization

- Nicholson, chapters 2 and 4, Pindyck and Rubinfeld, section 3.3 and appendix to chapter 4

A Useful Alternative: Revealed Preference

- Nicholson, chapter 5, pp. 151-154, Pindyck and Rubinfeld, section 3.4

Comparative Statics of the Consumer Choice Problem: The Slutsky Equation

- Nicholson, chapters 5 and 6, Pindyck and Rubinfeld, chapter 4

Choice With Endowments: Savings and Labor Supply

- Nicholson, chapter 23

Choice Under Uncertainty

The Basics: Probability and Expected Utility

- Nicholson, chapter 9, Pindyck and Rubinfeld, sections 5.1 and 5.2, Milgrom and Roberts, chapter 7

Risk Aversion, Diversification and Insurance

- Nicholson, chapter 9, Pindyck and Rubinfeld, section 5.3, Milgrom and Roberts, chapter 7

Risky Business: Investments With Uncertain Payoffs

- Nicholson, chapter 9, pp. 265-266, Pindyck and Rubinfeld, section 5.4, Milgrom and Roberts, chapter 14

A Quick Review of the Neoclassical Firm

- Nicholson, chapters 11-13, Pindyck and Rubinfeld, chapters 6-8

Market Structure

Monopoly: The One and Only

- Nicholson, chapter 19, Pindyck and Rubinfeld, chapters 10 and 11

Imperfect Competition

- Nicholson, chapter 20, Pindyck and Rubinfeld, chapter 12

Let's Play: An Introduction to Game Theory

- Nicholson, chapter 21, Pindyck and Rubinfeld, chapter 13

What Do You Know: Information and Markets

3

Efficient Markets: A Perfect World

- Nicholson, chapters 16 and 17, Pindyck and Rubinfeld, chapter 16, Milgrom and Roberts, chapter 3

Why Is Information Different?

- Nicholson, chapters 10 and 18

Information and Actions: The Moral Hazard Problem

- Nicholson, chapter 10, pp. 274-278, Pindyck and Rubinfeld, sections 17.3 and 17.4, Milgrom and Roberts, chapter 6

Information and Selection: Lemons and Signals

- Nicholson, chapter 10, pp. 278-285, Pindyck and Rubinfeld, sections 17.1 and 17.2, Milgrom and Roberts, chapter 5

Applications (given time, interests, and energy of class and instructor)

Alternative Theories of the Firm

- Nicholson, chapter 14, Milgrom and Roberts, chapter 7-9 and 15

Alternative Forms of Markets: Auctions and Asset Markets

- Paul Milgrom, "Auctions and Bidding: A Primer," *Journal of Economic Perspectives* Summer 1989, pp. 3-22

- Orley Ashenfelter, "How Auctions Work for Wine and Art," *Journal of Economic Perspectives* Summer 1989, pp. 23-36

- Peter M. Garber, "Famous First Bubbles," *Journal of Economic Perspectives* Spring 1990, pp. 35-54

Law and Economics

- Criminal behavior, Liability Law

Other Forms of Externalities

- Nicholson, chapter 25, Pindyck and Rubinfeld, chapter 18

4

Prof. Steve Pischke
Fall 1994

14.03
Applied Intermediate Microeconomics
Quiz 1
October 6, 1994

You have 80 minutes to complete this quiz. The quiz has one page and consists of four questions. You have to answer any three out of these four. Each question carries the same weight. The questions are listed in roughly increasing order of difficulty. If you attempt all four, indicate clearly which answers you wish to be graded; otherwise three answers will be chosen for grading at random. It is recommended that you read all the questions before you start. Show your work since partial credit will be awarded.

Good luck!

1. We have shown in class that increasing a parking fine will do better in deterring false parking than the same proportionate increase in the probability of getting a ticket if drivers are risk averse. How does the analysis change if drivers are risk loving? Which has the greater deterrence effect in this case, increasing the fine or the probability of getting a ticket?

2. Liane has the following utility function over consumption this period c_1 and consumption in the future c_2:
$$U(c_1, c_2) = c_1 c_2$$
She has income y_1 this period and y_2 in the future, and she can borrow and lend at the interest rate r. Derive Liane's savings function (her supply function of funds to the capital market). Find the sign of the derivative of savings with respect to the interest rate. Does it depend on whether Liane is saving or borrowing?

3. You are a collector (of baseball cards, coins, or antique cars). Sometimes you buy items for your collection, sometimes you sell items in your collection to other collectors. Suppose you are currently "in equilibrium," i.e. you are neither buying nor selling items in your collection. Show that you will be better off if prices for your collectibles change by either going up or going down. Explain why this is the case.

4. Suppose an investor has wealth W and faces the opportunity to invest in a risky asset. If investing x dollars in the asset she receives $(1 + r_g)x$ in good times (which happen with probability p) and $(1 + r_b)x$ in bad times (with probability $1-p$) with $r_g > r_b > 0$. Show that a risk averse investor would increase the optimal amount x^* invested in the risky asset as the government imposes a tax on the investment return (so that an amount $tr_i x$ has to be paid to the government where t is the tax rate). Why does this happen?

1

14.03
Applied Intermediate Microeconomics
Quiz 1
Answer Key

1. The utility function is convex in this case. Therefore, following the analysis we did in class

$$FU'(W - F) > U(W - F) - U(W)$$

$$\Longleftrightarrow \frac{F}{U}\frac{\partial U}{\partial F} > \frac{p}{U}\frac{\partial U}{\partial p}$$

so that increasing the probability of getting a ticket lowers expected utility more, and therefore has a larger effect on deterring false parking. Alternatively, you can use the same graph as in class to show this:

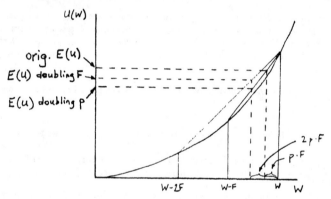

2. The budget constraint is

$$c_1 + \frac{c_2}{1+r} = y_1 + \frac{y_2}{1+r}$$

or

$$y_1 - c_1 - \frac{c_2 - y_2}{1+r} = 0$$

The Lagrangian for the problem is

$$L = c_1 c_2 + \lambda \left(y_1 - c_1 - \frac{c_2 - y_2}{1+r} \right)$$

The first order conditions are

$$\frac{\partial L}{\partial c_1} = c_2 - \lambda = 0$$

$$\frac{\partial L}{\partial c_2} = c_1 - \frac{\lambda}{1+r} = 0$$

1

in addition to the budget constraint. Combining these two yields

$$c_2 = (1 + r)c_1$$

Substitute this in the budget constraint to get

$$c_1 + \frac{(1 + r)c_1}{1 + r} = y_1 + \frac{y_2}{1 + r}$$

or

$$c_1 = \frac{1}{2}\left(y_1 + \frac{y_2}{1 + r}\right)$$

The savings function is given by

$$s = y_1 - c_1 = y_1 - \frac{1}{2}\left(y_1 + \frac{y_2}{1 + r}\right)$$

$$s = \frac{1}{2}\left(y_1 - \frac{y_2}{1 + r}\right)$$

The derivative of savings with respect to the interest rate is

$$\frac{\partial s}{\partial r} = -\frac{1}{2}\frac{-y_2}{(1 + r)^2} = \frac{y_2}{2(1 + r)^2} > 0$$

Savings increases as the interest rate rises independently of the level of savings; the result does not depend on whether Liane is a saver or a borrower.

3. Think of preferences over collectibles and other goods. Being in equilibrium means that you are currently making an optimal choice of both types of goods. Since you own the collectibles the budget constraint is going to pivot in your equilibrium point. A tilt in either direction lets you reach a higher indifference curve.

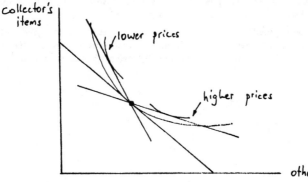

4. Note that wealth in the two states of the world is

$$W_g = W - x + (1 + r_g)x = W + r_g x$$

2

$$W_b = W - x + (1 + r_b)x = W + r_b x$$

As some of you noticed, to get a sensible solution to this problem we should actually have $r_g > 0 > r_b$; sorry for this typo. Introducing taxes means

$$W_i = W + r_i(1 - t)x$$

where $i = g, b$. The investor maximizes

$$E(U) = pU\left(W + r_g(1 - t)x\right) + (1 - p)U\left(W + r_b(1 - t)x\right)$$

The first order condition is

$$\frac{\partial E(U)}{\partial x} = pU'\left(W + r_g(1 - t)x\right)r_g(1 - t) + (1 - p)U'\left(W + r_b(1 - t)x\right)r_b(1 - t) = 0$$

which implies

$$pU'\left(W + r_g(1 - t)x\right)r_g + (1 - p)U'\left(W + r_b(1 - t)x\right)r_b = 0$$

Let x^* denote the level of investment when $t = 0$, implicitly this is given by

$$pU'\left(W + r_g x^*\right)r_g + (1 - p)U'\left(W + r_b x^*\right)r_b = 0$$

Let $\hat{x}$ denote the level of investment when $t > 0$, implicitly this is given by

$$pU'\left(W + r_g(1 - t)\hat{x}\right)r_g + (1 - p)U'\left(W + r_b(1 - t)\hat{x}\right)r_b = 0$$

Note that there is no difference in these two equalities when

$$x^* = (1 - t)\hat{x}$$

so this has to be the relationship between the amounts invested with no taxes and with taxes. It is obvious that $x^* < \hat{x}$ if $t > 0$.

What is happening here is that the taxes change the returns in the good state and the bad state proportionately. By scaling up the investment by a factor $1/(1 - t)$ the investor can recreate the same payoff that existed before the tax was imposed.

3

Prof. Steve Pischke
Fall 1994

14.03
Applied Intermediate Microeconomics
Quiz 2
November 17, 1994

You have 80 minutes to complete this quiz. The quiz has two pages and consists of four questions. **You have to answer any three out of these four.** Each question carries the same weight. If you attempt all four, indicate clearly which answers you wish to be graded; otherwise three answers will be chosen for grading at random. It is recommended that you read all the questions before you start. Show your work since partial credit will be awarded. No notes or books are allowed.

Good luck!

1. Suppose two duopolists compete in a market by setting prices (i.e. in the Bertrand fashion). Products are homogeneous so that consumers will always buy only from the cheaper firm. Demand is D units and independent of price at any price below P_o, and zero at higher prices. Both firms have constant average and marginal cost functions; firm A has $MC_A = c$, and firm B has $MC_B = d$, with $c < d < P_o$. What is the Nash equilibrium in this model?

2. A competitive industry is in long run equilibrium where all firms earn zero economic profits. All firms in the industry and potential entrants have identical U-shaped average cost curves. A large demand increase is being forecast for this industry. The business association for the industry starts to lobby Congress to adopt new environmental regulation for the industry. The business representatives argue the increase in demand could worsen pollution by the industry considerably. They suggest that any new plant in the industry should be equipped with expensive filters which would involve a different design than is common in existing plants. The main cost of this new equipment is related to keeping the filters clean which would raise the variable costs for plant equipped with filters but would leave fixed costs unchanged. Industry representatives also suggest that existing plants be exempted from this regulation since it would be very uneconomical to change the existing plants. Why would business leaders suggest that their own industry be subjected to environmental regulation? Explain why this makes sense using a graphical analysis.

3. The demand function for an industry is given by $Q = 100 - P$. There are five identical Cournot oligopolists in the market. Average and marginal cost for each firm is constant at \$4. Three of the firms are foreign suppliers importing their product into the domestic market. What quantity is supplied by each firm? Suppose that the government imposes an import quota (a quantity restriction on imports) equal to current imports. What happens to output of the domestic firms after the quota is imposed?

4. A monopolist supplies rides at an amusement park. The demand function for rides of a consumer is shown in the figure on the next page. The capital letters in the figure represent areas. The per unit cost of supplying rides has two components: c, the cost

1

of supplying the equipment, and d, the cost of printing and collecting tickets at each ride. Each per unit cost is independent of the number of rides offered at the park. The monopolist is considering two pricing policies:

- *Policy 1.* An entrance fee and a per unit charge for each ride.
- *Policy 2.* Just an entrance fee. (The advantage of this policy is that the firm can save on printing and collecting tickets.)

Using the information denoted in the graph, what is the entrance fee, per unit charge, total number of rides supplied, and total profits under each policy? Under what conditions will profits under policy 2 exceed profits under policy 1? What is the disadvantage of policy 2?

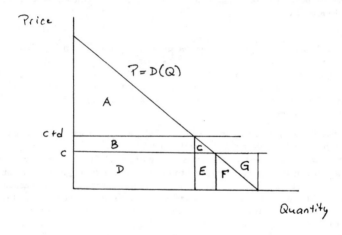

14.03
Applied Intermediate Microeconomics
Quiz 2
Answers

1. Firm A serves the entire market at a price $P = d - \epsilon$, i.e. just below the marginal cost of firm B. Firm B does not enter at prices below d. Why is this an equilibrium? Firm B has no incentive to enter the market. It would have to charge a price of at most P to sell anything. But profits at P are already negative for firm B. Firm A cannot do better by charging a different price either. If it charges a higher price firm B will enter and they have to split the market. If it charges a lower price, profits will be lower since the number of units it sells are limited by D (demand is inelastic).

2. In long run equilibrium, all firms will earn zero economic profits. Therefore, the price will be equal to minimum average cost, the lowest price at which firms in the industry are willing to operate. As demand increases, all firms will move up their supply (marginal cost) curves to serve the additional customers. Firms make positive profits now which would lead to entry of new producers. If the environmental regulation is such that only new entrants to the industry are subjected to the tighter pollution standards and have to install filters then costs will be higher for new entrants. In this case, new firms will only enter if the higher price covers the cost of the antipollution devices. Even after entry to the industry the price does not return to its old level but remains higher by the cost of the antipollution equipment. Therefore, old firms in the industry continue to make profits until their plants wear out and they have to build new plants themselves (which will also be subject to the more stringent environmental regulation).

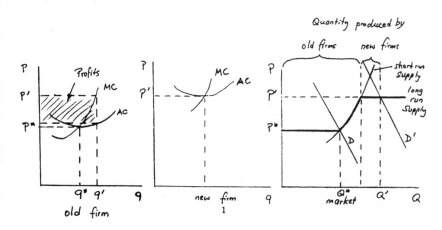

3. The inverse demand function is

$$P = 100 - Q$$

Profits for each oligopolist are

$$\pi = Pq_i - 4q_i = (100 - Q)q_i - 4q_i$$

The first order condition is

$$\frac{\partial \pi}{\partial q} = 100 - Q - q_i - 4 = 0$$

This gives the reaction function

$$96 - \sum_{j \neq i} q_j = 2q_i$$

Notice that this gives five equations in five unknowns. Since all firms are equal, four of those will yield symmetry conditions of the form

$$q_i = q_j$$

Using these we get

$$96 = 6q_i$$

or

$$q_i = \frac{96}{6} = 16$$

If the government imposes a quota on the three importers equal to their current market share the foreign firms cannot sell more than $3 \cdot 16 = 48$. What will the domestic firms want to do given that the importers sell a quantity of 48? The answer is simply that they will want to continue to sell 16 units each. This was a best response to the foreign firms selling 48 units before. So it is still a best response to the foreign firms selling 48 units. The quota only changes the reaction function outside the equilibrium but does not affect the equilibrium itself. Alternatively, you can get this answer by calculating the residual domestic demand curve and going through the Cournot problem again for the two domestic firms.

4. Under policy 1 the entrance fee is A and the charge per ride is equal to marginal cost $c + d$. Profits are A and the number of rides sold are given by the intersection of the demand function and the per unit charge $c + d$. Under policy 2 the entrance fee is $A + B + C + D + E + F$. The number of rides will be equal to the intersection of demand with the x-axis. Notice that consumers don't care about marginal cost. Once they are in the amusement park each ride is free so they consume up to their satiation point. Profits are $A + B + C + D + E + F - (C - E - F - G) = A + B + D - G$. Profits under policy 2 will be greater if $A + B + D - G > A$ or $B + D > G$. The disadvantage of policy 2 is that consumers take too many rides now. The firm would like to restrict them to the point where c intersects demand but the only way of doing that is selling costly tickets for each ride.

2

Prof. Steve Pischke
Fall 1994

14.03
Applied Intermediate Microeconomics
Final Examination
December 19, 1994

You have 3 hours to complete this exam. The exam has three pages and consists of three parts. The first part contains short answer questions, the second part an analytical question and the third part more open ended questions. The first section carries 30 points, the second part 40 points and third part 30 points. Within each section every question carries the same number of points. Everybody has to answer the question in part two. Parts one and three give you some choice. If you attempt more than the required number of questions clearly label which ones you wish to have graded. Show your work since partial credit will be awarded. Please write legibly.

Good luck!

Part I: Short Answer Questions (30 points)   Answer any *six* out of the following eight. Indicate whether the statement is true, false, or uncertain. If the statement is true, explain why. If the statement is false, explain why. If the statement is uncertain, give conditions under which it is true and those under which it is false. In any case, your answers should be short and to the point.

1. The Hicksian (or compensated) demand function for a normal good is steeper than the Marshallian (or uncompensated) demand function.

2. In the two-period model of savings a saver will always save less when the interest rate goes up.

3. A risk averse individual will always prefer the expected value of a gamble for sure over the gamble itself.

4. A firm with a constant returns to scale production function and no fixed costs has constant average and marginal costs.

5. A monopolist with constant marginal costs charging a two part tariff will generally set a per-unit price equal to marginal cost.

6. If average cost is increasing then marginal cost is also increasing. If marginal cost is increasing then average cost is increasing.

7. The adverse selection problem is more serious for insurance firms offering group health insurance to large employers rather than to small employers.

8. A monopoly produces 1 million units of a good. If a $10 per unit tax is imposed on the good, the profits of the monopolist will decrease by $10 million.

1

Part II (40 points)   Answer all parts of the following question.

9. American Widgetmakers sells widgets in a market where demand is given by

$$Q = 140 + A - P$$

Q is the quantity demanded, P is the price, and A is the level of advertising expenditures undertaken by the firm. Widgetmakers has a cost function of producing widgets $C(q_1) = 20q_1$. Furthermore, the cost of advertising to the firm is $C_A(A) = A^2$.

  (a) Assume Widgetmakers has a monopoly position in the market and does not undertake advertising. How much does it produce and what are its profits?

  (b) Continue with the assumption that Widgetmakers has a monopoly. How much does it produce when it sets both advertising and output optimally? How much does it advertise? What are its profits?

  (c) Now assume that a competitor, Taiwanese Widget Import and Export (TWIX), enters the market. TWIX has a cost function of selling in the American market given by $C(q_2) = 50q_2$ (because of transportation costs). Suppose the two firms compete as Cournot duopolists. TWIX does not advertise and takes the advertising level of American Widgetmakers as given. Find the output levels for the two firms, the level of advertising and profits for each firm.

  (d) Give the economic intuition why the levels of advertising differ between your answers in (b) and (c).

  (e) Suppose in addition to the assumptions in (c) that TWIX also has a fixed cost of 800 if it sells in the American Market at all. American Widgetmakers has no fixed costs. Suppose the two firms take the following decisions simultaneously: American Widgetmakers decides whether to advertise at the optimal level or not at all and TWIX decides whether to enter the American market or not. What is the Nash equilibrium outcome of this game?

Part III (30 points)   Answer *two* out of the following three questions. Feel free to make specific assumptions that help you to answer these questions but state any assumptions you make clearly.

10. The state legislature wants to subsidize day care. It considers two proposals. Under program 1 a family would receive a subsidy of s dollars for each day that the child attends an authorized day care facility. Under program 2 a family with a child registered in an authorized day care facility receives a lump sum subsidy. The state would spend the same amount of money on either proposal. Legislators find it hard to decide on one of the proposals because day care providers lobby for program 1 while parents lobby for program 2. Using indifference curves, show that more day care would be purchased under program 1. Show that parents' utility would be higher under program 2.

11. Explain why only low quality products may be sold in a market where manufacturers can produce different qualities but the quality level is hard to ascertain by consumers prior to purchase. Clearly explain how the possibility of offering warranties may affect the outcome. Should the government require all firms to offer warranties?

12. Many manufacturers feel that outside suppliers can produce parts and intermediate goods more cheaply than they can do themselves in house. But tying yourself to a supplier can create problems as well. Often it is not easy to switch quickly to different supplier, for example if parts need to be produced to the buyer's specifications. This means that a supplier, once establishing a relationship with a buyer, can raise its price, giving the buyer few options other than to pay the higher price in the short run. Of course, the buyer may terminate the relationship and look for another supplier for the coming year. Explain how the buyer may be able to induce the supplier not to "cheat" on the contract by offering a premium above the competitive price. Derive how large this premium has to be.

3

14.03
Applied Intermediate Microeconomics
Final Examination
Answer Key

Part I: Short Answer Questions

1. **True.** Hicksian demand reflects just the negative substitution effect while Marshallian demand reflects both the substitution and income effects, both of which are negative. Marshallian demand will therefore be more negatively sloped (flatter).

2. **False.** As the interest rate rises a saver will want to substitute away from first period consumption. But the saver is also richer (positive income effect) if savings is a normal good. We can't say whether current consumption will go up or down, and therefore we can't say what happens to savings either.

3. **True.** That's basically the definition of risk aversion.

4. **True.** Let $C = C(q, w, v) = wL + vK$ be the cost function. Increase q by a factor λ. This yields

$$C(\lambda q, w, v) = w\lambda L + v\lambda K$$

because constant returns to scale implies that you need to increase each factor input by λ to increase q by λ. This yields

$$C(\lambda q, w, v) = \lambda(wL + vK) = \lambda C(q, w, v)$$

which means C is linear in q; if C is linear then marginal and average cost are constant.

5. **False.** This is only true if all consumers are the same. If there are two types of consumers then the monopolist will want to set the entry fee according to the consumer surplus of the smaller consumer but raise the per-unit price above marginal cost to extract more surplus from the larger consumers.

6. **False.** If both average and marginal costs are U-shaped, then marginal cost cuts average cost from below at the minimum. Thus, average cost will be both decreasing and increasing over some range where marginal cost is increasing.

7. **False.** The adverse selection problem is worst if individuals buy insurance themselves. Once insurance is sold to groups formed for other reasons (like employment) the adverse selection problem will be less severe, and it will be less severe the larger the groups.

8. **False.** The monopolist will also reduce output, therefore profits will decrease by less than $10 million.

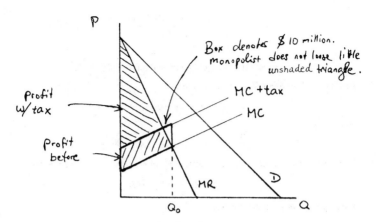

Box denotes $10 million.
monopolist does not loose little
unshaded triangle.

MC + tax

MC

profit w/ tax

Profit before

MR

D

Q_o

Part II

9. American Widgetmakers

(a) In this case demand is just $P = 140 - Q$ so that

$$\pi_1 = (140 - q_1)q_1 - 20q_1$$

The first order condition is

$$\frac{\partial \pi_1}{\partial q_1} = 140 - q_1 - q_1 - 20 = 0$$

which yields

$$120 = 2q_1 \Longleftrightarrow q_1 = 60$$
$$P = 140 - 60 = 80$$
$$\pi_1 = (P - MC)q_1 = (80 - 20)60 = 60^2 = 3600$$

(b) Now

$$\pi_1 = (140 + A - q_1)q_1 - 20q_1 - A^2$$

The first order conditions are

$$\frac{\partial \pi_1}{\partial q_1} = 140 + A - 2q_1 - 20 = 0$$

$$\frac{\partial \pi_1}{\partial A} = q_1 - 2A = 0$$

Substitute the first order condition for A into the first order condition for q_1 to get

$$120 + \frac{q_1}{2} - 2q_1 = 0$$

2

or
$$q_1 = 80$$
$$A = 40$$
$$P = 140 + 40 - 80 = 100$$
$$\pi_1 = (100 - 20)80 - 40^2 = 6400 - 1600 = 4800$$

(c) Profits for American Widgetmakers are
$$\pi_1 = (140 + A - q_1 - q_2)q_1 - 20q_1 - A^2$$

which yields
$$\frac{\partial \pi_1}{\partial q_1} = 140 + A - 2q_1 - q_2 - 20 = 0$$

The first order condition for A is still the same and substituting yields
$$120 + \frac{q_1}{2} = 2q_1 + q_2$$

which gives the reaction function
$$240 = 3q_1 + 2q_2$$

Profits for TWIX are
$$\pi_2 = (140 + A - q_1 - q_2)q_2 - 50q_1$$

The first order condition is
$$\frac{\partial \pi_2}{\partial q_2} = 140 + A - 2q_2 - q_1 - 50 = 0$$

Substituting in for A yields
$$90 + \frac{q_1}{2} = 2q_2 + q_1$$
$$180 = 4q_2 + q_1$$

Subtract this from twice the reaction function for American Widgetmakers to get
$$480 - 180 = 6q_1 - q_1 + 4q_2 - 4q_2$$
$$300 = 5q_1$$
$$q_1 = 60$$

Use either reaction function to find
$$q_2 = 30$$

and remember that
$$A = \frac{q_1}{2}$$

This gives
$$P = 140 + A - q_1 - q_2 = 140 + 30 - 60 - 30 = 80$$
$$\pi_1 = (80 - 20)60 - 30^2 = 3600 - 900 = 2700$$
$$\pi_2 = (80 - 50)30 = 900$$

3

(d) American Widgetmakers advertises less when there is competition because advertising shifts out market demand but American Widgetmaker can only capture part of the additional demand (part goes to the competitor). On the other hand, American Widgetmakers still pays for all the advertising. Marginal benefit of advertising has decreased while marginal cost has stayed constant, therefore American Widgetmakers does less advertising.

(e) You have calculated all the entries necessary to construct a payoff matrix for this game except the case where American Widgetmakers does no advertising and TWIX enters (if TWIX stays out it will make zero profits). Also notice that the addition of fixed costs only changes the level of profits TWIX earns but not the quantities or prices calculated above. For the remaining Cournot case the reaction functions are

$$120 = 2q_1 + q_2$$

and

$$90 = q_1 + 2q_2$$

They yield

$$q_1 = 50$$
$$q_2 = 20$$
$$P = 140 - 50 - 20 = 70$$
$$\pi_1 = (70 - 20)50 = 2500$$
$$\pi_2 = (70 - 50)20 = 400 - 800 = -400$$

Profits for TWIX when it enters and American Widgetmakers advertises were 900 from (c) minus the fixed costs of 800 leaving 100. The payoff matrix is

	TWIX	
	enter	stay out
advertise	2700,100	4800,0
don't advertise	2500,-400	3600,0

American Widgetmakers

Advertising is a dominant strategy for American Widgetmakers. When American Widgetmakers advertises TWIX will want to enter because it can make positive profits.

Part III:

10. The subsidy lowers the price of day care P_D to $P_D - s$. To parents this is just a regular price change. If they put their child in day care for D_A days originally and consumed at point A they will move to point B now and put the child in day care for D_B days. This costs the government $s \cdot D_A$. If they give this amount to parents in a lump sum subsidy the budget constraint moves right from its original position so that it also goes through point B but remains parallel to the original constraint. I.e. parents will just be able to buy the bundle at B with the lump sum subsidy as well. But this budget constraint has to intersect the indifference curve through B so parents can reach a

4

higher utility level at point C. Therefore parents prefer the lump sum subsidy. Point C necessarily involves less day care than point B. Therefore day care providers prefer the subsidy because it lets them sell more day care.

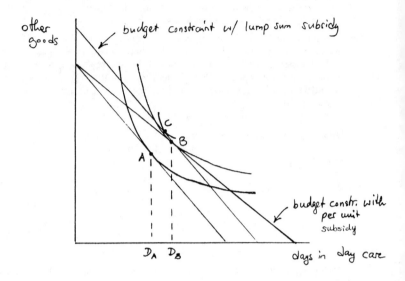

11. Assume that there are two levels of quality, high and low. They can be made at constant marginal and average cost c_h and c_l, repectively. Assume competitive firms offer both quality levels in the market and there are some consumers willing to buy the low quality good at price c_l and others who are willing to buy the high quality good at price c_h. If firms offered the two qualities at their marginal cost they would make no profit. A firm could make a profit by offering the low quality good at price c_h. But consumers will realize that firms have an incentive to do so, thus they will not buy any goods at a price above c_l (at which price they just expect the lowest quality). Now assume that manufacturers can offer warranties. A warranty guarantees replacement of the product if it breaks within a year. For simplicity, assume that high quality products never break while low quality product break with probability p. Thus, the costs of making the goods including the replacement costs for defectives are $(1 + p)c_l$ for the low quality and c_h for the high quality, where no replacements are ever needed. If $(1 + p)c_l > c_h$ only high quality producers have an incentive to offer warranties and charge a price of c_h. Low quality producers would have to offer warranties too if they wanted to conceal their low quality. But they can't get a price above c_h, so this is not worthwhile. Warranties act as a signal. The condition $(1 + p)c_l > c_h$ needed for a

5

separating equilibrium in the signalling case just says that the costs of sending the signal are so much higher for the low quality producers than for the high quality producers that separation is possible. If this condition is satisfied and the government required all firms to offer warranties the low quality producers would leave the market. This is not a good idea because there are consumers who would like to buy the low quality product at the cheaper price. These consumers will be worse off when warranties are required.

12. This is called a hold-up problem. The buyer makes an investment in an asset that is specific to the contract, e.g. instructing the supplier about the specifications needed for the part. Once the investment is made, this creates some rents. The suppliers can "hold-up" the buyer for these rents. The solution to this by offering a price premium is similar to the idea of price premia for high quality products which you analyzed in problem set 6, question 5. Suppose buyers have to make arrangement with suppliers one year in advance. The rents generated from the arrangement during year are R. Suppose the market for the part is otherwise competitive, i.e. other firms are willing to supply it at a price P. For simplicity assume the buyer only buys one part during the year. The maximum price the supplier can therefore charge is $P + R$. If it charged anything higher, the buyer would just shut down operations for a year. Suppose the buyer offers a price $P' > P$. If the supplier sells at this price the buyer will continue the relationship. The present value of profits for the supplier is therefore

$$PV(honest) = \sum_{i=0}^{\infty} \frac{P' - P}{(1+r)^i} = \frac{1+r}{r} (P' - P)$$

If the supplier cheats and asks for $P + R$ the buyer will pay the higher price for a year but discontinue the contract afterwards. The supplier is now scarred, and no one else will want to purchase from this firm any more. It therefore makes a profit of R once. Thus

$$PV(cheat) = R$$

In order to make it in the suppliers interest to behave honestly we have to have

$$PV(honest) > PV(cheat)$$

$$\frac{1+r}{r} (P' - P) > R$$

$$P' - P > \frac{r}{1+r} R$$

$P' - P$ is the value of the price premium. It has to be larger than the implied interest from cheating and getting the rent R once. The buyer has an interest to pay this premium and have an honest supplier rather than having to find a new supplier every year since this involves new spending on instructing the supplier about the correct specification for the part.

6

14.03
Applied Intermediate Microeconomics
Problem Set 1
Due Date: Tuesday, September 20, 1994

1. Consider the market for apartments in Cambridge. Assume that all apartments are alike, in equally desirable locations etc. Suppose there are 10,000 people in the Cambridge area who are willing to pay up to $1,200 rent for such a standard apartment, another 10,000 who are willing to pay up to $1,000 and a further 10,000 who are only willing to pay up to $800. In the short-run the number of apartments is determined by the existing housing stock and therefore fixed.

   (a) Draw the demand curve for the market for apartments in Cambridge. Draw the supply curve if the total number of apartments is 15,000. What is the equilibrium price? What is the equilibrium price if the total supply of apartments is 20,000? What if it is 20,001?

   (b) Does the market demand curve you constructed in (a) slope down? Why?

   (c) Discuss your results in (a): Which renter(s) determine the equilibrium price? What role do the preferences of other potential renters play? In your discussion, think about the following scenario: what changes if the first set of potential renters was willing to pay up to $1,600? What if they were willing to pay only $900?

2. After the unification with the west, East German consumers indicated when asked on a survey that they preferred Mercedes cars to Volkswagens. Yet, sales of Volkswagens in the east were far higher than sales of Mercedes. Use the model of consumer choice to explain this phenomenon.

3. Explain why two indifference curves cannot intersect. Which assumption of the model of consumer choice would be violated if they did?

4. There are two ways of keeping in touch with your friends across the country, letters and phone calls (well, I guess your friends don't have e-mail). Suppose a 3-minute phone call costs $1.50 and a letter costs 30 cents. You have $60 to allocate between phone calls and letters. Now suppose the phone company institutes a new calling option where you pay a lump sum of $30 and you get $60 worth of phone calls (an callers are free to purchase many of those $30 bundles of calls). Under the new plan you can either pay per call or use the option of paying a lump sum for your calls.

   (a) Draw your budget constraint under the old and under the new plan.

   (b) Draw the indifference curves for the following individuals:

      1. a deaf-mute who considers phone calls worthless and only writes letters under the old and under the new plan

1

2. an individual who makes the same number of (non zero) phone calls and writes the same number of letters under the old and under the new plan.

5. Beth is an MIT student. She has one more week (168 hours) to go before the due date of her 1.00 project and a 14.03 quiz. She can spend this time either on preparing the 1.00 project or on studying economics. (This question is making the simplifying assumption that MIT students do nothing else than work for their courses). Both the project and the quiz are worth 100 points and Beth's goal is to maximize the total points received in both courses. She figures that a good approximation for her productivity on the computer project is given by

$$P_c = 30 + 5\sqrt{h_c}$$

where P_c are points earned on the project by spending h_c hours on it. Similarly, for hours spent studying economics

$$P_e = 20 + 15 \ln h_e$$

(a) How should Beth allocate her hours?

(b) What are the implicit "prices" in this problem?

6. Suppose Max's utility function over two goods x and y has the form

$$U(x, y) = x^a y^b$$

(a) What is the formula for the indifference curve at $U = 10$ if $a = 2$ and $b = 1$. Prove that this indifference curve is downward sloping. Is it convex?

(b) Write down the total differential for U.

(c) Calculate dy/dx for $dU = 0$; i.e. derive the marginal rate of substitution (slope of the indifference curve) at an arbitrary point (x, y).

(d) Now consider the transformation of Max's utility function given by

$$V(x, y) = \ln U(x, y)$$

Show that the marginal rate of substitution is the same as in (c).

(e) Suppose the price of x is p_x, the price of y is p_y, and the Max has income I. Derive Max's demand functions for x and y.

(f) For the good y, derive the own-price elasticity, the cross-price elasticity (i.e. the elasticity of demand with respect to p_x), and the income elasticity. Is the demand function downward sloping? Is y a normal good?

(g) Suppose instead of maximizing utility, Max tries to minimize his expenditure necessary to achieve utility level U^*. Set up the optimization problem and solve it. In what sense does your result differ from (e), in what sense is it similar?

2

14.03
Applied Intermediate Microeconomics
Problem Set 2
Due Tuesday, October 4, 1994

1. House prices fell dramatically in many regions of the US in the late 1980s. Analyze the effect of this change in house prices on the consumption of housing and other goods by various groups of consumers: renters, owner-occupants, and landlords. Assume that both housing and other goods are normal. Assume that the change in house prices will be reflected in rents as well.

   (a) Draw the budget constraint before and after the change in house prices for renters. Assume that it is impossible to move quickly, so that renters can only adjust their consumption of other goods in the short run but they can't adjust their consumption of housing. What will happen to their consumption of other goods? Are they better or worse off? What will happen to consumption of housing and other goods in the long run when people can move to different apartments?

   (b) Draw the budget constraint before and after the change in house prices for home owners who live in their own house. What will happen to their consumption in the short run and in the long run? Are they better or worse off?

   (c) Draw the budget constraint before and after the change in house prices for land-lords. Assume that landlords get all their income from renting out housing. What will happen to their consumption in the short run and in the long run? Are they better or worse off?

   (d) Who gained and who lost from the fall in housing prices? Carefully distinguish renters, owner occupants and landlords as well as movers and non-movers.

2. (Problem 9.8 in Nicholson) A farmer believes there is a 50-50 chance that the next growing season will be abnormally rainy. His expected utility function has the form

$$0.5 \ln Y_{NR} + 0.5 \ln Y_R$$

where Y_{NR} and Y_R represent the farmer's income in the states of "normal rain" and "rainy". Suppose the farmer must choose between two corps that promise the following payoffs

Crop	Y_{NR}	Y_R
Wheat	\$28,000	\$10,000
Corn	\$19,000	\$15,000

   (a) Which crops will he plant if he can only plant one crop on his whole field?

   (b) Suppose the farmer can choose to plant half his field with each crop. Would he choose to do so? Explain your result.

   (c) What mix of wheat and corn would provide maximum expected utility to this farmer?

   (d) Would wheat crop insurance, available only to farmers who grow only wheat, which costs \$4,000 and pays off \$8,000 in the event of a rainy growing season, cause this farmer to change what he plants under (a)-(c)?

Prof. Steve Pischke
Fall 1994

14.03
Applied Intermediate Microeconomics
Problem Set 3
Due Tuesday, October 25, 1994

1. Many airlines offer frequent flyer programs to their customers. Members of these programs receive free flights after using the airline for a minimum number of miles (typically 20,000 to 25,000). The free flight awards are typically subject to blackout dates (i.e. the award flights cannot be taken around Thanksgiving or Christmas) and capacity restrictions (i.e. only a certain number of seats are available for awards per flight). Many airlines offer additional bonuses like first class check-in and free upgrades to business or first class when seats are available to travelers who fly 25,000 miles or more with the airline in a calendar year.

   Why are airlines giving away tickets for free? What are the costs to the airlines of running these programs? What are the benefits to the airlines? What type of travelers do you think the airlines are targeting most (occasional flyers, who fly once a year; moderate travelers flying 20,000 miles a year; or frequent travelers flying more than 100,000 miles a year)?

2. John's lawn mowing service is a small business that acts as price taker. The prevailing market price is \$10 per acre. John's costs are described by the cost function

$$C(q) = 0.125q^2 + 5q + 10$$

   where q is the number of acres that John mows in a week.

   (a) How many acres does John mow and what is his weekly profit?

   (b) John's greedy father decides to charge John for the use of the family lawn mower. He considers four different schemes of charging John for the mower: a flat charge of \$20 per week, a charge equal to 50% of John's profits, a charge of \$1 per acre mowed, a charge of 10% of John's revenues. For each scheme, calculate how many acres John mows, his weekly profits and the amount John's father collects. Which charges result in the same outcome and why? Which scheme would John prefer? Which his father if he wanted to collect as much as possible from his son?

   (c) In order to break the hold of John's greedy father over the struggling son, the government is thinking of instituting an income subsidy plan for the poor lad. Two plans are under consideration: a flat grant of \$40 and a grant of \$2 per acre. Which of these plans will John prefer? Does it depend on how his father charges him for the lawn mower? Which plan is more costly to the government?

3. At the end of August, a manufacturer receives an order from a retailer for q^* widgets that the firm must deliver by November 1. Let $C = C(q)$ be total monthly cost of producing q units in that month, $C'(q) > 0$ and $C''(q) > 0$. Let h be the inventory cost of storing one widget for a month. The firm has no other orders to fill during this period.

1

(a) How will the firm decide how many units to produce in September and how many to produce in October? Derive the result both algebraically and graphically. Explain why it is not efficient to produce half the order in September and half the order in October.

(b) Derive the comparative statics result for the changes in the production amounts in September and October as the inventory cost h increases. Again, derive your result both algebraically and graphically.

4. A few years out of MIT you are running a small company. In July, you signed a contract to deliver q^* units by the end of December of the following year at price P''. Your production capacity is backed up till the end of the year and the new order will use all of your capacity for next year. Your cost function is

$$C(q) = F + aq$$

where your short run marginal cost a depends mostly on materials prices. Your company must pay a local franchise tax of T dollars per year if you receive any revenues. If you don't receive any revenues the tax may be waived.

A few months after signing the contract the price of your raw materials increases thus raising your marginal cost to $b > a$. You also notice that $b > P''$. Your contract does not include an inflation clause that lets you raise your selling price. Your attorney advises you that by not fulfilling your contract you will be liable for any excess the customer has to pay above P'' for buying the good elsewhere. You know that without extensive effort at searching for the best price this means that the customer would be paying a price P' which is well above P''.

In December of this year another customer approaches you with an order of q^* units to be delivered a year hence. This new customer is willing to pay P^*, where $P' > P^* > b$. Your capacity only allows you to fulfill one of the contracts but not both.

(a) If you decide not to fulfill the old contract, under what conditions do you decide to take the new contract?

(b) What should you do to minimize your losses for the year, fulfill the old contract, take the new contract or shut down for the year? How do the values of F, T, and b affect your choice?

5. The market for caviar is dependent on the weather. If the weather is good and many fancy parties take place the price is $30 per pound. If the weather is bad the price is only $20 per pound. Caviar produced in one week will not keep till the next. Sturgeon General, Inc., a small caviar producer has the following cost function

$$C(q) = 0.5q^2 + 5q + 100$$

where q is weekly caviar production. Production decisions have to be made before the weather (and therefore the price) is known. Good and bad weather both occur with probability 0.5.

2

(a) How much caviar should Sturgeon General produce if it wishes to maximize expected profits? What are expected profits going to be? How much caviar would the firm produce if the price was $25, the average price, for sure instead. Would the firm prefer the average certain price?

(b) Suppose the owner of the firm has a utility function of the form

$$U = \sqrt{\pi}$$

where π is weekly profits. How much caviar should the firm produce to maximize expected utility? What is expected utility going to be? How much caviar would the firm produce if the price was $25 for sure. Would the owner prefer the average certain price?

(c) Suppose that high quality weather forecasts become available for free. The forecast predicts weather for the week accurately and is available before production decisions have to be made. How much caviar should Sturgeon General produce if it wishes to maximize expected profits? What are expected profits going to be? Would the firm prefer the average certain price now? How much caviar would the firm produce now if it maximized expected utility of the owner? What is expected utility going to be? Would the firm prefer the average certain price in this case?

(d) Explain the different results you have obtained in (a)-(c).

3

14.03
Applied Intermediate Microeconomics
Problem Set 4
Due Tuesday, November 8, 1994

1. Some critics contend that US automobile producers pursue a strategy of planned obsolescence: that is they produce cars that are intended to become obsolete in a few years. Would that strategy make sense in a monopoly market? How might the production of obsolescence depend on market demand? How would oligopolistic competition affect the profitability of the strategy?

2. Many video stores offer two alternative plans for renting movies:

   • A two-part tariff: You pay an annual membership fee (say $20), and then you pay a low price per rental of each film (say $2)

   • A straight rental fee: You pay no membership fee but a higher price per rental (say $4).

   What is the logic behind the two-part tariff in this case? Why offer the customer a choice of two plans rather than a simple two-part tariff?

3. (Nicholson, problem 20.2) A monopolist can produce at constant average (and marginal) costs of $AC = MC = 5$. The firm faces a market demand curve given by

$$Q = 53 - P$$

   (a) Calculate the profit-maximizing price-quantity combination for this monopolist. Also calculate the monopolist's profits.

   (b) Suppose that a second firm enters the market. Let q_1 be the output of firm 1 and q_2 the output of firm 2. Market demand is now give by

$$q_1 + q_2 = 53 - P$$

   Assuming that firm 2 has the same costs as firm 1 calculate the profits of firms 1 and 2 as functions of q_1 and q_2.

   (c) Suppose (after Cournot) that each of these two firms chooses its level of output so as to maximize profits on the assumption that the other's output is fixed. Calculate each firm's reaction function, which expresses desired output of one firm as a function of the other's output.

   (d) On the assumptions in part (c), what is the only level for q_1 and q_2 with which both firms will be satisfied (what q_1, q_2 combination satisfies both reaction curves)?

   (e) With q_1 and q_2 at the equilibrium level found in part (d), what will be the market price, the profits of each firm, and the total profits earned?

1

(f) Suppose now that there are n identical firms in the industry. If each firm adopts the Cournot strategy towards all its rivals, what will be the profit-maximizing level of output for each firm? What will be the market price? What will be the profits earned by each firm and the total profits earned in the industry? (All these will depend on n.)

(g) Show that when n approaches infinity, total industry output, market price, and industry profits approach those that would prevail in perfect competition.

4. Suppose a firm facing a downward sloping demand curve for its product can shift that demand curve outward by undertaking an advertising campaign that involves a certain level of fixed costs (that is, the level of advertising does not depend on the amount produced). Show that if the firm is a monopoly this advertising campaign will definitely increase the amount the monopoly chooses to produce.

5. You are an executive for Super Computer, Inc. (SC), which rents out super computing time. SC receives a fixed rental payment in exchange for the right to unlimited computing at rate of P dollars per hour. SC has two types of potential customers of equal number, 10 businesses and 10 academic institutions. Business customers each have a demand function

$$Q = 50 - P$$

where Q is hours of processing time per month and academic institutions each have a demand function

$$Q = 40 - P$$

The marginal cost to SC of additional computing is 2 dollars per hour, no matter what the volume.

(a) Suppose you can separate business and academic customers. What rental fee and usage fee would you charge to each group? What are your profits?

(b) Suppose you are unable to separate the two groups of customers and you charged a zero rental fee. What usage fee maximizes your profits? What are your profits?

(c) Again suppose you are unable to separate the two groups of customers but you now set a two-part tariff. That is you set one rental fee and one usage fee paid by both types of customers. What usage and rental fee will you set? What are your profits? (Hint: Write down profits as we did in class and notice that the idea of the two part-tariff is to extract all the consumer surplus from the smaller group of consumers. That implicitly leaves only the usage fee as decision variable.)

6. Analyze the world oil market and the behavior of the OPEC cartel using the price leadership model. World demand for oil in millions of barrels is given by

$$W = 160 - P$$

and noncartel (competitive) supply is

$$S = -80 + 2P$$

OPEC's marginal production cost is 20.

2

(a) Write down an expression for the demand function D which the OPEC cartel faces.

(b) Sketch the world demand curve W, competitive supply S, OPEC's net demand D, and OPEC's marginal revenue curve. Indicate OPEC's production, OPEC's optimal price, and non-OPEC production in the diagram.

(c) Suppose non-OPEC oil resources start running out thus making non-OPEC supply more expensive. Assume this involves only a shift in the intercept of the non-cartel supply curve. Indicate on a new diagram how the various curves will shift. How does OPEC's optimal price change? What happens to quantities?

3

Prof. Steve Pischke
Fall 1994

14.03
Applied Intermediate Microeconomics
Problem Set 5
Due Tuesday, November 22, 1994

1. Consider the following "Peanuts" episode:

[*Editor's Note: Because of copyright issues, we at Eno River Press are unable to reprint the "Peanuts" cartoon which originally appeared in the problem set. We have, however, provided below a comprehensive account of the sequence of events depicted in the censored comic.*]

The cartoon begins with Lucy kneeling on a field, holding a football in position for an impending kick. "Charlie Brown," she cajoles, "I'll hold the ball and you come running up and kick it."

Charlie Brown eyes Lucy warily. Her history of duplicity, reflects Brown, suggests that any dealings with her should be approached with circumspection. "Nope," he states flatly. "I refuse! You'll pull the ball away at the last minute and I'll come crashing down and kill myself!"

"But you can't back out now...the programs have already been printed," Lucy counters, thrusting a flyer into Brown's cartooned paw.

Brown reads, "At one o'clock Lucille Van Pelt will hold the football and Charles Brown will run up and kick it."

This appeal to the pragmatist Brown is impossible to resist. "She's right," he muses, "If the programs have already been printed, I can't back out now."

Brown takes a running start. Aflame with enthusiasm, he yells, "This year I'm gonna kick this ball clear out of the universe!"

Predictably, Lucy removes the ball at the moment of truth, and Brown smacks the ground with a WHAM! Lucy approaches the prostrate line drawing. "In every program, Charlie Brown, " she gloats, "There are always a few last minute changes."

 (a) Draw a game tree to depict the interaction of Lucy and Charlie.

 (b) Does Charlie have a dominant strategy? Does Lucy? What is the Nash equilibrium of this game?

2. Colonel Blotto and Count Baloney are facing each other in a war. Colonel Blotto has four companies available that he can distribute among two locations in three different

1

ways: (1,3), (2,2), and (3,1). Count Baloney has only three companies and can distribute them among the same two locations in two different ways: (2,1) and (1,2). If both commanders send an equal number of companies to a location there is a standoff and each of them obtains a payoff of zero. If $m > n$ companies meet at a location the commander sending more companies wins and receives a payoff of n, while the loosing commander gets $-n$. Each player's total payoff is determined by the sum of the payoffs at the two locations.

(a) Assume both commanders have to send out their companies simultaneously. Draw the payoff matrix of this game. Explain why there is no Nash equilibrium in pure strategies in this game. Determine a mixed-strategy Nash equilibrium (this can be easily done by looking at the payoff matrix, no fancy math is needed).

(b) Colonel Blotto obtains permission from his general to concentrate all his armies in one location (i.e. the additional strategies (4,0) and (0,4) are now allowed).

    1. If Baloney is unaware of this change in the game and continues to play his equilibrium strategy from (a), does Blotto benefit from his additional options?

    2. Now suppose that Blotto finds out about the additional strategies. Show that there are still no Nash equilibria in pure strategies in the new game and determine a mixed-strategy Nash equilibrium. Does Blotto benefit in this new equilibrium from his additional choices?

(c) (Back to the original set of strategies.) Suppose that Count Baloney can delay dispatching his companies until he obtains information through his scouts about the location of Blotto's companies. Draw the game tree for this new game. If Blotto knows about the scouts, what is the unique subgame perfect equilibrium? Does Blotto loose from the enemy's knowledge of his location? How would this change if Blotto had the (4,0) and (0,4) strategies available?

3. Amy and Bert are given a cake by their parents which they have to split between themselves. If they can't agree how to split the cake it will be taken away from them again. Each of them likes to get as large a piece of the cake as possible. Suppose they use the following bargaining mechanism: Amy offers a particular split of the cake; then Bert decides whether to accept this split or whether to decline, in which case the whole cake goes back to the parents.

(a) What is the only subgame perfect division of the cake?

(b) How does the equilibrium change if there is an additional stage to the game as follows: first, Bert starts by offering a split and Amy can either accept or make a counteroffer. Now Bert can either accept or decline, in which case the cake is lost.

4. Two prisoners are playing the classical one-shot prisoner's dilemma game.

(a) Suppose the prisoners find a way to communicate between their prison cells by knocking on the walls using morse code. How would this change the outcome of the game?

(b) Suppose the prisoners will be able to retaliate after their prison term is over if only one of them confesses. Which feature of the game would this affect? How would that change the outcome? Could this result in a Pareto efficient outcome (i.e. shorter prison sentences for both)? What condition has to be met for this to be true?

5. Defendo has decided to introduce a revolutionary new video game, and as the first firm in the market, it will have a monopoly position for at least some time. In deciding what manufacturing plant to build, it has the choice of two technologies. Technology A is publicly available and will result in annual costs of:

$$C_A(q) = 10 + 8q$$

Technology B is a proprietary technology developed by Defendo itself. It involves higher fixed costs, but has lower variable costs:

$$C_B(q) = 60 + 2q$$

Defendo's CEO must decide which technology to adopt. Annual market demand for the new product is $P = 20 - Q$, where Q is total industry output.

(a) Suppose that Defendo were certain that it would maintain its monopoly position during the entire product life span. Which technology should it adopt? What would be Defendo's profits given that choice?

(b) Suppose Defendo expects its archrival, Offendo, to consider entering the market shortly after Defendo introduces its new product. Offendo will have only access to technology A. If Offendo enters the market the two firms will compete à la Cournot and arrive at the Cournot-Nash equilibrium.

1. If Defendo adopts technology A and Offendo enters the market, what will be the profits for each firm? Would Offendo choose to enter?

2. If Defendo adopts technology B and Offendo enters the market, what will be the profits for each firm? Would Offendo choose to enter?

3. Which technology should Defendo adopt?

(c) Calculate social welfare (the sum of consumer surplus-the area between the demand function and price-and profits) under monopoly and in the outcome under (b) when Offendo threatens to enter the market. What happens to the equilibrium price? What does this tell us about the effect of *potential* competition?

6. Three contestants, A, B, and C, each have a balloon and a pistol. They fire at each other's balloon in turn. When a balloon is hit its owner is out. When only one balloon remains, its owner is the winner, and receives a $1,000 prize. At the outset, the order in which the players take shots is determined randomly. At their turn, each player can choose any remaining balloon as target. Everyone knows that A is the best shot and always hits the target, B hits the target with probability 0.9, and C hits with probability 0.8. If all players behave rationally, what are their expected winnings? Which player has the highest probability of winning? Explain why.

14.03
Applied Intermediate Microeconomics
Problem Set 6
Due Tuesday, December 6, 1994

1. When Medicare and Medicaid (government medical insurance programs, the first covers all retirees, the second covers all poor mothers) were proposed, the projected cost was based upon medical expenses at that time (that is, when these programs did not exist). After they had been in effect for several years, it was clear that they were far more expensive than expected, even allowing for rising prices due to inflation. Explain why these programs turned out to be much more expensive than expected.

2. (Nicholson, problem 10.4) Blue-eyed people are much more likely to lose their expensive watches than are brown-eyed people. Specifically, there is an 80% chance that a blue-eyed individual will lose a $1,000 watch during a year, but only 20% chance that a brown-eyed person will. Blue-eyed and brown-eyed people are equally represented in the population.

   (a) If an insurance company assumes that blue-eyed and brown-eyed people are equally likely to buy watch loss insurance, what will the actuarially fair insurance premium be?

   (b) If blue-eyed and brown-eyed people have preferences of the form

$$U(W) = \ln(W)$$

   and current wealth $W = \$10,000$ each, which individuals will buy watch insurance at the premium calculated in (a)?

   (c) Given your results from part (b), will the insurance premium be correctly computed? What should the premium be? What will be the utility for each type of person?

   (d) Suppose that an insurance company charged different premia for blue-eyed and brown-eyed people. How would these individuals' utilities compare to those computed in parts (b) and (c)?

3. Many consumers view a well-known brand name as a signal for quality and will pay more for a brand-name product (e.g. Bayer aspirin instead of generic aspirin). Can a brand name provide a useful signal of quality? Why or why not?

4. An insurance company is considering issuing three types of fire insurance policies: (i) complete insurance coverage, (ii) complete coverage above and beyond a $10,000 deductible, and (iii) 90% coverage of all losses. Which policy is more likely to create moral hazard problems? Which policy is least likely to create such problems?

1

5. A competitive industry can produce either a high quality or a low quality product. Average cost functions for both types of products are U-shaped and average costs for high quality products are higher at every level of output than average costs of low quality products. The quality of a product cannot be ascertained by customers before purchasing it. Customers know that the low quality level is the minimum quality they will get in the market. A court will not penalize a seller which delivers a lower quality product than promised. Consumers will always find out about the quality of a product after buying it and will not patronize sellers who deceive them in the future. Consumers are also assumed to understand what the costs of the low and high quality product are. We want to find out what type of equilibria can exist in this market.

(a) Draw the marginal and average cost curves for both product qualities. On your graph denote the price P_h and quantity a firm would sell in the long run (i.e. after entry competes away economic profits) if only high quality products were sold in the market and that was known to everyone. Also denote the price P_l and quantity if only low quality products were sold in the long run.

(b) Assume a firm promises to deliver a high quality product but cheats and delivers the low quality good. Using the appropriate areas in your graph from (a), what is the one period profit for this firm while it deceives customers? What is the PV of profits for this firm?

(c) Compare your result in (b) to the PV of profits for a firm always delivering the high quality product at price P_h. What is the PV of profits for a firm producing the low quality product at price P_l? What will firms do given the profits of these various strategies. What should consumers do if they understand how this market works? What is the outcome in equilibrium?

(d) The problem in (c) is that firms who actually deliver the high quality product will not make enough profits. If consumers understand this, they may be willing to pay a premium above P_h for the high quality product, say P'. Repeat your analysis from (a) and (b) assuming that firms producing a high quality product can receive $P' > P_h$. What is the PV of honestly supplying the high quality product now? What is the PV of cheating (announcing high quality but delivering low quality). What is the PV of supplying low quality honestly? Under what condition will firms prefer to supply the high quality product honestly? (Note that this is very similar to the analysis we have used to ask whether cooperation is possible in the infinitely repeated prisoners' dilemma.)

(e) Discuss informally how consumers' preferences for the high and the low quality good and firm's relative costs of producing the two qualities will determine when an equilibrium exists where firms honestly produce the high quality good.

2

Prof. Steve Pischke
Fall 1994

Applied Intermediate Microeconomics
Practice Exercises on Game Theory
(with Answers)

1. Determine the Nash equilibrium in the following game. Why is it a Nash equilibrium?

		left	right
	up	5,2	3,3
A	down	4,3	2,4

(header: B)

2. Consider the following game:

		left	right
	up	3,3	5,4
A	down	4,5	2,2

(header: B)

(a) What are the pure strategy Nash equilibria of this game? Why?

(b) Suppose this game is changed to a sequential game where A moves first. Draw the appropriate game tree. What are the Nash equilibria of the sequential game? Which of these are subgame perfect equilibria?

(c) What is the maximum amount A might be willing to pay to have the game changed from a simultaneous to a squential game?

3. "Odd man out" is an extension of "matching pennies" for three players. (I guess, these days it would be more politically correct to call this "odd person out.") Each player turns up heads or tails simultaneously. If all three turn up either heads or tails, nobody wins. If two players turn up heads and one tails, then tails pays one dollar to each of the other players. Similarly, if two of them turn up tails and one heads. (The odd man out looses.)

(a) What are the two pure strategy Nash equilibria in this game?

(b) What happens to the structure of the game if the "odd man out" wins and receives one dollar from each of the other two players?

(c) Why does this game have Nash equilibria while matching pennies doesn't?

4. Two players are engaged in an infinitely repeated prisoner's dilemma.

(a) Suppose both players play tit-for-tat. What happens if one of them makes a mistake in one period and fails to cooperate but both players play tit-for-tat again from then on?

(b) Is "never cooperate" a subgame perfect equilibrium strategy for both players?

5. The Wave Energy Technology (WET) company has a monopoly on the production of vibratory waterbeds. Demand for these beds is relatively inelastic; at a price $1,000 per bed, 25,000 beds can be sold, while at a price of $600 per bed, 30,000 will be sold. WET has an existing production plant capable of producing up to 25,000 beds. We will assume that the variable costs of these beds are zero. Suppose a would-be entrant to this industry could always be assured of half the market but would have to invest $10 million in a new plant. The entrant would always sell at the same price as WET.

   (a) Construct the payoff matrix for WET's strategies (P=1,000, P=600) against the entrant's strategies (enter, don't enter). Does this game have a (pure strategy) Nash equilibrium?

   (b) Suppose WET could invest $5 million in building a plant to produce a total of 40,000 beds. Would this be a profitable strategy to deter entry?

   (c) Suppose demand was more elastic so that 40,000 beds would be sold at a price of $600 instead. Would it be profitable for WET to build a new plant now?

6. The following story is told about the invention of Russian Roulette. Two officers in the army of the Czar, call them Alexej and Boris, were competing for the affection of a Muscovite maiden. They agree that they should not press their claims simultaneously. In order to decide who should withdraw from the competition they settle the matter in the following way. In the original story a six-shooter is loaded with one bullet and the barrel is spun. To simplify things we will say it's a four-shooter (a revolver that can hold four bullets). The two officers then alternate in taking turns starting with Alexej. When it is his turn, a player may either chicken out (call this strategy D) or set the revolver to his head and pull the trigger (A). Chickening out and death disqualify a player from further pursuit of the lady. Each player distinguishes three alternative outcomes: love, death, and humiliation. Each of them ranks love (being allowed to woo the lady) highest (say at 1) and death the lowest (say at 0). Humiliation gives intermediate utility of a for Alexej and b for Boris with $0 < a < 1$ and $0 < b < 1$. The two officers maximize their expected utlity.

   (a) Each player moves at most twice. What are the three strategies each player has?

   (b) Construct a payoff matrix for the simultaneous move game in these three strategies using the expected utility values of each potential outcome as entries.

   (c) Which strategy can you eliminate because it is dominated? Explain in words why.

   (d) Suppose $a = 0.2$ and $b = 0.2$. Construct the payoff matrix and find the Nash equilibrium.

   (e) Suppose $a = 0.2$ and $b = 0.8$. Construct the payoff matrix and find the Nash equilibrium.

   (f) Suppose $a = 0.8$ and $b = 0.8$. Construct the payoff matrix and find the Nash equilibrium.

   (g) Compare your results in (d), (e), and (f). How do players' optimal strategies change as they and their opponent become more reckless (i.e. they dislike insult more, reflected in lower values of a and b)? Comment.

1. Consider the game

		B	
		left	right
A	up	5,2	3,3
	down	4,3	2,4

Playing "up" is a dominant strategy for A. Playing "right" is a dominant strategy for B. Since plays of dominant strategies lead to a Nash equilibrium, up/right has to be the only one.

2. Consider the game

		B	
		left	right
A	up	3,3	5,4
	down	4,5	2,2

(a) This game is only slightly harder to solve. Start in some corner, say up/left. Is this an equilibrium? No, A would prefer to play down as a response to B playing left; and B would prefer to play right in response to A playing up. So consider A playing down next. B playing left is a best response now, and we found already that A playing down is a best response to B playing left. So down/left is a Nash equilibrium. We also have to consider the opposite corner, up/right, because there may be other Nash equilibria. Indeed, similar reasoning establishes that up/right is also a Nash equilibrium. The only corner we haven't considered is down/right. This cannot be an equilibrium since we know already that the best responses to the opponent's strategy get us into the down/left or up/right corners, since those were equilibria. (This last sentence just says that there can't be a Nash equilibrium in one corner of the game if the two adjacent corners contain equilibria. But careful, this only works when players aren't indifferent between two outcomes.)

(b) The sequential game has the form:

(a) Nash strategies involve making choices for all possible (and impossible) contingencies, i.e. B has to decide what to do at each of the upper and lower nodes, even for plays that won't happen in equilibrium. Thus, B's strategies are to play left at the top node and left at the bottom node, left at top and right at bottom.

1

right at top and left at bottom, and right at both nodes. A, of course, has just two strategies, up and down. This can be arranged again into a table

		B			
		left, left	left, right	right, left	right, right
A	up	3,3	3,3	5,4	5,4
	down	4,5	2,2	4,5	2,2

The three Nash equilibria are marked by boxes. Notice that there can be no Nash equilibrium involving B's strategy left, right: A's best response would be to play up, but left, right isn't B's best response to up. The only perfect equilibria are the ones involving A playing up and B responding by playing right. In the other Nash equilibrium, B would have an incentive to deviate from it's Nash strategy if A actually played up, rather than down. Left isn't an optimal response in the subgame where A plays up.

(b) The worst equilibrium for A in the simultaneous move game will leave A with a payoff of 4. In the sequential game A will get 5 in (the perfect) equilibrium. Thus A would be willing to pay at most 1 to have the game changed.

3. "Odd man out"

(a) The Nash equilibria are that all players play heads or all players play tails. In this case, everyone gets zero. It is easy to see that no *single* player has an incentive to deviate. If you are the only one changing your strategy, you will be the odd man out and you loose two dollars. It is also easy to see that there are no other Nash equilibria. Any other plays of the game involve one player being the odd man out. This player always has an incentive to deviate and play what the other two are doing as that would raise his payoff from -2 to zero.

(b) If the odd man (the player doing something different from the other two) wins rather than looses the situation will be turned around compared to (a). The six possible plays where one player behaves differently from the other two (these are HTT, THT, TTH, HHT, HTH, THH) are Nash equilibria. The odd man wins and wouldn't want to change his strategy. Each of the others doesn't gain by switching because he still looses (because the roles of heads and tails are also reversed). All players playing tails or heads is not an equilibrium because each player has an incentive to deviate and become the (winning) odd man.

(c) Matching pennies differs from this because there is something special about two players. If your opponent wins in matching pennies, you are all the other players. So by changing your strategy, you can avoid loosing, which is also true if all other players would change their strategies simultaneously in odd man out (but being the *only* one who changes in odd man out doesn't help you). Similarly, in a play where both do the same you can win by switching to a different strategy while in odd man out that doesn't work either. Notice that the crucial step is in going from two to three players. Odd man out can easily be played by a larger (odd) number of people like five or seven without changing the set of Nash equilibria any further.

2

4. Infinitely repeated prisoner's dilemma

(a) The game will enter a cycle where both players alternate between cooperation (C) and deviating (D) but they are not synchronized. One player will always play C while the other plays D. This happens because each player does what the other player did in the last period.

(b) **Yes.** Would either player want to deviate from that strategy? No, because if I am the only player who cooperates this is detrimental to my payoff. I have no chance of moving the play to cooperation because the other player will continue to not to cooperate (the prescribed strategy in the candidate equilibrium).

5. WET

(a) The payoff matrix is

		Competitor	
		enter	stay out
WET	$P = 1000$	12.5,2.5	25,0
	$P = 600$	9,-1	15,0

The entries are constructed as follows: If the competitor doesn't enter then WET sells 25,000 beds for $1,000 each making $25 million or 25,000 beds (the capacity limit) for $600 each making $15 million. (Revenues equal profits here since all fixed costs to WET are sunk and variable costs are zero.) Staying out, the competitor makes zero. If the competitor enters, and WET charges the high price, the market is split. WET gets half of the $25 million while the competitor gets the other half after paying the $10 million fixed cost for the plant. If WET charges the low price, they each sell 15,000 beds at $600 for a revenue of $9 million. Charging the high price is a dominant strategy for WET, and the best response to the high price strategy for the other firm is to enter the market. Thus, total demand is split between the two firms at the high price. Notice that WET would really prefer to charge the low price and have the competitor not enter but that isn't a credible threat (if the competitor enters anyway WET would give in and revert to the high price where they both do better).

(b) We add two new options to WET's strategies

			Competitor	
			enter	stay out
WET	don't invest	$P = 1000$	12.5,2.5	25,0
	don't invest	$P = 600$	9,-1	15,0
	build new plant	$P = 1000$	7.5,2.5	20,0
	build new plant	$P = 600$	4,-1	13,0

The top part of the payoff matrix is still the same. The bottom part has similar entries but WET gets $5 million less because building a new plant is costly. The only exception is the cell where WET builds the plant, charges the low price,

3

and the competitor stays out. Now WET can serve the whole market (sell 30,000 beds) and therefore make revenues of $18 million. So the cell entry is $13 million since we have to subtract the $5 million from that. It is easy to see that this does not change anything. Don't invest and charge $P = 1000$ remains a dominant strategy.

(c) If demand for beds was 40,000 at $600 we would get

			Competitor	
			enter	stay out
	don't invest	$P = 1000$	12.5,2.5	25,0
WET	don't invest	$P = 600$	12,2	15,0
	build new plant	$P = 1000$	7.5,2.5	20,0
	build new plant	$P = 600$	7,2	19,0

There are three changes here in the $P = 600$ rows. If WET doesn't invest and the competitor enters then the total market size is 40,000, so payoffs for both increase. Nothing happens in that row if the competitor stays out because WET is at maximum capacity. If WET builds the new plant and the competitor enters, we again get an increase in payoffs because the market is larger. If the competitor stays out and WET has the new plant it can sell 40,000 beds now at the low price for a revenue of $24 million, leaving $19 million in profits. This still does not help WET. Not building the new plant and charging the high price remains a dominant strategy. In addition, entering is now a dominant strategy for the competitor. We still end up with the same equilibrium.

6. Russian Roulette

(a) A strategy is a combination of actions taken at each turn when a player receives the revolver. The strategies are AA, AD, and DD. Notice that DA is not different from DD because the game ends when one player plays D, so DD just denotes D in the first round.

(b) The payoff matrix is

		Boris		
		DD	AD	AA
Alexej	DD	$a, 1$	$a, 1$	$a, 1$
	AD	$\frac{3}{4}, \frac{1}{4} + \frac{3}{4}b$	$\frac{1}{4} + \frac{1}{2}a, \frac{3}{4}$	$\frac{1}{4} + \frac{1}{2}a, \frac{3}{4}$
	AA	$\frac{3}{4}, \frac{1}{4} + \frac{3}{4}b$	$\frac{1}{2}, \frac{1}{2} + \frac{1}{4}b$	$\frac{1}{2}, \frac{1}{2}$

Finding these payoffs is mostly just tedious cranking through the algebra of what the probabilities are that one of the officers dies along the way. The top row is easy. If A chickens out immediately he get a, while B gets the lady. Turn to the next row and look at the cell AD, DD. A takes a chance by pulling the trigger, he has a 3/4 chance of living and wooing because B will chicken out if A lives. In this case B gets $b3/4$ but there is also a 1/4 probability that A dies, leaving the lady to B. So this one was pretty easy too. The next cell, with plays

4

247

AD, AD is slightly more complicated. Again there is a 1/4 chance that A dies, leaving expected payoffs 0, 1/4. If A wins (which happens with probability 3/4) only two empty slots are left in the revolver so the probability of dying for B when he pulls the trigger is now 1/3. Expected payoffs for the case when B dies, which happens with probability $(3/4) \cdot (1/3) = 1/4$, are 1/4, 0. If B lives (which happens with probability $(3/4) \cdot (2/3) = 1/2$) A will chicken out in the next round to get a. This allows B to woo for 1. The expected values of this outcome are $a/2, 1/2$. Adding up the payoffs from the three possible outcomes in this case we get $(1/4) + (a/2)$, $(1/4) + (1/2)$ or $(1/4) + (a/2)$, 3/4. The next cell in this row will have the same payoff because A chickens out in the second round, so whether B would have responded by chickening out or pulling the trigger doesn't matter any more because the game ends before B's last choice. Finally, you can construct the bottom row analogously.

(c) Boris' strategy AA is dominated by AD. This makes sense. If B gets the revolver after three klicks, no empty slot can be left in the revolver, the bullet must be next. If he plays A, he dies for sure. Given that he values humiliation higher than death, he is better off chickening out at this stage.

(d) Again, it's pretty mindless algebra now. The payoff matrix for $a = b = 0.2$ is

		Boris		
		DD	AD	AA
Alexej	DD	0.2, 1	0.2, 1	0.2, 1
	AD	0.75, 0.4	0.35, 0.75	0.35, 0.75
	AA	0.75, 0.4	0.5, 0.55	0.5, 0.5

It is easy to see that AA is a dominant strategy for A and AD is a dominant strategy for B.

(e) The payoff matrix for $a = 0.2, b = 0.8$ is

		Boris		
		DD	AD	AA
Alexej	DD	0.2, 1	0.2, 1	0.2, 1
	AD	0.75, 0.85	0.35, 0.75	0.35, 0.75
	AA	0.75, 0.85	0.5, 0.7	0.5, 0.5

A still has the dominant strategy AA while B has a new dominant strategy DD.

(f) The payoff matrix for $a = b = 0.8$ is

		Boris		
		DD	AD	AA
Alexej	DD	0.8, 1	0.8, 1	0.8, 1
	AD	0.75, 0.85	0.65, 0.75	0.65, 0.75
	AA	0.75, 0.85	0.5, 0.7	0.5, 0.5

A now has a new dominant strategy DD just like B. Here you have an example of a game where you definitely don't want to move first.

5

(g) The results can be summarized in the following table

	a	b	A's strategy	B's strategy
both reckless	0.2	0.2	AA	AD
A reckless, B cautious	0.2	0.8	AA	DD
both cautious	0.8	0.8	DD	DD

Recall from expected utility theory that a implies that Alexej is indifferent between humiliation on the one hand and getting to pursue his love with probability a and death with probability $1 - a$ on the other hand. A lower a and therefore accepting death with a higher probability in the above tradeoff means more reckless behavior. Reckless players always start by choosing the chance of winning the maid (at the risk of loosing their life) while cautious players are always willing to give up, go to the officers club and, sit there alone. The preferences of the officers clearly matter to the outcome of the game. Also notice that when both players are reckless there is a 3/4 probability that one of them dies while they will both live if they are both cautious.

6

Brown University

Economics 144
Economic Theories of Firms   U

Professor Louis Putterman   Spring, 1994
Robinson Hall 206, x3837
Office Hours: Tues., 12-12:50, Th., 2:40-3:20, and by appointment.

Description: This course examines theories of why firms exist,
        their internal organizations and employment relations,
        questions of ownership and control, efficiency versus conflict
        approaches to understanding firm organization and contractual
        relations, and alternative organizational forms, such as
        employee ownership.

Prerequisites: Economics 111 or 113.

Requirements and Grading: Midterm and final exams. Possibility of
        paper assignment to be determined by Mid-February.

Reading: Much of the assigned reading is contained in the book,
        The Economic Nature of the Firm: A Reader (Cambridge U.
        Press, 1986), edited by the instructor, hereafter referred to
        as Reader.* Copies may be purchased at Brown Bookstore. Other
        readings will be on reserve at Rockefeller Library.

Syllabus

   1.   The nature of firms; intermediate micro "theory of the
         firm" and "micro" views.

         Friedman, "The Methodology of Positive Economics," Essays
         in Positive Economics, 1953.

         Putterman, "The Economic Nature of the Firm: Overview,"
         in Reader, especially pp. 1-19.

   2.   Why are there firms/why is there not just on big firm?

         Coase, "The Nature of the Firm," in Reader.

         Marglin, "What Do Bosses Do?" in Reader.

         Hayek, "The Use of Knowledge in Society," in Reader.

         Williamson, "The Limits of Firms: Incentive and
         Bureaucratic Features," Ch. 6 in The Economic
         Institutions of Capitalism, 1985.

         (Other background reading, which may be skimmed: Marx,
         Goldberg, and Chandler chapters in Reader.)

* Note: a revised edition of this book will appear in 1996.

3. Internal organization: the monitoring problem

    Alchian and Demsetz, "Production, Information Costs, and Economic Organization," in Reader.

    Bowles, "The Production Process in a Competitive Economy: Walrasian, neo-Hobbesian, and Marxian Models," in Reader.

    Shapiro and Stiglitz, "Equilibrium Unemployment as a Worker Discipline Device," *American Economic Review*, 1984.

    Leibenstein, "Allocative Efficiency and X-Efficiency," and "The Prisoners' Dilemma in the Invisible Hand," in Reader.

    Edwards, excerpts from *Contested Terrain*, in Reader.

    Akerlof, "Labor Contracts as Partial Gift Exchange," *Quarterly Journal of Economics*, 1982.

4. Internal organization: job ladders, etc.

    Williamson, Wachter and Harris, "Understanding the Employment Relation: The Analysis of Idiosyncratic Exchange," in Reader.

    Simon, "A Formal Theory of the Employment Relationship," in Reader.

    Freeman, "Individual Mobility and Union Voice in the Labor Market," in Reader.

    Baker, Jensen and Murphy, "Compensation and Incentives: Practice vs. Theory," *Journal of Finance*, 1988.

    (Dumaine)   "Who Needs a Boss?" *Fortune*, May 7, 1990.

5. Quasi-rents and coalitions

    Alchian, "Specificity, Specialization, and Coalitions," *Journal of Institutional & Theoretical Economics*, 1984.

    Nelson and Winter, excerpt from *An Evolutionary Theory of Economic Change* in Reader.

    FitzRoy and Mueller, "Cooperation and Conflict in Contractual Organizations," *Quarterly Review of Economics and Business*, 1984.

6. Asset specificity and governance structures

Klein, Crawford and Alchian, "Vertical Integration, Appropriable Rents, and the Competitive Contracting Process," in Reader.

Williamson, "Transaction-Cost Economics: The Governance of Contractual Relations," *Journal of Law and Economics*, 1979.

7. The managerial agency problem and financial markets

Jensen and Meckling, "Theory of the Firm: Managerial Behavior, Agency Costs, and Ownership Structure," in Reader.

Fama, "Agency Problems and the Theory of the Firm," in Reader.

Manne, "Mergers and the Market for Cooperate Control," in Reader.

Fama and Jensen, "Organizational Forms and Investment Decisions," *Journal of Financial Economics*, 1985.

Jensen, "Eclipse of the Public Corporation," *Harvard Business Review*, Sept.-Oct. 1989.

8. Ownership and control

Williamson, "Corporate Governance," *Yale Law Journal*, 1984.

Fama and Jensen, "Separation of Ownership and Control," *Journal of Law and Economics*, 1983.

Demsetz, "The Structure of Ownership and the Theory of the Firm," *Journal of Law and Economics*, 1983.

Putterman, "Ownership and the Nature of the Firm," *Journal of Comparative Economics*, 1993.

9. Nonprofit firms

Ben-Ner and Hoomissen, "Nonprofit Organizations in the Mixed Economy: A Demand and Supply Analysis," *Annals of Public and Cooperative Economics*, 1991.

10. Socialist firms

Furubotn and Pejovich, "Property Rights and the Behavior of the Firm in a Socialist State: The Example of Yugoslavia," *Zeitschrift für Nationalokonomie* (Journal of Economics), 1982.

Kornai, "The Soft Budget Constraint," *Kyklos*, 1986.

11. Profit-sharing, participation, cooperatives

Each student will read Blinder's introduction (pp. 1-13) and select any two of the five papers in Blinder, ed., Paying for Productivity (see above).

Mitchell, Levin, and Lawler, "Alternative Pay Systems, Firm Performance, and Productivity."

Weitzman and Kruse, "Profit Sharing and Productivity."

Conte and Svejnar, "The Performance Effects of Employee Ownership Plans."

Levine and Tyson, "Participation, Productivity, and the Firm's Environment."

Hashimoto, "Employment and Wage Systems in Japan and Their Implications for Productivity."

Rosner and Putterman, "Factors Behind the Supply and Demand for Less Alienating Work, *Journal of Economic Studies*, 1991.

University of Chicago
Microeconomics
S. Rosen   Economics 303
Spring, 1995   Reading List

I. Background.

G. Stigler The Theory of Price any edition. (read this or any good undergraduate text so you maintain an overview of the material and don't get bogged down in details).

H. Varian, Microeconomic Analysis (standard, modern, dull exposition of demand, production and cost duality. Deaton and Muellbauer is more elegant and interesting, but only covers demand).

M. Friedman, "Methodology of Positive Economics," in Essays on Positive Economics University of Chicago Press, 1966, 1955, (classic paper on logical positivist economic methodology. Some feel it is normative, on how economics should be done).

D. McCloskey, "The Rhetoric of Economics" Journal of Economic Literature 21, (June 1983): 481-517 ("post modernist" approach to method, makes Milton look like Paradise Lost).

II. Introduction. The Gains From Trade.

A. Smith, The Wealth of Nations, Book 1, Ch. 1-6 (specialization and division of labor).

A.A. Young, "Increasing Returns and Economic Progress," Economic J. 1928 (pregnant elaboration of Smith but birth has still not entirely materialized).

R. Coase, "The Nature of the Firm," Economica, 1938 (nonmarket division of labor and Transactions Costs).

F.A. von Hayek, "The Uses of Knowledge in Society," AER, 1945 (evolutionary approach to market and the division of labor: "spontaneous coordination").

G.J. Stigler, "The Division of Labor is Limited by the Extent of the Market," JPE 1951 (classic ind. org. paper on possible empirical content of specialization. Some are still looking).

R. Jones, "The Structure of Simple General Equilibrium Models," JPE 1965 (outstanding exposition of model fundamental for int. trade, pub. finance and much more. The 2x2x2... model. Read only 2x2 part here).

III. Costs and Supply

J. Viner, "Costs Curves and Supply Curves," AEA Readings in Price Theory (classic paper on average and marginal long-run and short-run cost).

E.A.G. Robinson, The Structure of Competitive Industry, (excellent elementary book on the nature of costs--a quick read)

S. Rosen   Economics 303
Spring, 1995   Reading List

A.A. Alchian, "Costs and Outputs," in Abramovitz, The Allocation of Economic Resources, (interesting ideas on short- and long-run costs, capital utilization).

M. Mussa, "External and Internal Adjustment Costs and the Theory of Aggregate and Firm Investment," Economica, 1977 (connection between adjustment costs and rising supply price of investment goods, Q-theory. U. of C. economists must know this).

G. Stigler, "Production and Distribution in the Short Run," AEA Readings in the Theory of Income Distribution (how production and costs might be accommodated to stochastic variation in demand for output).

IV. Selected Topics in the Theory of the Firm

J. Tirole, The Theory of Industrial Organization, pp. 15-62 (outline of modern information-based theory).

J. Robinson, "Rising Supply Price," in AEA Readings in Price Theory (classic statement about why industry supply price must be increasing in general equilibrium).

G. Becker and G. Stigler, "Law Enforcement, Malfeasance and Compensation of Enforcers," Journal of Legal Studies, 1974 (basic solution to agency problem:front money).

R.E. Lucas, "On the Size Distribution of Business Firms," Bell Journal. 1978 (some economics of the extensive margin).

S. Rosen, "Authority, Control and the Distribution of Earnings," Bell Journal. 1982 (assigning heterogeneous workers to hierarchical levels: economic rent).

V. Spatial Economics

G. Becker, "A Theory of the Allocation of Time," Economic Journal 75, (Sept. 1965): 493-517 (classic analysis of the household as a firm)

K. Lancaster, "A New Approach to Consumer Theory," J. Political Economy 1966 (basic spatial model of demand theory with combinable characteristics).

M. Jensen, "Capital Markets: Theory and Evidence," Bell Journal. 1972. Read the first part and the appendix (relationship between CAPM and product "characteristics").

C. Tiebout, "A Pure Theory of Local Government Expenditure," J. Political Economy, 1954 (classical statement of how residential mobility sets up a form of competition for local public goods. Broader implications for competition).

S. Rosen, "Hedonic Prices and Implicit Markets," J. Political Economy, 1974 (market equilibrium theory of noncombinable differentiated goods with competitive firms).

2

S. Rosen   Economics 303
Spring, 1995   Reading List

H. Hotelling, "Stability in Competition," Econ. J., 1929 (there is a famous error in this remarkable paper, but it doesn't really matter whether you find it.)

VI. Social Costs, Property Rights and Prices

F. Knight, "Some Fallacies in the Interpretation of Social Cost," Quarterly J., 1924 (first precise statement of externalities as failure of property right systems. "mathematically perfect," but no math in it)

R. Coase, "The Problem of Social Cost," J. Law and Econ., 1960 (most comprehensive statement of property rights and externalities--The Coase Theorem).

J.E. Meade, "External Economies and Diseconomies in a Competitive Situation," Econ. J. (excellent exposition of Pigouvian tax solutions to externalities).

A. Plant, "Economic Theory Concerning Patents for Inventions," Economica, 1934 (unusual perspective on intellectual property rights, namely that none are needed!).

G. Loury, "Market Structure and Innovation," Quarterly J., 1979 (patent races. Note how Poisson arrivals simplifies the problem).

H.S. Gordon, "The Economic Theory of a Common Property Resource," J. Political Economy, 1954 (common pool resource problems--overfishing, land rushes, rent-seeking).

J.S. Chipman, "External Economies of Scale and Competitive Equilibrium" Quarterly Journal of Economics 84, (August 1970): 347-385. (customary scholarly treatment of an important problem. See also elementary treatment by M. Friedman in his price theory notes).

TECHNOLOGY, INNOVATION, AND ECONOMIC GROWTH

F. M. Scherer
Fall Semester 1994

Suggested paperback purchases (marked P) are Martin Baily
and Alok Chakrabarti, <u>Innovation and the Productivity Crisis</u>
($8.95); Thomas Kuhn, <u>The Structure of Scientific Revolutions</u>
($5.95); and F. M. Scherer, <u>Innovation and Growth</u> ($10.95). All
should be available at the main Coop bookstore. The Course
Materials Distribution Office will provide a collection of
duplicated materials (marked C). Other items (marked R) will be
available on reserve, as will a backup copy of most recommended
purchase materials.

Two-thirds of the seminar grade will be assigned to a term
paper, the written version of which will be due January 16. The
papers will also be summarized orally in class the weeks of
December 5 and 12. Although other topics are possible following
consultation, it is suggested that the term paper be a case study
of how some scientific or technological innovation came into
being. One-third of the grade will be assigned to an in-class
midterm examination the week of November 7.

Readings with an asterisk (*) are of lower priority than
those without.

Week
beginning:

Sept. 19   Technological Change, Productivity Growth, and
              Economic Welfare.

   Baily and Chakrabarti, <u>Innovation and the Productivity
Crisis</u>, Chapters 1 and 2 (P).

   Williamson, "Productivity and American Leadership: A Review
Article," <u>Journal of Economic Literature</u>, March 1991, pp. 51-
68 (C).

   McKinsey Global Institute, <u>Manufacturing Productivity</u>,
Executive Summary (C).

   "Modern Wonders," <u>The Economist</u>, Dec. 25, 1993, pp. 47-51
(C).

   *Mokyr, <u>The Lever of Riches</u>, Chapters 1, 7, and 10 (R).

Sept. 26   Research, Innovation, and Productivity Growth.

   Solow, "Technical Change and the Aggregate Production
Function," <u>Review of Economics and Statistics</u>, August 1957,
pp. 312-320 (C).

   Baily and Chakrabarty, <u>Innovation and the Productivity
Crisis</u>, Chapters 3-6 (P).

Scherer, <u>Innovation and Growth</u>, Chapters 3, 14, 15, and 16 (P).

*Griliches, "Productivity, R&D, and Basic Research at the Firm Level in the 1970s," <u>American Economic Review</u>, March 1986, pp. 141-154 (R).

*Nelson, "U.S. Technological Leadership: Where Did It Come From, Where Did It Go?" in Scherer and Perlman, eds., <u>Entrepreneurship, Technological Innovation, and Economic Growth</u>, pp. 25-50 (R).

Oct. 3   Market Forces, Economic Stimuli, and the Innovative Response.

Nelson, "The Economics of Invention," <u>Journal of Business</u>, April 1959, pp. 101-107 only (C).

Schmookler, "Economic Sources of Inventive Activity," <u>Journal of Economic History</u>, March 1962, pp. 1-20 (C).

Binswanger and Ruttan, <u>Induced Innovation: Technology, Institutions and Development</u>, Chapters 2 and 3 (R).

Arthur, "Positive Feedbacks in the Economy," <u>Scientific American</u>, February 1990, pp. 92-99 (C).

*Rosenberg, <u>Perspectives on Technology</u>, pp. 260-279 and 339-340 (R).

*Mokyr, <u>The Lever of Riches</u>, Chapter 11 (R).

**Grossman and Helpman, "Endogenous Innovation in the Theory of Growth," <u>Journal of Economic Perspectives</u>, Winter 1994, pp. 23-44 (R).

Oct. 10   The Economics of Basic Science.

National Science Board, <u>Science and Engineering Indicators: 1993</u>, Chapter 5 (C).

Paula Stephan article for <u>Journal of Economic Literature</u> (C).

Kuhn, <u>The Structure of Scientific Revolutions</u>, Chapters II, III, VI, and VII; rest optional (P).

National Science Foundation, <u>Technology in Retrospect and Critical Events in Science</u>, Introduction and Parts I and II (C).

Sherwin and Isenson, "Project Hindsight," <u>Science</u>, 23 June 1967, pp. 1571-1577 (C).

*Chapters by Merton (3, 4, and 28) and Shryock (6) in Barber and Hirsch, <u>The Sociology of Science</u>, pp. 33-88, 98-110, and 447-485 (R).

*de Solla Price, <u>Little Science, Big Science</u>, Chapters 2 and 3 (R).

*Hounshell and Smith, <u>Science and Corporate Strategy</u>, Chapter 12 (R).

Oct. 17   Managing and Financing Industrial R&D.

National Science Board, <u>Science and Engineering Indicators: 1993</u>, Chapter 4 (C).

Scherer, <u>Innovation and Growth</u>, Chapters 1, *2, and 4 (P).

Mansfield, <u>Industrial Research and Technological Innovation</u>, Chapter 3 (R).

Roberts, <u>Entrepreneurs in High Technology</u>, Chapters 1, 4, 5, and 9 (R).

Twiss, <u>Managing Technological Innovation</u>, Chapters 5 and 6 (R).

*Nelson, "Uncertainty, Learning, and the Economics of Parallel R&D Efforts," <u>Review of Economics and Statistics</u>, November 1961, pp. 351-364 (R).

*Hounshell and Smith, <u>Science and Corporate Strategy</u>, Chapter 13 (R).

*Mansfield et al., <u>The Production and Application of New Industrial Technology</u>, Chapters 2 and 8 (R).

*Marschak et al., <u>Strategy for R&D</u>, Chapters 2 and 4 (R).

Oct. 24   The Patent System.

Scherer and Ross, <u>Industrial Market Structure and Economic Performance</u>, pp. 621-630 (R).

Scherer, <u>Innovation and Growth</u>, Chapter 7 (P).

Mansfield et al., "Imitation Costs and Patents," <u>Economic Journal</u>, December 1981, pp. 907-918 (C).

Deardorff, "Welfare Effects of Global Patent Protection," <u>Economica</u>, February 1992, pp. 35-51 (C).

*Levin et al., "Appropriating the Returns from Industrial R&D," <u>Brookings Papers on Economic Activity</u>, 1987, no. 3, pp. 783-820 (R).

*Gort and Klepper, "Time Paths in the Diffusion of Product Innovations," <u>Economic Journal</u>, September 1982, pp. 630-653 (R).

*Merges and Nelson, "On Limiting or Encouraging Rivalry in Technical Progress: The Effect of Patent Scope Decisions," manuscript, May 1991 (R).

Oct. 31   Firm Size, Market Structure, and Innovation.

Scherer, "Schumpeter and Plausible Capitalism," <u>Journal of Economic Literature</u>, September 1992, pp. 1416-1433 (reprints).

Scherer, <u>Innovation and Growth</u>, Chapters 5, 6, *8, 11, and 13 (P).

Utterback, <u>Mastering the Dynamics of Innovation</u>, Chapter 2 (R).

*Nelson and Winter, "The Schumpeterian Tradeoff Revisited," <u>American Economic Review</u>, March 1982, pp. 114-132 (R).

*Barzel, "Optimal Timing of Innovations," <u>Review of Economics and Statistics</u>, August 1968, pp. 348-355 (R).

*Geroski, "Innovation, Technological Opportunity, and Market Structure," <u>Oxford Economic Papers</u>, July 1990, pp. 586-602 (R).

Nov. 7   Cooperation in R&D. Noncooperative Midterm
                Examination.

Jorde and Teece, "Innovation and Cooperation: Implications for Competition and Antitrust," <u>Journal of Economic Perspectives</u>, Summer 1990, pp. 75-96 (C).

Martin, "Public Policies Toward Cooperation in Research and Development: the European Union, Japan, the United States," manuscript, April 1994 (C).

Werner and Bremer, "Hard Lessons in Cooperative Research," <u>Issues in Science and Technology</u>, Spring 1991, pp. 44-49 (C).

Hane, "The Real Lessons of Japanese Research Consortia," and "Interview: Sematech's William J. Spencer," <u>Issues in Science and Technology</u>, Winter 1993-94, pp. 56-68 (C).

Nov. 14   Government Science and Technology Policy: I.

Branscomb, "Toward a U.S. Technology Policy," <u>Issues in Science and Technology Policy</u>, Summer 1991, pp. 50-55 (C).

Freeman, <u>Technology Policy and Economic Performance</u>, Chapters 1, 2, pp. 55-64, pp. 79-90, and Chapter 5 (R).

Nelson, <u>National Innovation Systems</u>, Chapters 1, 2 (R).

Hall, "R&D Tax Policy During the Eighties: Success or Failure," NBER Working Paper No. 4240 (C).

Stever, Lederman, and Penzias, "Very Large Science," <u>Issues in Science and Technology</u>, Summer 1985, pp. 47-68 (C).

Sobel, "Longitude?" <u>Harvard Magazine</u>, March-April 1994, pp. 44-52 (C).

*Beltz, "Lessons from the Cutting Edge: The HDTV Experience," <u>Regulation</u>, vol. 16, no. 4 (1994), pp. 29-37 (R).

*Robyn et al., "Bringing Superconductivity to Market," <u>Issues in Science and Technology</u>, Winter 1988-89, pp. 38-45 (R).

*Phillips, Kornberg, and Roberts, "British Science and Technology," <u>Issues in Science and Technology</u>, Winter 1987, pp. 73-90 (R).

*Brown and Daneke, "Photovoltaics: How Japan Won," <u>Issues in Science and Technology</u>, Spring 1987, pp. 69-77 (R).

Nov. 21   Government Science and Technology Policy: II.

Burnett and Scherer, "The Weapons Industry," in Walter Adams, ed., <u>The Structure of American Industry</u>, eighth ed., Chapter 11 (R).

Snow, <u>Science and Government</u> (R).

Sapolsky, <u>The Polaris System Development</u>, Chapters 1, *2, 3, *5, and 8 (R).

Berkowitz, "Can Defense Research Revive U.S. Industry?" <u>Issues in Science and Technology</u>, Winter 1992-93, pp. 73-81 (C).

*Lichtenberg, "The Private R&D Investment Response to Federal Design and Technical Competitions," <u>American Economic Review</u>, June 1988, pp. 550-559 (R).

*DeGrasse, <u>Military Expansion, Economic Decline</u>, pp. 9-52 (R).

*McNaugher, <u>New Weapons, Old Politics</u>, Chapters 1, 2, and 8 (R).

Nov. 28   Technology and Competitiveness.

Scherer, "Competing for Comparative Advantage through Technological Innovation," reprints.

National Science Board, <u>Science and Technology Indicators: 1993</u>, Chapter 6 (C).

"Foreign Passports, U.S. Doctorates," <u>Issues in Science and Technology</u>, Spring 1991, pp. 86-87 (C).

Archibugi and Pianta, "Specialization and Size of Technological Activities in Industrial Countries," in Scherer and Perlman, eds., <u>Entrepreneurship, Technological Innovation, and Economic Growth</u>, pp. 65-85 (R).

Westphal, Kim, and Dahlman, "Reflections on the Republic of Korea's Acquisition of Technological Capability," in Rosenberg and Frischtak, ed., <u>International Technology Transfer: Concepts, Measures, and Comparisons</u>, pp. 167-221 (R).

*Mansfield et al., "Overseas Research and Development by US-based Firms," <u>Economica</u>, May 1979, pp. 187-196 (R).

*Mowery, "Helping Workers Adjust," <u>Issues in Science and Technology</u>, Fall 1987, pp. 22-27 (R).

*de Solla Price, <u>Little Science, Big Science</u>, Chapter 1 (R).

Claremont Graduate School

Economics 317   G

Professor Rodney T. Smith   *Pitzer Hall 208*
1993 Spring Semester   *Extension 2818*

Office Hours

M	3:00 - 4:00
Tu	9:00 - 11:00
by appointment	

Purpose of Course

Improve the ability of students to use formal modelling in micro-economics and provide an introduction to game theory. Emphasis on comparative-statics analysis with applications in demand theory, theory of the firm, and economic organization.

The course is divided into three parts. Part I will explore simple applications and extensions of price theory (4 weeks). Part II will examine Becker's seminal applications of price theory to "non-market" behavior (4 weeks). Part III will introduce non-cooperative game theory and explore economic applications.

Class Meetings

MW 9:00 - 10:15
F (lab section to be organized by Nancy Lumpkin)

The lab section will provide a forum for discussion of problem sets (see below), lectures, and readings.

Course Requirements

Grades will be awarded on the basis of performance on weekly problem sets, term paper, and final examination. The fifteen problem sets will receive a collective weight of 40 percent, the term paper 30 percent, and the final examination 30 percent. Each Monday, I will handout a problem. Students will turn in the problem at the Friday lab section. A hand-out on the term paper will be distributed on Wednesday, March 3.

Required Books

Gary S. Becker, *The Economic Approach to Human Behavior* (University of Chicago Press)

Robert Gibbons, *Game Theory for Applied Economists* (Princeton University Press)

H. Scott Bierman and Luis Fernandez, *Game Theory with Economic Applications* (Addison-Wesley).

Reading List

Please read the material before the indicated date. Copies of all articles can be found on reserve at Honnold Library.

I. Explorations in Micro-Economic Theory

Week 1 -- Introduction to Course and Application of Duality Theory and Envelope Theorem

Monday, January 18   Introduction to course

Wednesday, January 20   Rodney T. Smith, "Water Transfers, Irigation Districts and the Compensation Problem," *Journal of Policy Analysis and Management*, (1989)

Week 2 -- Economics of Product Safety

Monday, January 25   Walter Oi, "The Economics of Product Safety," *Bell Journal of Economics and Management Science* (Spring 1973)

Wednesday, January 27   Richard Posner and William Landes, "A Positive Economic Analysis of Products Liability," *Journal of Legal Studies* (1985)

Week 3 -- The Modern Theory of the Corporation

Monday, February 1   Michael Jensen and William Meckling, "Theory of the Firm: Managerial Behavior, Agency Costs and Ownership Structure," *Journal of Financial Economics* (1976)

Wednesday, February 3   Jensen and Meckling continued.

Week 4 -- The Modern Theory of the Corporation continued

Monday, February 8   Walter Oi, "Hetergeneous Firms and the Organization of Production," *Economic Inquiry* (1983)

Wednesday, February 10   Oi continued.

II. Application of Price Theory to Non-Market Activity

Week 5 -- Economics of Enforcement

Monday, February 15   Gary Becker and George Stigler, "Law Enforcement,
                                             Malfeasance, and Compensation of Enforcers," *Journal
                                             of Legal Studies* (1974).

Wednesday, February 17   Becker, Chapter 4

Week 6 -- Allocation of Time

Monday, February 22   Becker, Chapters 4 and 6

Wednesday, February 24   Becker Chapter 5

Week 7 -- Economics of Marriage

Monday, March 1   Becker, Chapter 11

Wednesday, March 3   Becker, Chapter 11 continued

Week 8 -- Social Interactions

Monday, March 8   Becker, Chapter 12

Wednesday, March 10   Becker, Chapter 12 continued and Chapter 13

Week 9   **Spring Break**

III. Game Theory

Week 10 -- Introduction to Game Theory and Nash Equilibrium

Monday, March 22   Bierman and Fernandez, Chapters 1 - 4

Wednesday, March 24   Bierman and Fernandez, Chapter 5

Week 11 -- Static Games of Complete Information

Monday, March 29   Gibbons, Chapter 1, §1.1 - §1.2

Wednesday, March 31   Bierman and Fernandez, Chapters 11, 13
                                             Gibbons, Chapter 1, §1.3 - §1.4

Week 12 Dynamic Games of Complete Information

Monday, April 5   Bierman and Fernandez, Chapter 6
                                         Gibbons, Chapter 2, §2.1 - §2.2

Wednesday, April 7   Bierman and Fernandez, Chapter 23
                                         Gibbons, Chapter 2, §2.3

Week 13 -- Dynamic Games of Complete Information Continued

Monday, April 12   Bierman and Fernandez, Chapters 24 and 25

Wednesday, April 14   Gibbons, Chapter 2, §2.4 - §2.5

Week 14 -- Static Games of Incomplete Information

Monday, April 19   Bierman and Fernandez, Chapter 17

Wednesday April 21   Gibbons, Chapter 3, §3.1 - §3.2

*Week 15 -- Static Games of Incomplete Information Continued and Dynamic Games of
Incomplete Information*

Monday, April 26   Bierman and Fernandez, Chapters 21, 22
                                         Gibbons, Chapter 3, §3.3 - §3.4

Wednesday, April 28   Gibbons, Chapter 4, §4.1 - §4.2B

Week 16 -- Dynamic Games of Incomplete Information continued

Monday, May 3   Gibbons, Chapter 4, §4.2C - §4.3B

Wednesday, May 5   Gibbons, Chapter 4, §4.3C - §4.4

CLAREMONT GRADUATE SCHOOL

ECO 314   MICROECONOMICS II

WILLIAM STUBBLEBINE

COURSE OUTLINE

I. **COURSE DESCRIPTION.** Extensions of microeconomic theory — consumer theory, firm theory, and markets — to situations involving many periods, and uncertainty. Introductions to general equilibrium, externality, and welfare economics.

II. **REQUIRED TEXTS.**   Nicholson, W. Microeconomic Theory. 5th ed. New York: Dryden, 1992.
    and

    Stigler, G. J. The Theory of Price. 4th ed. New York: Macmillan, 1987.
    and

    Briet, Hochman, and Saueracker. Readings in Microeconomics. St. Louis: Times Mirror/Mosby, 1986.

III. **ADDITIONAL SOURCES.**   Frank, R. H. Microeconomics and Behavior. 2nd ed. New York: McGraw-Hill, 1994.

    Hirshleifer, J. and A. Glazer. Price Theory and Applications. 5th ed. Englewood Cliffs: Prentice Hall, 1992.

    Silberberg, E. The Structure of Economics. 2nd ed. New York: McGraw-Hill, 1990.

    Varian, H. Microeconomic Analysis. 3rd ed. New York: Norton, 1992.

III. **HOURS.** Class: MW 12 (Noon)—1:10 p.m. Location: P5 at CMC.

    Office: MW 10:30—11:30 a.m. and 1:30—2:30 p.m. and by appointment through Ext. 8012.

    Location: Adams Hall 212 at CMC.

IV. **PROBLEM SETS AND SHORT PAPERS.** There will be several problem sets and/or short papers assigned to complement the lectures and text assignments.

V. **TERM PROJECT.** There will be a team term project to be introduced on/about 6 March and due on 3 May (the last day of class).

VI. **EXAMINATIONS.**

    Midterm Examination: On/About 8 March (Introduction through Factor Markets).

    Final Examination: On/About 10 May from Noon-3. (Note: Final Examination is comprehensive.)

VII. **OUTSIDE READINGS.** From time to time, the instructor may assign additional reading and/or practice material. To the extent possible, all such material will be available either through the Reserve Book desk at Honnold Library or through class.

VIII. **GRADING.** The Midterm Examination, the Problem Sets (taken together), and the Term Project each counts as one-fifth — for a total of three-fifths — of the course grade. The Final Examination counts as two-fifths of the course grade.

IX. **LATE PROBLEM SETS AND EXAMINATIONS.** Late Problem Sets will not be accepted and make-up Examinations will not be administered.

X. **REVIEW SESSIONS.** Ms. Chu-Shin Li will be available for assistance.

(Continued)

266

COURSE OUTLINE (Continued)

XI. READINGS. [F: Frank — H: Hirshleifer — N: Nicholson — S: Stigler — V: Varian | B: Briet et al]

Introduction and Review [F:1-2; H:1-2; N:1-2; S:1-2; V:26-27]

Consumer Behavior and Demand [F:3-5⊕7-8; H:3-5; N:3-7; S:3-6; V:7-10]
Rationality [H:1/7-12; N:3/74; S:4/52-56]
All-or-None Demand Curves and Implied Property Rights [S:4/70]
Marginal Evaluation Curves [B:5/Buchanan-Stubblebine(458+/Ref:Hicks)]
Offer curves [N:8/233-237; V:9]
Multiple Constraints [H:5/136-144; N: 23/681-693]
    [B:2/Stigler-Becker(78+)⊕3/Becker(186+)⊕Barzel(218+)]

Firm Behavior and Cost [F:9-10; H:11⊕6; N:11-12⊕14; S:7-10; V:1⊕4-6]
Production [H:11/284-305; N:11; S:8-9]
Cost [H:6; N:12; S:7-8 | Buchanan: Cost and Choice (1969)]

Competitive Industry [F:11; H:7; N:13⊕15; S:5⊕11; V:2-3⊕13 | B:3/McNulty(302+)]
Zero-Profit Theorems (#1, #2, and #3)
Joint Product [Marshall: Principles of Economics Book V:6⊕MathApp:Note 14-21]

Monopoly [F:12; H:8; N:19; S:12; V:14 | B:4/Lerner(313+)]
Natural Monopoly [N:19/559-566]
Regulation [N:19/573-585 | B:4/Demsetz(344+)⊕Briet-Elzinga(351+)]
Multi-market Pricing [H:8/227-233; N:19/566-573; S:4/72-74⊕12/210-215]
Multi-plant Firm [H:6/161-163; B:4/Patinkin(327+)]
Quality [H:9]
Transfer Pricing [B:2/Hirshleifer(139+)]
Monopolistic Competition [H: 8/233+⊕9; N: 20]

Factor Markets [F:15; H:11-12; N:22-23; S:12/215-218/⊕15-19; V:18]
    [B:3/Arrow(232+)⊕Gordon(258+)⊕Spence(289+)]
Profit-Max Conditions under 4 conditions of seller-buyer competition and monopoly
Elasticity of Substitution [N:11/307+; S:15]

Multi-Period
Consumer Theory [H:14; N:24; S:19; V:19]
Producer Theory [F:16; N:24 | B:3/Stigler(176+)]

Uncertainty
Consumer Theory [F:6; N:9⊕10; S:6/103-106; V:11]
    [B:2/Strotz(51+)⊕Thaler(92+)⊕3/Akerlof(276+)⊕Pauly(284+)]
Producer Theory [H:10; N:18⊕21; V:20⊕25]

General Equilibrium [N:16; V:17⊕21]

Efficiency and Pareto Optimality [F:17; H:7/188+⊕13⊕15-16; N:8⊕17⊕26; S:20/320-324; V:22]
    [B:2/Leibenstein(149+)⊕4/McNulty(302+)⊕5/Arrow(377+)⊕Bator(389+)]

Externality, Property Rights, and Public Goods [F:18-19; H:15-16; N:25; S:7/117-122; V:23-24]
    [B:3/Cheung(246+)⊕5/Coase(414+)⊕Samuelson(441+)⊕Buchanan(449+)
        ⊕Buchanan-Stubblebine(458+)⊕Hochman-Rogers(468+)]

END

Economics 11

INTERMEDIATE MICROECONOMICS

Fall Semester, 1994
Larry Westphal

Office hours at Trotter 206:
Tuesdays, 2 - 4 pm; and by appointment.

Purchase Required: You are to purchase a text, workbook, and "reader:"

- text -- Heinz Kohler, Intermediate Microeconomics: Theory and Applications,
  3rd edition;
- workbook -- that which accompanies Kohler's text;
- reader -- William Breit, Harold M. Hochman, and Edward Saueracker, eds.,
  Readings in Microeconomics, 1986; this book is not available in the
  bookstore (arrangements for its purchase will be discussed in the first
  class session).

Purchase Optional: If you are interested in learning the calculus based
foundations of microeconomics, you should think seriously about purchasing --
for use as a supplementary text:

- Binger, Brian R., & Elizabeth Hoffman, Microeconomics with Calculus, 1988.
  Note: three copies of this text are on General Reserve at McCabe; as with
  any item on General Reserve, copies can be obtained at the Circulation Desk.

References (available at library): In addition to the items just listed, you
are strongly encouraged to consult -- as supplementary texts -- other textbooks
which differ in expositional style and/or substantive content and level.
Indeed, it is an excellent(!) idea to read a second text in its entirety, to
help solidify your understanding. If you are not that ambitious, you may
nonetheless on occasion find Kohler opaque and so want to find another, more
communicative (to you, at least) exposition. Some excellent alternatives are
listed below. Unless otherwise indicated, books listed below are shelved
either in the stacks or on honors reserve (consult Tripod).

A. Introductory textbook:

    Unlike the other references listed below, the following is an introductory
    textbook of the encyclopedic, yearlong course variety. Such introductory
    textbooks often provide particularly illuminating introductions to basic
    concepts and are thus likely to prove especially helpful. They are, in a
    very real sense, the intelligent student's first line of defense in seeking
    clarification! For your convenience, the Reading Assignment sheet at the
    end of this syllabus indicates parallel chapters (read appendices also!)
    in this text.

    Baumol, W.J. & A.S. Blinder, Economics: Principals & Policy, 5th ed., 1991.
      Note: several copies of this text are on General Reserve at McCabe.

B. Don't require or use calculus:

1. Supplemental study guide, found useful by past students having difficulty:

    Salvatore, D., 1992 Schaum's Outline of Theory and Problems of Micro-

economic Theory, 3rd ed.
Note: three copies of this text are on General Reserve at McCabe.

2. Somewhat less difficult (hence less coverage) and considerably "wordy-er."

   Mansfield, E., Micro-economics: Theory / Applications, 8th ed., 1994.
   Note: three copies of this text are on General Reserve at McCabe.
   Mansfield, E., Applied Microeconomics, 1st ed., 1994.
   Note: one copy of this text is on General Reserve at McCabe.

3. Quite close in coverage and level to Kohler:

   Maddala, G.S., & E. Miller, Microeconomics: Theory and Applications, 1988.
   Eaton, B. Curtis, & D.F. Eaton, Microeconomics, 1988.

4. Somewhat more difficult; follows the conventional approach:

   Hirshleifer, J., Price Theory and Applications, 1984,88.
   Pindyck, R.S. & D.L. Rubinfeld, Microeconomics, 1989.

5. Somewhat more difficult; approach the material `unconventionally:'

   Varian, H.R., Intermediate Microeconomics: A Modern Approach, 1987,90.
   McCloskey, D.N., The Applied Theory of Price, 2nd ed., 1985.

C. Classic textbooks (none is comparable in coverage to Kohler; but each is well worth looking at or even reading in its entirety):

   Marshall, A., Principles of Economics, 8th ed.
   Scitovsky, T., Welfare and Competition, rev. ed., 1971.
   Stigler, G.J., The Theory of Price, 3rd ed., 1966.

D. Useful calculus refresher:

   Chiang, A.C., Fundamental Methods of Mathematical Economics, 1974,84.

E. Require and use calculus:

1. Comparable to Binger & Hoffman, but assumes more calculus knowledge:

   Nicholson, W., Microeconomic Theory: Basic Principles and Extensions, 1985,92.

2. Considerably more advanced than Binger & Hoffman; close to a graduate text:

   Henderson, J.M., & R.E. Quandt, Microeconomic Theory: A Mathematical Approach, 3rd ed., 1980.

Weekly lab assignments: "Self-examination" -- through posing and answering questions as well as through problem solving -- is the central ingredient of learning. Thus: you are expected to complete the workbook that accompanies Kohler in its entirety. Two things are done to help enforce this expectation:

- questions worth approximately 40 percent of each exam grade are based on -- "inspired by" -- the problems in the workbook;
- each "lab" session is a recitation period in which individual students are asked to present answers to problems in the workbook as well as on each week's handout (distributed in class on the preceding Wednesday).

Note that the workbook contains answers to all questions and problems that it poses. Correspondingly, the emphasis in recitation is on the reasoning employed to arrive at answers.

Most weeks, one article from Breit is to be read; you are to select the one article from among those indicated for the week (you are, of course, free to read them all!). Week 11 is an exception: you must ALSO (i.e., in addition to one other article) read the article by Bator. You will undoubtedly find some of the readings in Breit to be rather hard going. That's to be expected! Indeed, most of them require careful, thoughtful reading; many of them, more than once. (Some have mathematics, but the central ideas in each article are accessible without following the mathematics -- close attention to the words will suffice!) Such reading is a superb vehicle of learning. Thus, the weekly handout will include study questions on that week's Breit readings and:
- the long essay questions on each exam will be taken from these study questions (with ample choice to assure that you will have read at least one of the articles at issue);
- the study questions will be fair game for asking at the recitation periods. In addition, for each article, a student will be chosen at random (from among those who read the article) to give a brief synopsis of the entire article for the benefit of those who chose to read something else.

There will also be a small amount of additional supplementary reading taken from elsewhere; this reading is distributed the week before it is to be done, as part of the week's handout.

Several -- the number depends on student demand -- of the recitation periods will be calculus drill sessions; the mechanics will be discussed at the beginning of the semester. Also to be discussed are the mechanics of assuring that all students who wish to work in small study groups (of six or fewer students) are assured of being able to do so (group work in preparation for recitation periods and for the exams is strongly! encouraged).

Copies of past examinations are on file in McCabe Library: All students are strongly encouraged to look at these examinations. Why? Because roughly half of the mid-term and final exams is taken from previous exams. Note that the instructor will not discuss any past exam questions with students, either individually or collectively. (The binder containing the exams has an index showing all exams that should be contained within it; please tell the Econ. Dept. secretary immediately if you find that there are missing exams. Thanks.)

For students experiencing difficulty: Students who are finding it difficult to absorb and master the material from the required readings should consult one or more of the references listed previously to determine whether supplementary reading can resolve their problems. Likely to be particularly useful in this regard are the texts by Baumol & Blinder and Mansfield or the study guide by Salvatore, all of which are on General Reserve in McCabe. If difficulty persists, students are strongly encouraged to discuss the problems that they are having with the instructor as soon as it is apparent that the problems are persistent. If warranted, some form of tutoring will be arranged. Tutoring will most likely be by one of the two Teaching Assistants in the course: Julia Stock and Kendrew Witt. (Unlike in previous years, the TAs will not conduct regular clinics. They will instead be available primarily if not only to help study groups to tutor students having particular difficulty.)

NotaBene: The most effective way to arrange for supplementary instructional assistance is through the instructor rather than through the Dean's Office; the

TAs can make initial arrangements to assist study groups, but they can not offer tutoring without the instructor's approval.

Grades will be determined on the following basis:

- exams during term   40 percent weight
- final exam   50   "   "
- recitation   10   "   "

There are two exams during the term, a required mid-term and an optional take-home. The optional exam is for students who -- for any reason -- are not satisfied with their performance on the required exam. It is also meant to be an aid in studying for the final exam. You are free either to take or not to take the optional exam; either way, your grade on exams during the term will not be less than your grade on the required exam. Your grade on exams during the term will, however, be raised if you submit a completed optional exam and your grade on it is higher than your grade on the required mid-term -- your grade on exams during the term will then be the average of your grades on the required and optional exams. Note that the optional exam is not graded on a curve, unlike the required exam and the final.

Policy regarding Plagiarism and Cheating

See the Student Handbook's statement regarding Academic Honesty. Cases of suspected plagiarism and cheating on exams will be reported to the Dean's Office for judicial action. In addition, the instructor has the automatic policy that any student whom he considers, on the basis of evidence available to him, to have engaged in plagiarism or cheating in any individually assigned work (i.e., in this course, exams) will automatically receive No Credit for the course.

Wk	Week of	Kohler | Baumol & Blinder [Binger] chapters: Topic(s) / Breit, et al. *
1	9/ 6	1#,2 | 2,3,4;21 [1-5]: Introduction, Consumer Choice ix, Introduction
2	9/13	9,10 | n.a. [19,20]: Choice under Uncertainty EITHER 176, Information OR 78, DeGustibus
3	9/20	3 | 22 [6,8,9]: Consumer Demand EITHER 35, Marshallian demand OR 186, Time
4	9/27	4 | 23 [10]: Theory of the Firm EITHER 124, Advances OR 203, InformationCosts
5	10/ 4	5# | 24 [11,12]: Competitive Supply EITHER 131, ShortRun OR 149, X-Efficiency
6	10/18	6 | 25 [13]: Competitive Equilibrium EITHER 1, Organization OR 302, Competition
7	10/25	Catch-up and Review; Mid-Term Required mid-term exam is on Thursday, Oct. 27; covers weeks 1 through 6. There are no lab section meetings on the 28th.
8	11/ 1	7 | 27 [15]: Monopoly Equilibrium EITHER 313, Monopoly OR 344, Utilities
9	11/ 8	8,15 | 28;31,32 [16]: Imperfect Competition EITHER 139, TransferPricing OR 327, Multiple-plant
10	11/15	11,12A$ | 35,36 [17]: Labor Markets; Rent ONE OF: 232, Discrimination; 258, Unemployment; 289, Signaling
11	11/22	13#@,14 | 26,37 [7,14]: General Equilibrium; Efficiency, Equity 389, Analytics AND 246, Contractual OR 468, Redistribution
12	11/29	16 | 29,34 [21]: Market Failures ONE OF: 377, Issues; 414, Social cost; 441, Public expenditure
13	12/ 6	12 | n.a. [18]: Capital Theory EITHER 276, Lemons OR 284, Moral hazard Optional take-home exam (distributed Tuesday, Nov. 22) is due at beginning of class on Thursday, Dec. 8

Final exam date/time to be announced, covers entire semester

NOTES:
* Articles in Breit are referenced as follows: number of first page, some key word(s) in title.
# Chapter appendix in Kohler workbook may be omitted at student's discretion.
$ There is no associated Kohler workbook chapter.
@ Excluding PROBLEMS section in Kohler workbook.
NotaBene: Kohler assignments include doing the questions and problems in the corresponding workbook chapters. Additional questions and problems will also be distributed.

University of British Columbia

Economics 306
Intermediate Microeconomics II

Spring 1995

John Weymark
Buchanan Tower 1021

Texts: A. Feldman, *Welfare Economics and Social Choice Theory*.
S. Bierman and L. Fernandez, *Game Theory with Economic Applications*.

Examinations

There will be two midterms and a final exam. Both midterms will be held in the regular class hour. The first midterm examination will be held on Friday, February 3. The second midterm examination will be held on Friday, March 3.

Grades

Midterm No. 1:	30 marks
Midterm No. 2:	30 marks
Final Exam:	40 marks
	100 marks

Problems

Students are expected to do the problems at the end of the chapters in both of the texts. For each topic, I will point out which are the most important problems. Problems will not be marked.

Outline

1. General Equilibrium and Welfare Economics

   Feldman, Chapters 2 - 4.
   W. Hildenbrand and A. Kirman, *Introduction to Equilibrium Analysis* (1976), Chapter 1.
   K. J. Arrow and F. Hahn, *General Competitive Analysis* (1971), Chapter 8, Section 2.
   T. Koopmans, *Three Essays on the State of Economic Science* (1957), Chapter 1, Sections 4 and 5.

2. Externalities

   Feldman, Chapter 5.
   D. M. G. Newberry, "Externalities: The Theory of Environmental
   Policy", in G. A. Hughes and G. M. Heal, eds., *Public Policy and the
   Tax System* (1980).

3. Extensive and Normal Form Games

   Bierman and Fernandez, Chapters 1, 4 and Chapter 3, Section 2.

4. Equilibria in Normal Form Games

   Bierman and Fernandez, Chapters 11, 13, 16.
   M. D. Intriligator, *Mathematical Optimization and Economic Theory*
   (1971), Chapter 8, Section 5.

5. Equilibria in Extensive Form Games

   Bierman and Fernandez, Chapter 5.

6. Expected Utility Theory

   Bierman and Fernandez, Chapter 2.
   J. A. Weymark, "A Reconsideration of the Harsanyi–Sen Debate on
   Utilitarianism", Section 2, in J. Elster and J. E. Roemer, eds.
   Interpersonal Comparisons of Well-Being (1991).

7. Uncertainty and Asymmetric Information

   W. Nicholson, *Microeconomic Theory: Basic Principles and
   Extensions, Fifth Edition* (1992), pp. 256 - 261.
   H. Gravelle and R. Rees, *Microeconomics, Second Edition* (1992), pp.
   569 - 571 and Chapter 20.
   D. M. Kreps, *A Course in Microeconomic Theory* (1990), Chapter 17,
   Section 1 and Chapter 18, Section 1.

UNIVERSITY OF BRITISH COLUMBIA
ECONOMICS 600
(MICROECONOMICS I)

FALL 1994   **JOHN WEYMARK**

TEXT: G. Jehle, *Advanced Microeconomic Theory.*

SUPPLEMENTARY TEXTS: G. Debreu, *Theory of Value.*
R. Cornes, *Duality and Modern Economics.*

READING LIST

1. Background Mathematics

K. Binmore, *Foundations of Analysis: A Straightforward Introduction, Book 1: Logic, Sets, and Numbers,* Chapters 1–4.

C. Simon and L. Blume, *Mathematics for Economists,* Chapter 12 and Section A1.3.

G. Jehle, *Advanced Microeconomic Theory,* Chapters 1–2.

G. Debreu, *Theory of Value,* Chapter 1.

W. Hildenbrand and A. Kirman, *Introduction to Equilibrium Analysis,* Mathematical Appendix III.

2. Consumer Theory

G. Jehle, *Advanced Microeconomic Theory,* Chapters 3–4.

G. Debreu, *Theory of Value,* Chapter 4.

D. Kreps, *A Course in Microeconomic Theory,* Chapter 2.

K. Arrow and F. Hahn, *General Competitive Analysis,* Sections 4.1–4.2, 4.6.

R. Cornes, *Duality and Modern Economics,* Chapters 2–4.

W. E. Diewert, Duality Approaches to Microeconomic Theory, in K. Arrow and M. Intriligator, eds., *Handbook of Mathematical Economics, Volume II,* Sections 1–4, 8–9.

H. Varian, The Nonparametric Approach to Demand Theory, *Econometrica* 50, 1982, pp. 945–973.

3. Competitive Producer Theory

G. Jehle, *Advanced Microeconomic Theory,* Chapter 5.

G. Debreu, *Theory of Value,* Chapter 3.

D. Kreps, *A Course in Microeconomic Theory,* Chapter 7.

K. Arrow and F. Hahn, *General Competitive Analysis,* Chapter 3.

R. Cornes, *Duality and Modern Economics,* Chapter 5.

W. E. Diewert, Duality Approaches to Microeconomic Theory, in K. Arrow and M. Intriligator, eds., *Handbook of Mathematical Economics, Volume II,* Section 10.

4. Competitive General Equilibrium

G. Jehle, *Advanced Microeconomic Theory*, pp. 309–320, 326–334.

G. Debreu, *Theory of Value*, Chapter 5.

D. Kreps, *A Course in Microeconomic Theory*, pp. 187–198, 206–216.

K. Arrow and F. Hahn, *General Competitive Analysis*, Chapter 2.

D. Duffie and H. Sonnenschein, Arrow and General Equilibrium Theory, *Journal of Economic Literature* **27**, 1989, Sections I–II.

C. Bliss, *Capital Theory and the Distribution of Income*, Chapter 3.

F. Fisher, *Disequilibrium Foundations of Equilibrium Economics*, Chapter 2.

5. First-Best Welfare Economics

G. Jehle, *Advanced Microeconomic Theory*, pp. 303–309, 320–326, 335–350.

G. Debreu, *Theory of Value*, Chapter 6.

W. Hildenbrand and A. Kirman, *Introduction to Equilibrium Analysis*, Chapter 1.

D. Kreps, *A Course in Microeconomic Theory*, pp. 199–205.

K. Arrow and F. Hahn, *General Competitive Analysis*, Chapter 8.

D. Duffie and H. Sonnenschein, Arrow and General Equilibrium Theory, *Journal of Economic Literature* **27**, 1989, Section III.

T. Koopmans, *Three Essays on the State of Economic Science*, pp. 1–54.

6. Social Choice Theory

G. Jehle, *Advanced Microeconomic Theory*, Chapter 8.

C. Blackorby, D. Donaldson, and J. Weymark, Social Choice with Interpersonal Comparisons: A Diagrammatic Introduction, *International Economic Review* **25**, 1984, pp. 327–356.

M. Le Breton and J. Weymark, An Introduction to Arrovian Social Welfare Functions on Economic and Political Domains, in N. Schofield, ed., *Social Choice and Political Economy*, forthcoming.

Williams College

Undergraduate, Upper Level Econ Majors

Spring 1995
Economics 354

Gordon Winston

PERSPECTIVES ON ECONOMIC THEORY

Objectives of the course:

The course is designed to show, through a set of selected subjects, how and how far current theory often goes beyond the level of Economics 251-252. Those courses give a solid textbook grounding in economic theory -- most of it established for half a century or so -- and they do it with as little confusing ambiguity as possible. The result is a clear, concise treatment of the essentials of modern economic theory. But it inevitably leaves one with a sense that, even theoretically, the world can't possibly be as simple as that. It's not.

While the actual issues chosen for study vary somewhat from year to year to reflect the interests and/or research of the instructor, their unifying theme is simply that they go well beyond the elementary conventional wisdom of economics and ask you to view the stuff of textbook theory with some greater distance. There is less coherence among these issues than in the micro or macroeconomic theory courses. Certain themes will appear and reappear in this syllabus -- time, uncertainty, irrationality, and motivations -- but their recurrence reflects more the preoccupations of the profession (and instructor) than a systematic development. Some of the readings are new; some are classics; some are middle aged. Choices among subjects are hard so there may be further changes during the semester.

The issues are inevitably abstract -- it's theory -- and sometimes fairly mathematical in presentation. What you should concentrate on in each reading is (a) what the author does or tries to do -- how those observations modify the 251-252 view of economics -- and (b) how he or she does it -- what are the logic and arguments.

The bias is toward microeconomic theory -- the way people behave as consumers, workers, managers. But since microeconomics and macroeconomics describe the same reality, this is all relevant to -- if not dead center within -- macroeconomic questions. And occasionally, at least, we'll touch on macro questions like unemployment.

Organization

The format for the course is suggested by its objective. Seminars will have assigned readings and assigned student discussants. Discussants will be responsible for giving a brief summary of the relevant 251-252 theory and of what is being done in the assigned readings -- again, what the author is doing and how it modifies the world according to 251-2. These summaries should typically take no more than five minutes each -- you should assume that everyone's read the material so it needs only comment and context. The balance of each seminar session, then, will be devoted to discussion of the issues.

There are two assumptions underlying this approach: (1) that everyone will in fact have read the material for the day including a review of the relevant parts of 251-252 with enough care to know, at least, what he or she didn't understand so it can be raised in the discussion and (2) that lecture-type presentations of the theory are not part of it. Note that bracketed readings are optional -- it won't be assumed they've been read.

The student responsibility inherent in this is heavy but it's worked well in the past. It should again.

Grading

The source of the grade for the course is also suggested by the format. There will be an hour test (20% of the course grade) and a final exam (30%). No paper. The rest of the grade will rest explicitly on the assigned oral summary (performance as "presenter") and on involvement in class discussion -- evidence of reading, understanding, thinking, and participation -- (25% each). Tests will cover both the reading and discussions.

Readings

Most reading will be from xeroxed journal articles which will be available soon in Seeley House, at a price. In addition, you should buy

Arrow, Kenneth J. The Limits of Organization (Norton, 1974)
Sen, Amartya K. Poverty and Famine (Oxford, 1981)
Axelrod, Robert. The Evolution of Cooperation (Basic, 1984)

They are all paperbacks.

278

I. INTRODUCTION

Feb 3   Hahn, "The Next Hundred Years," The Economic Journal, 1991

II. INFORMATION AND UNCERTAINTY

Feb. 8   Stigler, "The Economics of Information," Journal of Political Economy, 1961

               Akerlof, "The Market for 'Lemons,' Quality Uncertainty and the Market
               Mechanism," Quarterly Journal of Economics, 1970

Feb. 10   Arrow, The Limits of Organization, Chapters 1-2

Feb. 15   Arrow, Chapters 3-4

III. PREFERENCES AND RATIONALITY

Feb. 17   Sen, "Rational Fools: a Critique of the Behavioral Foundations of Economic
               Theory," Philosophy and Public Affairs, 1977

               March, "Bounded Rationality, Ambiguity, and the Engineering of Choice," The
               Bell Journal of Economics, 1978

Feb. 22   Tversky and Kahneman, "Judgment under Uncertainty: Heuristics and Biases,"
               Science, 1974

               Tversky and Kahneman, "The Framing of Decisions and the Psychology of
               Choice," Science, 1981

Feb. 24   Scitovsky, "How to Bring Psychology Back into Economics," Middlebury
                  Conference, October, 1985

               Frank, Passions within Reason, Chapter 1 "Opportunism and the Commitment
               Problem"

Mar. 1   Simon, "How to Decide What to Do," The Bell Journal, 1978

Cohen and Axelrod, "Coping with Complexity: The Adaptive Value of Changing Utility," American Economic Review, 1984

[Akerlof and Dickens, "The Economic Consequences of Cognitive Dissonance," American Economic Review, 1982]

[Goleman, "Assessing Risk: Why Fear May Outweigh Harm," The New York Times, Feb. 1, 1994, p. c1.

Mar. 3   Schelling, "Egonomics, or the Art of Self-Management," The American Economic Review, May, 1978.

Winston, "The Reasons for Being of Two Minds," Journal of Law, Economics, and Organization, 1985 (Note that this comments on a different Schelling article, so don't worry that they don't seem to relate.)

Winston, "Addiction and Backsliding: A Theory of Compulsive Consumption," Journal of Economic Behavior and Organization, 1980

IV. TIME, ACTIVITIES, AND DISCOUNTING THE FUTURE

Mar. 8   Michael and Becker, "On the New Theory of Consumer Behavior," Swedish Journal of Economics, 1973

Winston, "Activity Choice," The Journal of Economic Behavior and Organization, 1987

Mar. 10   Strotz, "Myopia and Inconsistency in Dynamic Utility Maximization," Review of Economic Studies, 1955-56

Winston and Woodbury, "Myopic Discounting: Empirical Evidence," in Frantz, Singh, and Garber, Handbook of Behavioral Economics, Vol.2B 1991.

[Benartzi and Thaler, "Myopic Loss Aversion and the Equity Premium Puzzle," NBER Wkng Pa. 4369.]

V. THE THEORY OF ECONOMIC THEORY

Mar. 15   Friedman, "The Methodology of Positive Economics," from Essays in Positive Economics, 1955

Schön, "Preparing Professionals for the Demands of Practice," Chapter 1 in Educating the Reflective Practitioner,

Mar. 17   **HOUR TEST (Timing?)**

SPRING BREAK

Apr. 5   Hirshleifer, "The Expanding Domain of Economics," American Economic Review, 1985

Winston, "Three Problems with the Treatment of Time in Economics," in Winston and Teichgraeber, The Boundaries of Economics, 1987

VI. ENTITLEMENT THEORY AND FAMINE

Apr. 7   [Review Ec 251 on a full general equilibrium -- Bator is one of the best.]

Sen, Poverty and Famine, Chapters 1 and 5, 6 and 10

VII. RELATIONSHIPS, CONTRACTS, AND FAIRNESS

Apr. 12   Simon, "A Formal Theory of the Employment Relation," Econometrica, 1951 (and in Models of Man)

Telser, "A Theory of Self-enforcing Agreements," Journal of Business, 1980

Apr. 14   Klein and Leffler, "The Role of Market Forces in Assuring Contract Performance," JPE, 1981

Kahneman, Knetsch, and Thaler, "Fairness as a Constraint on Profit Seeking: Entitlements in the Market," American Economic Review, 1986.

Apr. 19   Akerlof, and Janet Yellen, "Fairness and Unemployment,"
                 AER, May, 1988

                 McPherson and Winston, "The Economics of Academic Tenure," Journal of
                 Economic Behavior and Organization, 1983

IX. WHY FIRMS? WHY NON-PROFIT FIRMS?

Apr. 21   Alchian-Demzets, "Production, Information Costs and Economic
                 Organization," AER, 1972

                 Williamson, The Economic Institutions of Capitalism, Chapter 1

Apr. 26   Nelson and Winter, "Firm and Industry Response to Changed Market
                 Conditions: an Evolutionary Approach," Economic Inquiry, 1980

                 Hansmann, "The Role of Nonprofit Enterprise," in Rose-Ackerman, The
                 Economics of Nonprofit Institutions

VIII. GENDER IN ECONOMICS

Apr. 28   Sen, "Gender and Cooperative Conflicts," Ch. 8 in Tinker,
                 Persistent Inequalities: Women and World Development. (Long, so two
                 presenters can divide it.)

May 3   Folbre and Hartman, "The Rhetoric of Self Interest and the Ideology of
                 Gender," in Klamer, McCloskey, and Solow, The Consequences of
                 Economic Rhetoric,

                 Folbre, "Guys Don't Do That: Gender Groups and Social Norms," AEA
                 Meetings, 1992

[Brown-Kruse & Hummels, "Gender Effects in Laboratory Public Goods Contribution: Do Individuals Put Their Money Where Their Mouth Is?" JEBO, December 1993]

X. COOPERATION AND MORALITY

May 5   Axelrod, The Evolution of Cooperation, Chapter 1 and 2

May 10   Axelrod, Chapters 3 and 4
               [Axelrod, Chapter 5]

May 12   "The Place of Ethics in the Theory of Production," in Boskin ed. Economics and Human Welfare

               McPherson, "Limits on Self-Seeking: the Role of Morality in Economic Life," in Colander, Neoclassical Political Economy

Pomona College
Spring 1992

Economics 162
M W 2:45-4:00
Frank C. Wykoff

ADVANCED MICROECONOMIC ANALYSIS

REQUIRED READING

Silberberg, Eugene, The Structure of Economics, A Mathematical Analysis, Second Edition, McGraw Hill, New York, 1990

RECOMMENDED READING

Becker, Gary, The Economic Approach to Human Behavior, The University of Chicago Press, Chicago, 1976

Coase, Ronald H., The Firm, The Market and The Law, The University of Chicago Press, Chicago, 1988.

Deaton, Angus and John Muellbauer, Economics and Consumer Behavior, Cambridge, University Press, 1983.

Henderson, James M. and Richard E. Quandt, Microeconomic Theory, Third Edition, McGraw Hill, 1990.

Hey, John D., (ed.), Current Issues in Microeconomics, St. Martin's Press, New York, 1989.

Hirshleifer, Jack, Economic Behavior in Adversity, The University of Chicago Press, 1987.

COURSE DESCRIPTION

We begin with the basic models used to analyze behavior of individual economic agents. This will involve a detailed analysis of the budget constraint and preference orderings. Various aspects of these topics will be studied by each students who will write a short, two page **paper** on household behavior. The specific topics may be theoretical, empirical or conceptual.

It will take us about three weeks to complete our discussion of the foundations of economic analysis of individual decision makers. This will include discussion of preference orderings (satiation, transitivity, completeness, etc.), budget constraints and objective functions.

We will learn to apply the Lagrangian method of optimization subject to constraints. We will derive income and substitution effects, the Slutsky equations leading to the first law of demand. We will examine the limits of behavior imposed by theory. Some of this will be applied to index number theory. Each student will write a short **paper** applying one of the tools learned so far in the course.

We will branch out from this system into risk aversion and expected utility, Euler's theorems, dynastic (altruistic) models, compensating variation, the winner's curse, separability, moral hazard and adverse selection. Each student will write a two page paper on an application of the theoretical models discussed in this section.

Next we turn to producer behavior. Here we will learn modern duality theory which will firm up our understanding of linear homogeneity, homogeneity degree zero, revealed preference, own and cross elasticities, additivity, adding up restrictions. We will examine specific utility and production functions including the Cobb Douglas, Leontief, and Stone Geary. We will turn then to flexible functional forms including the Generalized Leontief and the Transcendental Logarithmic. Again, each student will write a short paper on some application of business theory, either individual producer or business or market situation.

We will review derivation of various cost curves. We then turn to market systems: competition, oligopoly and monopoly. General equilibrium analysis of Walrasian type systems will be studied. The Coase theorem will be studied with its implications for traditional economic analysis. This will afford us another opportunity for a paper by each student.

We will be extending the analysis at this point to various forms of market failure and papers may deal with a very wide range of subjects from inadequate information, public goods, externalities, monopoly, etc. We will also discuss regulation and government failure. Here again applications may come from urban problems such as poverty, housing, homelessness, congestion, pollution, etc.

COURSE GRADING PRACTICES

Your course grade will be determined roughly as follows:*
  Papers   60%
  Exams   40%
*The instructor's subjective assessment of your progress, effort, class room participation, and exceptional performances on papers or exams can effect your course grade as well.

Final Exam: _____

OFFICE HOURS:
MonWedTh 4:00-5:00
or by appointment with
Ms. Carolyn Williams
x8303

Economics 269   **G**

Microeconomic Analysis

About the Course

This course is primarily for M.A. students in economics and graduate students in other related fields. The technical requirement of the course elevates from intermediate microeconomics (Economics 149/249) by introducing more rigorous mathematical tools. It also differs from the Ph.D microeconomic core sequence (Economics 301/302) by exploring more application topics. Lectures and homeworks will draw heavily from the Varian's textbook. Prerequisites are intermediate microeconomics, multivariable calculus and elementary linear algebra.

Required Text

(V1) Hal R. Varian (1992): Microeconomic Analysis, 3rd ed., Norton: New York.

Background Books

(V2) Hal R. Varian (1992): Intermediate Microeconomics, 3rd Edition, Norton: New York.

Steven E. Landsberg (1992): Price Theory and Applications, 2nd Edition, The Dryden Press.

Office Hours

My office is room 203 in the SS building. Phone #: 660-1821. Office hours are W 1:30 - 3:00pm. If these hours conflict with your schedule, please contact me for special appointments.

Course Requirement and Grading

The requirements for the course include problem assignments, a short class presentation, a midterm and a final exam. Problem sets will be assigned along with the lectures and they will be graded with a "+", "0" or "-". Late homeworks will not be accepted. A combined score on the assignments will contribute 10% to the course grade. The presentation might be a small theoretical or empirical exploration, a discussion or critique of the existing literature, or an analysis of a journal or a newspaper article. It might also take the form of a research prospectus within the general scope of microeconomics. The class presentation will count for 10% of the course grade, the midterm 30% and the final 50%. There will be no make up exams.

Course Outline

1. Theory of the Firm

   Varian's, Chapters 1-6
   Landsberg, Chapters 5, 6
   Applications: growth accounting.

2. Demand Analysis

   Varian's, Chapters 7-11
   Landsberg, Chapters 3, 4, 17

   Applications: optimal taxation, work decisions, welfare programs.

3. Market Structure

   Varian's, Chapters 13-16
   Landsberg, Chapters 1, 2, 7, 10, 11

   Applications: cost-benefit analysis, minimum wage legislation.

4. Welfare, Public Goods and Externality

   Varian's, Chapters 17, 21-24
   Landsberg, Chapters 8, 12, 13

   Applications: social benefits of education.

ECONOMICS READING LISTS, COURSE OUTLINES, EXAMS, PUZZLES & PROBLEMS
Compiled by Edward Tower, *Duke University & The University of Auckland*, September 1995

Volume 1 Microeconomics Reading Lists, 287 pp.
including Experimental, Games, General Equilibrium, Technology, Innovation, & Growth

Volume 2 Microeconomics Exams, 309 pp.

Volume 3 Macro I: Macro, Money, & Financial Economics Reading Lists, 269 pp.

Volume 4 Macro II: Macroeconomics Exams 304 pp.

Volume 5 Macro III: Advanced Macro, Monetary & Financial Economics Exams, 303 pp.

Volume 6 Mathematical Economics, Game Theory,
Computational Economics & Applied General Equilibrium, 252 pp.

Volume 7 Econometrics Reading Lists, 246 pp.

Volume 8 Econometrics Exams, 280 pp.

Volume 9 Industrial Organization & Regulation Reading Lists, 291 pp.

Volume 10 Industrial Organization & Regulation Exams with Transport Economics Reading Lists, 292 pp.

Volume 11 Labor Economics Reading Lists, 289 pp.

Volume 12 Labor Economics Exams with Demography Reading Lists, 247 pp.

Volume 13 International Economics Reading Lists, 293 pp.

Volume 14 International Economics Exams, 288 pp.

Volume 15 Development I: Reading Lists, 263 pp. *including Human Resources, Institutions, Macro Policy,
Public Choice, Project Evaluation & Public Finance in LDCs*

Volume 16 Development II: National Economies, Comparative, Transition & Planning, 219 pp.
including Asia, China, Japan, Europe

Volume 17 Development III: Exams, 197 pp.
including V.W. Ruttan's Reference List on Technology & Development

Volume 18 Public Economics I: Taxation & Expenditure Reading Lists, 278 pp.

Volume 19 Public Economics II: Taxation and Expenditure Exams, 272 pp.

Volume 20 Public Economics III: Public Choice, Political Economy, Peace & War, 246 pp.
compiled by Jurgen Brauer, Ronald Friesen & Edward Tower

Volume 21 Public Economics IV: Urban, Rural, Regional; Law & Crime; Health, Education, 280 pp.

Volume 22 Environmental & Natural Resource Economics, 332 pp.

Volume 23 Agricultural Economics & Agriculture in Economic Development, 214 pp.

Volume 24 Economic History, 286 pp.

Volume 25 History of Economic Thought, 237 pp.

The price of each volume is $24. The discount price of the complete set of 25 Economics volumes is $395. A special offer for individuals buying economics volumes: Buy 2 volumes at the regular price, and get additional volumes for $20 each when ordering directly from Eno River Press. Please add $3/order for shipping on all orders. Additional postage charges are: US first class and Canadian air @ $3/volume; other foreign air @ $6/volume.

5876